Codin' for the Web

A Designer's Guide to
Developing Dynamic Web Sites

CHARLES WYKE-SMITH

New Riders

Codin' for the Web
A Designer's Guide to Developing Dynamic Web Sites
Charles Wyke-Smith

New Riders
1249 Eighth Street
Berkeley, CA 94710
510/524-2178
800/283-9444
510/524-2221 (fax)

Find us on the Web at: www.newriders.com
To report errors, please send a note to errata@peachpit.com

New Riders is an imprint of Peachpit, a division of Pearson Education

Editor: Wendy Sharp, Judy Ziajka
Production editor: Andrei Pasternak
Technical editor: Austin Markus
Indexer: Julie Bess
Compositor: WolfsonDesign
Cover design: Aren Howell
Cover image: Veer
Interior design: Mimi Heft

ISBN 0-321-42919-2

9 8 7 6 5 4 3 2 1

Printed and bound in the United States of America

To my nephew James.

Acknowledgements

Three excellent programmers helped me greatly with this book. The first is Austin Markus of Ithus Digital (www.ithus.com) who has been working with me as a programming consultant for years. He originally helped me plan what would be in this book and contributed code, ideas and general encouragement as I was getting under way. Later in the process, when Peachpit asked if I had suggestions for a Technical Editor, I recommended Austin and he has done a great job in that role, and I am very grateful to him for his attention to detail and the many improvements he has made to this book.

Tamara Fredrikson, Technical Lead at Nacio where I worked until recently has also been a huge help, especially with SQL and database related issues, and with the set up of development servers and databases.

Scott Miles of TurboAjax (www.turboajax.com), who knows more about PHP than anyone I know, endured innumerable phone calls and IMs and provided me with support both moral and technical at all hours of the day and night.

At Peachpit, I first I'll mention my editors Wendy Sharp and Judy Ziajka (who stepped in when Wendy endured a nasty illness); they were both patient and supportive as I wrangled the chapters and tried to balance my work and writing obligations, and their editorial skills have improved every page of this book. Thank you both.

On the business side, I want to thank Peachpit's publisher Nancy Ruenzel, Executive Editor Nancy Davis and Acquisitions Editor Michael Nolan for asking me back to write another one, and for their help behind the scenes as this book came together.

On the design team, Production Editor Andrei Pasternak has again done a great job managing the transformation of my manuscript into this book, and thanks go to compositor Owen for his obsessive attention to the details of the layout, Aren Howel for the cover design, and Mini Heft for the design of the interior pages.

Murray Goldenberg, CFO of Nacio, was very flexible with my work schedule as I wrote this book and I sincerely thank him for that, and for two great years at Nacio. In Nacio's production group, I want to mention Creative Director Clark Heist, production manager Bobbi-Michelle Wehrfritz, designer Richard Grove, and our wunderkind intern Emily Stark, who at age 18 is already a highly skilled programmer.

Steve Haney, Dave Klienberg, Allan Lees, Geoff Lucas and Demetrio Cuzzocrea are colleagues and all round great guys, and I am grateful for both their friendship and business advice.

Thanks goes to the readers of "Stylin' with CSS" who turned it into a minor best-seller, and whose positive emails inspired me to write this book. It is very gratifying to know that so many people found Stylin' useful and I appreciate the daily feedback, errata, and URLs that I receive.

A heart-felt mention goes to my father Ted, an accomplished painter and writer, who encouraged me in more ways than he will ever know, and to my mother Sheila, whose creativity and joy for life is missed by us all. My brother John, sisters Caroline and Angela, nephew James and my Aunt Nina are far away in England but close to my heart.

Finally, I'll thank my wonderful wife Beth, who has once again endured many weekends of taking care of the chores, children and bookkeeping while I wrote. My daughters Jemma and Lucy are a constant joy to me and I will take this opportunity to tell them once again how much I love them, and their mother.

—Charles Wyke-Smith, October 7, 2006

About the Author

Photo–Lowell Downey, Art and Clarity, Napa, CA

Charles Wyke-Smith has been creating Web sites since 1994. Through his consulting company, BBd (www.bbd.com), he provides Web design and user experience services to corporate, nonprofit, and e-commerce companies. An accomplished speaker and instructor, Wyke-Smith has also taught multimedia and interface design and spoken at many industry conferences. He wrote the best-selling Stylin' with CSS: A Designer's Guide.

Contents

On the Codin' Web site:

Introduction

When I first learned HTML in the mid 90s, I was amazed, like everyone else, how easy it was to create a Web page and publish information. However, I was disappointed when I discovered that I couldn't easily have user-submitted form data e-mailed to me and had to resort to the intricacies of Perl, the original server-side scripting language. In short, it was easy to send information to a user's Web browser, but getting information back from the user was much more difficult.

Over the intervening 12 or so years, that situation has not really changed. Forms continue to be the primary method by which visitors send data to the Web sites they use, and if you want your visitors to be able to communicate with your site, you have to learn a server-side programming language such as PHP or .NET so you can capture, process, and store that data. Of course, we all became designers so we wouldn't have to do nerdy stuff like math and computer programming, but today's Web sites are more like applications and less like online brochures—the approach that set the commercial development of the Web in motion. Today's Web designers must accept that designing code is as much part of the job as designing graphics.

My previous book, *Stylin' with CSS*, showed how to separate content from its onscreen presentation through the use of style sheets, and many readers who worked thorough that book wrote to me and said something like, "Okay, I have the interface programmed—now how can I e-mail the form data?" or "create a members-only area of my site?" or "save e-mail addresses in a database?" In each case, the underlying question was "How can I create a two-way exchange of data between my site and my visitors?"

In my efforts to recommend resources to help in this regard, I discovered that it can be hard to find a book to bridge the gap between knowledge of front-end HTML and CSS coding and a language like PHP. So when I decided to write a book about server-side programming, I made a few decisions early on.

First, I wanted *Codin'* to focus on learning and writing code, but I also wanted to lay some groundwork for those of you who have some experience creating Web pages, but may not understand how a Web page, Web server, and database interact and may need a starter course on XHTML and CSS. To this end, I have created two introductory chapters, Chapters A and B, that are not in the book but are freely available for download from the *Codin'* Web site, at http://www.codinfortheweb.com.

Chapter A covers three-tier architecture, the model in which these three components work together, and provides some background on the workings of databases.

If you have not used XHTML (a reformulation of HTML) and CSS to create Web pages that conform to Web standards, you can check out Chapter B, which discusses the use of Web standards to create a page template, ready for use in later chapters.

Depending on your skill level, you may want to download these two bonus chapters and skim them before starting this book.

Another decision I made was to use the PHP scripting language and the associated mySQL database throughout the book; both are open source (free) and are widely available and ready to use as part of numerous ISPs' hosting packages that can cost only a few dollars a month.

I've tried to keep the book's examples as understandable as possible, while at the same time showing the reader how to create functionality that is practical and useful. This means that although we start simple, each chapter builds on the last, and by the end you will be developing some moderately complex projects.

Chapter 1 covers basic programming concepts and techniques using PHP, although much of this knowledge can be readily transferred to any programming language you might wish to learn.

Forms are the primary method by which site visitors communicate with you (or your client), the site owner, so Chapter 2 shows you how to validate and process forms and store form data in text files.

Chapter 3 explains how to create a database and build database tables in which to store and manage the data from the forms created in Chapter 2.

Chapter 4 discusses how to create a simple content management system that enables you to add lists of links and associated information to your Web site

In Chapter 5, you see how to use cookies to enable a password-protected members-only site area.

Chapter 6 shows you how to integrate all of this functionality into a complete Web site.

Throughout, I have tried to illustrate the basic concepts of code development so that you can confidently start to create other functionality you might need.

PHP is a powerful language, and it can take years to learn to make full use of its capabilities. In writing an introductory book like this, I have often had to strike a balance between the most technically correct way to write something and the simplest and most understandable way to write something. Where the choice had to be made, I have chosen simplicity. Experienced programmers may look at some of the examples in this book and say, "I could have written that with half the number of lines of code," but my response might be that only someone with their level of skill could easily make sense of such code. My goal has been to write examples that are readable, and if a couple extra lines were needed to achieve that, so be it. As you gain experience and confidence, you will soon see how to pack down your code into the most economical expressions.

The other balancing act has revolved around security. We hear about well-known sites being hacked from time to time, and companies invest huge sums to protect their online assets from vandalism and criminal activity. Online forms are an open door to Web site attacks unless we ensure that the data entered into them is in a valid format (an e-mail address, not code that reads your database, for example), and I show how to validate form data in Chapter 4. Most Web sites do not warrant Fort Knox–like security protection, and so except for showing some basic techniques that protect from the most common kinds of hacking, I decided not to obfuscate the functional aspects of the code with the layers of security that some sites employ. Unless you are dealing with sensitive personal information such as medical records or social security numbers, your exposure is probably low, but I recommend that you take the security advice scattered throughout *Codin'* and if in doubt, get advice from an Internet security expert.

The toughest decision I made was not to cover JavaScript in this book. While server-side applications like PHP have been a mainstay of the Web for many years, JavaScript is today taking on a new and important role with the advent of AJAX: asynchronous JavaScript and XML. AJAX is not actually a programming language but a coding technique that combines JavaScript, CSS, XHTML's Document Object Model (DOM), and XML to enable the browser to request data from the server and update the page's content without reloading the page. AJAX enables Web sites to work more like regular desktop applications and is fundamentally changing both the way sites work and the way users experience the Web. Because of the broad scope of JavaScript's new role as the core technology of AJAX and the fact that you need the kinds of skills shown in this book before tackling AJAX-based projects, I decided to focus in *Codin'* on programming the server-side middleware and database and perhaps I will write a book on JavaScript and AJAX sometime in the future.

I hope that *Codin' for the Web* will empower you to create Web sites that are economical and easy to maintain, and most of all to create sites that are online two-way streets, where you can provide useful content to your visitors, discover their needs and interests through the data they submit back to you, and deliver appropriate pages back to them in response.

I can't provide full-on technical support for your coding efforts, but as *Stylin'* readers have discovered, I try to answer all the mail I get and be as supportive as my time allows. You can submit questions and comments via the *Codin'* Web site, and I love to get URLs of sites that my books have helped readers produce, so keep them coming.

Although coding can be frustratingly slow at first, if you just keep writing code, you will build your skills fast and be able to turn your site design ideas into interactive reality, and maybe even hard, cold cash. And now, it's time to start codin'...

Technical Notes

Sample files of all the code in *Codin' for the Web* is available at www.codinfortheweb.com. You will find it very helpful to view this code as you read the associated chapters of the book. Also, I recommend that you use the downloadable code examples rather than copying the code from the book. Your work will be much quicker, and any errors found in the book will be corrected in the downloadable code.

To be able to upload and view the code examples, you need a Web server running PHP and mySQL, an HTML or PHP editor in which to develop your code, and an FTP client to move files between your local machine and the server. A basic Linux-package hosting account, from an ISP such as GoDaddy (www.godaddy.com), is the easiest way to obtain access to a ready-to-go PHP- and mySQL-enabled server, at a cost of a few dollars per month.

Adobe Dreamweaver provides a complete development environment for editing your code, and includes an FTP client, for around $400; I highly recommend the investment, and you can read more about Dreamweaver in online Chapter B. If you want to go the low-or-no-expense route, you can use HTML or PHP editors such as Alleycode for the PC (www.alleycodesoftware.com) or Taco HTML

Edit for the Mac (www.tacosw.com); both are shareware so you can get them for free, but make a donation if you use them and so gain useful karma. Good free FTP clients are harder to find, but I recommend the FTP client SmartFTP for the PC (www.smartftp.com) or Yummy for the Mac (www.yummysoftware.com), which are in the $25 to $40 price range—a minimal investment for a tool that you will use every few minutes during your programming sessions.

I have also provided some guidance on this Web site about getting set up to work through each example; in every case, you will need to upload the appropriate PHP files onto the Web server via FTP.

You also will have to create database tables on the mySQL database to work with some of the code examples, but I have provided simple SQL scripts that you can run on the database that will create the required tables automatically, and I also provide step-by-step instructions for creating database tables in Chapter 3.

The code samples, downloadable from the *Codin'* Web site, are heavily commented to help you understand how the code works. If you display the code samples in one of the code editors mentioned previously, the comments will be displayed in a different color from other parts of the code so you can easily see what is code and what is comment.

In the code examples in the book, these comments have been moved out of the flow of the code and turned into margin notes alongside each line, for added readability.

Code in this book is shown in The Sans Prime Mono, like this:

```
$myText = "This is a code sample";
```

When showing how a code element is structured, I indicate the kind of data that is required in italics, like this:

```
echo (data to add to output);
```

When you write the example in your code, you will replace the italicized text with appropriate data—for example:

```
echo ("Hello, world!");
```

All the code examples are written in PHP4, although the recently released PHP5 is slowly becoming more widespread. Two of the most talked about features of PHP5 are the new one-line function for writing to a file and, of far more consequence, improved object-oriented programming (OOP) capabilities (see the end of Chapter 1 for a brief description of OOP). However, I have used the ubiquitous

PHP4 for all the examples in this book, and they will run on a PHP5 server, too.

Note that some servers require the extension .php to be present at the end of PHP file names, and some require the .php4 extension. Your Web server's administrator can easily make either or both work for you, but if you are hosted by an ISP, you may need to adopt whichever works on that server.

Any errata, or additional information that I decide is needed after the book goes to press, will be added to the *Codin'* Web site, so check in there from time to time.

CHAPTER 1

Coding Principles

CREATE A SIMPLE MAILING SYSTEM

Switch from XHTML to PHP

Create a variable to store data

Build an array of names and e-mail addresses in the variable

Loop through the elements of the array

Create a customized e-mail for each person

Use PHP's mail function to send the e-mail

Print an onscreen confirmation for each e-mail sent

Switch back to XHTML

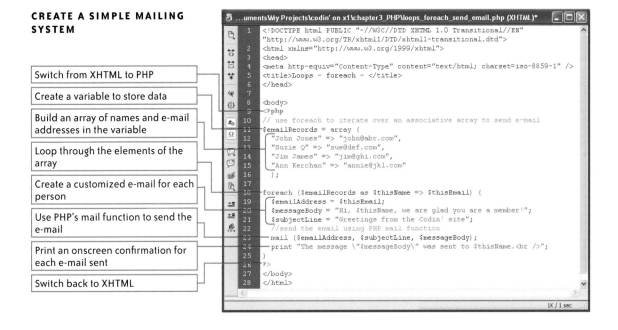

```
...uments\My Projects\codin' on x1\chapter3_PHP\loops_foreach_send_email.php (XHTML)*

1   <!DOCTYPE html PUBLIC "-//W3C//DTD XHTML 1.0 Transitional//EN"
    "http://www.w3.org/TR/xhtml1/DTD/xhtml1-transitional.dtd">
2   <html xmlns="http://www.w3.org/1999/xhtml">
3   <head>
4   <meta http-equiv="Content-Type" content="text/html; charset=iso-8859-1" />
5   <title>Loops - foreach - </title>
6   </head>
7
8   <body>
9   <?php
10  // use foreach to iterate over an associative array to send e-mail
11  $emailRecords = array (
12     "John Jones" => "john@abc.com",
13     "Suzie Q" => "sue@def.com",
14     "Jim James" => "jim@ghi.com",
15     "Ann Kerchan" => "annie@jkl.com"
16  );
17
18  foreach ($emailRecords as $thisName => $thisEmail) {
19     $emailAddress = $thisEmail;
20     $messageBody = "Hi, $thisName, we are glad you are a member!";
21     $subjectLine = "Greetings from the Codin' site";
22     //send the email using PHP mail function
23     mail ($emailAddress, $subjectLine, $messageBody);
24     print "The message \"$messageBody\" was sent to $thisName.<br />";
25  }
26  ?>
27  </body>
28  </html>

                                                          1K / 1 sec
```

"Real" programming languages can collect data from users and from sources such as files and databases and provide outputs based on the processing of those inputs. Using this definition, XHTML and CSS aren't real programming languages; they serve as data inputs that your browser uses to determine what to display, but they can't vary their responses based on user input.

The key attribute of a programming language is the ability to perform tests on data and then vary its output depending on what that data is. A good example of this is a login where the code checks the supplied password against the password stored in the database. If there is a match, then the user is logged in, and if not, the user is asked to try again.

JavaScript, PHP, Ruby, Perl, Java, C++, and a host of other programming languages have this test-and-respond capability that XHTML and CSS do not.

While each programming language has features that differentiate it from others, common concepts include variables, operators, conditional tests, loops, functions, arrays, and objects. Once you get these concepts in your mind, you can start to combine them to write useful scripts. Using PHP as an example, we'll take a look at these building blocks of code that are common to virtually every programming language.

To follow along with this chapter, you need to have the sample files on your computer and be able to upload them to a Web server running PHP so you can view them in a Web browser.

How PHP Works

The basic purpose of PHP is to generate XHTML. You can think of a PHP script (a file with the extension .php) as a recipe for an XHTML file.

Every time a page with the extension .php is requested from the server—by the user's typing a URL, clicking a link, or submitting a form—the PHP script within the requested page runs, and an XHTML page is generated (**Figure 1.1**).

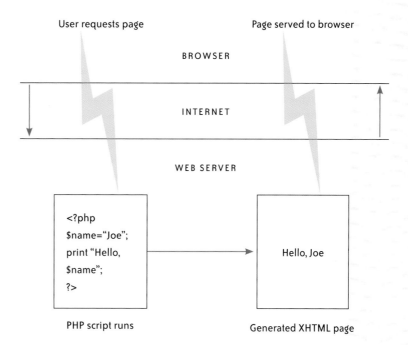

FIGURE 1.1 Each request for a PHP page (with a .php extension) generates an XHTML page that is served back to the requesting browser.

This sparkling new XHTML page is passed back over the Internet to the requestor's browser, where it is displayed. The user never sees the PHP in the script, only the resultant XHTML that the PHP script generates.

A PHP script is made up of a combination of XHTML, which is added as is directly to the generated XHTML page, and PHP, which is first processed and then replaced with the results it generates.

To illustrate, let's look at this simple example.

```
<p>Welcome, <?php echo $user_name; ?>, to our Web site!</p>
```

This example shows a line of XHTML code with a PHP tag in the middle of it. The PHP script would output `<p>Welcome,` verbatim to the generated XHTML file, but when it encounters `<?php`, it shifts gears and starts to interpret the code as PHP. It continues to do this until it encounters `?>`, when it shifts back to treating the code as XHTML and writing it directly into the page.

Code between `<?php` and `?>` does not get passed to the generated output but is instead replaced with the results of the PHP code being run through the PHP interpreter. In our example here, assuming that the variable `$user_name` is set to the value `Lucy`, the resultant XHTML would be:

```
<p>Welcome, Lucy, to our Web site!</p>
```

The programmer's key task, therefore, when writing PHP scripts, is to ensure that the XHTML that the PHP script generates is valid XHTML that the browser can successfully display. With this simple objective in mind, let's look at the elements that make up PHP code.

Variables

If coding is about creating code to work on our data, then the first thing we need to do is to get that data organized so our code can work on it. Data, in the form of all kinds and combinations of numbers and text, comes from databases, files on disk, and user inputs such as forms, and to manipulate that data with our code, we first need to get it into the computer's memory.

Every programming language can obtain and manage a part of the RAM (random access memory) of the computer on which it is running. It does this by dynamically (that is, as needed) organizing memory into containers called *variables* and putting data into them; the data in a variable is referred to as the variable's *value*. Variables are so named because your code can vary the values in them as it runs**.** Once the program has the required data in variables, it can perform a variety of processes on those variables at blinding speed: updating them, testing for specific data within them, and performing complex operations on them. For this reason, creating, managing, and eventually disposing of variables is a key skill in programming.

We'll now create and then display variables, to see how variables work. What makes variables powerful, however, is that the code can test, combine, and change their values as it runs and generate XHTML based on this changing data set. We will soon see this process in action.

Creating Variables

In programming languages of yore, creating variables was a two-step process: first declare (create) the variable and then, with a separate line of code, put the initial data into it. In modern programming languages, this process has been reduced to a single step; to *initialize* (create and put a starting value into) a variable in PHP called `userName` and containing the text string `"Lucy"`, for instance, we simply write this:

```
$userName = "Lucy";
```

PHP variables always begin with the dollar sign: `$`.

Type the name of the variable you want to create and enter `=` to set it to the value you want it to contain; the variable is created if it doesn't already exist. If the variable does already exist, its value is changed to this new value.

Naming Variables

A variable name must be a single word—that is, it can contain no spaces or dashes (a dash is written with the key to the right of 0). Although you can name a variable with just a single letter, it is well worth the effort to give variables meaningful names so you can more easily decipher your code in the future.

To this end, use either of these two common conventions for naming variables:

- To run several words together as one word, and in lieu of spaces, lead off with a lowercase letter and capitalize the second and subsequent words. In programmer parlance, this is known as camelCase, presumably because of the little humps created by the capitalized letters.

  ```
  $highUserScores
  ```

  ```
  $totalStateTax
  ```

- Put an underscore between each word, like this:

  ```
  $high_user_scores
  ```

  ```
  $total_state_tax
  ```

  Unlike dashes and spaces, underscores are seen as part of a word, so to PHP, the preceding examples are a single word.

You can use either approach—whichever you prefer (I use the first approach).

Also, because there are three main types of variables—local, global, and property variables—some programmers write global variables like this:

$gMyGlobalVariable

and property variables like this:

$pMyPropertyVariable

This differentiates them from local variables. You can decide whether you need to do this. All the variables we will use in this book are local variables unless otherwise noted; we will see why they are called this shortly.

Note that variable names are case sensitive, so $myScore, $Myscore, and $MyScore would (confusingly) be seen by PHP as three different variables—another good reason to adopt a consistent naming scheme.

Using print and echo

Let's use a basic XHTML template to see variables in action. Remember that the XHTML between the <body> and </body> tags determines what appears onscreen. To write the content of variables (or anything from PHP for that matter) in the page source code, we must use either print or echo.

Both print and echo can be used to output code to the browsers, but there is a subtle and usually irrelevant difference between them. Print can't do this:

```
echo "This", "that", "the
other";
```

Echo can't do this:

```
$var = print "Words in your
browser!";
```

In other words, print can be used in a more complex expression, but echo cannot.

CODE 1.1: variables1.php

Set the variable $userName to the value "Lucy";

```php
<?php

$userName = "Lucy";

?>

<!DOCTYPE html PUBLIC "-//W3C//DTD XHTML 1.0 Transitional//
EN" "http://www.w3.org/TR/xhtml1/DTD/xhtml1-transitional.
dtd">

<html xmlns="http://www.w3.org/1999/xhtml">

<head>

<meta http-equiv="Content-Type" content="text/html;
charset=iso-8859-1" />

<title>Codin' for the Web - PHP Variables</title>

</head>
```

```
<body>
```

Write out the user name ──┤ `<p><?php echo $userName; ?></p>`

```
</body>

</html>
```

This code sends the following to the browser:

```
<!DOCTYPE html PUBLIC "-//W3C//DTD XHTML 1.0 Transitional//
EN" "http://www.w3.org/TR/xhtml1/DTD/xhtml1-transitional.
dtd">

<html xmlns="http://www.w3.org/1999/xhtml">

<head>

<meta http-equiv="Content-Type" content="text/html;
charset=iso-8859-1" />

<title>Codin' for the Web - PHP Variables</title>

</head>

<body>
```

Displays the user name in the browser ──┤ `<p>Lucy</p>`

```
</body>

</html>
```

Note the following points about this example:

- XHTML code that is not within `<?php` and `?>` tags is written as is to the output—PHP code does not appear in the output at all.

- You can write PHP code before the `<html>` tag, enabling you to perform all necessary processing before you start to write out the page.

- If you view the source code in the browser, you can visually check that PHP is generating the output you expect.

- You can switch to PHP anywhere within the XHTML, but, between the `<?php  ?>` tags, if you want PHP to add XHTML code to the output, you must use echo or print.

Viewing Source Code

It's interesting to observe that anyone can see your XHTML, CSS, and JavaScript code—all a person needs to do is choose View Source in the browser's View menu to see the XHTML. A shortcut to view code is to right-click (Windows) or Option-click (Mac) and choose View Source from the pop-up menu.

In the head of the XHTML, you can also see the relative paths to any CSS and JavaScript files. If the source code of a page at www.somesite.com/products.htm has `<link type="text/css" media="screen" href="css/site.css" />` as the link to the CSS, then you know that you can view the CSS with the URL www.somesite.com/css/site.css. The same applies to JavaScript URLs in script tags. Some browsers display the CSS and JavaScript code, and others ask you to download it. Either way, you get it. This process is a great way to quickly obtain code that works and build your coding skills. Everybody does it, so don't feel guilty—this is the Web, after all—but be nice and add comments to credit the original site from which you obtain code snips, and respect Creative Commons and other copyright notices.

Your PHP code cannot be viewed in the output that is sent to the browser. Because PHP code is not sent to the browser but is processed on the server, it can be viewed only by someone who can, by fair means or foul, access the Web server. Thus, when you write in PHP, you effectively prevent anyone viewing or copying your efforts.

Specifying the Type of Data

Variables can hold several types of data. In more hard-core programming languages, such as Java, you have to decide what type of data a variable will hold (a string of text or an integer, for example) as you declare it. Such a language is referred to as "strongly typed." JavaScript and PHP are both weakly typed—that is, you don't have to declare what type of data is held in variables, and both languages, for example, will happily attempt to add an integer to a number stored as a text string, but in fact will just print both values, as illustrated here:

```
$myNum = 5;

$myString= "7";

print (myNum + myString);
```

Outputs: 57

Weakly typed languages are easier to learn as you don't have to keep track of what type of data can be stored in each variable. However, they also allow you to do absurd things accidentally, such as add a number to a word, which, as shown, is unlikely to return a meaningful result.

Numeric Variables

Numeric variables holds numbers, as you might imagine.

```
$totalCost = 200;

$thisItemCost = 15;
```

The $totalCost variable holds the value 200, and the $thisItemCost variable holds the value 15. You can perform math operations on the contents of numeric variables by using their names in the calculation, as shown in this example:

```
$totalCost = 200;

$ThisItemCost = 15;

print ($totalCost + $thisItemCost);
```

Outputs: 215

Be aware that there are various types of numbers. Most common are integers, which are whole numbers such as 4 and 15,768, and floating-point numbers, which have numbers after a decimal point, such as 1.14 and 0.88876. The accuracy of mathematical operations is greatly affected by the kind of number, and the number of floating numbers (to the right of the decimal point) that you use.

Another type of numerical variable is a Boolean, whose value can be only 1 or 0. A Boolean variable is commonly used to store the state of something that has only two possible values, such as TRUE or FALSE or Yes or No—for example, whether a check box is checked or unchecked.

Numeric variables will accept any type of number you store in them, but it's important that you, as the programmer, be aware of the types of numbers your variables hold.

Operators

Operators are the symbols that go between numbers and expressions in our code to specify operations such as addition, subtraction, multiplication, and division, and comparisons such as greater than, equal to, and less than.

An operator performs some operation on the operands—the data elements on either side of it. For example, although we don't often think about the mechanics of it in this way, the – operator (subtraction) causes the number to its right to be subtracted from the number to its left, as shown:

```
print 104 - 78;
```

Outputs: 26

The – operator is said to have *right associativity*, because the right side acts on the left. However, as you will see, this concept of "the right side affects the left side" runs through the logic of our code.

Assignment Operator

In PHP, the = operator is used to set the expression to its left to the value of the expression to its right and is not used to mean "equal to." If you want to check whether two things are equal in PHP, you use ==, the equality operator, like this:

```
if ($a==$b) {print "The
same!";}
```

The = assignment operator also has right associativity: the right value is assigned to the element on the left.

```
$total = 100;
```

Whenever you see this structure, you know that the left expression will be set as the result of the evaluation of the right expression. Because functions (we'll discuss functions very soon) return their result to you in this way, it's important to understand this simple but crucial point.

Math Operators

The basic math operators are +, -, *, and / for addition, subtraction, multiplication, and division respectively.

$total is set to 1615 ── $total = 4845 / 3;

PHP evaluates the expression on the right side of the = operator before setting the variable on the left to the evaluated result.

So now it should be easy to understand this example, which performs some basic math on variables to calculate the volume of a box:

CODE 1.2: Part of operators1.php4

```
$boxHeight=6;

$boxWidth=12;

$boxLength=9;


$boxCubicInches = $boxHeight * $boxWidth * $boxLength;

$boxCubicFeet = $boxCubicInches/144;

print "This box is $boxCubicInches cubic inches";

print " or $boxCubicFeet cubic feet.<br  />";
```

Outputs: This box is 648 cubic inches or 4.5 cubic feet.

Comparison Operators

Comparison operators allow us to compare two values. The result is always a Boolean 1 or 0, meaning TRUE or FALSE.

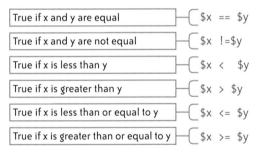

True if x and y are equal	`$x == $y`
True if x and y are not equal	`$x !=$y`
True if x is less than y	`$x <  $y`
True if x is greater than y	`$x > $y`
True if x is less than or equal to y	`$x <= $y`
True if x is greater than or equal to y	`$x >= $y`

Here is an example of the use of a comparison operator in an `if` statement:

```
if ($x < $y) print "It is true that x is less than y.";
```

Increment and Decrement Operators

The increment and decrement operators are `++` and `--`.

Often, you need to use a variable as a counter. Each time some process occurs, you add 1 to the counter: `x++` is equivalent to `x=x+1`. Such a counter might help you process several sequential items of data.

Depending on whether you want to use the number before or after you increment, put the operator before or after the expression. Note the difference in the output of these two bits of code:

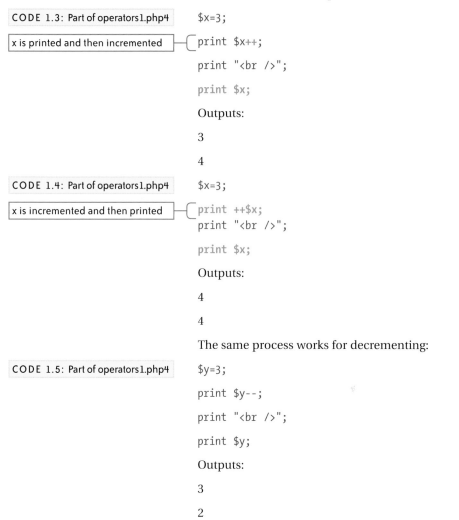

CODE 1.3: Part of operators1.php4

x is printed and then incremented

```
$x=3;
print $x++;
print "<br />";
print $x;
```

Outputs:

3

4

CODE 1.4: Part of operators1.php4

x is incremented and then printed

```
$x=3;
print ++$x;
print "<br />";
print $x;
```

Outputs:

4

4

The same process works for decrementing:

CODE 1.5: Part of operators1.php4

```
$y=3;
print $y--;
print "<br />";
print $y;
```

Outputs:

3

2

Concatenating (Joining) Operator

The . (dot) operator joins, or concatenates, several values into one string.

```
$firstName = "Dave";

$lastName = "Matthews";

print $firstName." ".$lastName." is a singer/songwriter.";
```

Outputs: Dave Matthews is a singer/songwriter.

Note here we use three . operators to join "Dave", a text string containing a space (highlighted), "Matthews", and the text string " is a singer/songwriter." (which has a space at the start of the string) to get the required output.

We can use the same kind of shorthand as for incrementing and decrementing with this operator also:

```
$a = "together";
```

Same as $a = $a."ness"; ──┤

```
$a .= "ness";

print $a;
```

Outputs: togetherness

Operator Precedence and Parentheses

An important fact to understand about operators is their order of precedence. When multiple operators appear in a single expression, precedence determines the order in which the operations are performed. As always, an example helps explain—what's the answer to this sum?

6 + 2 * 4

Is it 32 (8 times 4) or is it 14 (6 plus 8)? The answer depends on whether you multiplied or added first. In this case, PHP, and all other programming languages that I know of, would return the answer 14 because multiplication takes precedence over addition. Thus, even though * is the second operator in this example, the multiplication is performed first: 2 times 4 equals 8, and 8 plus 6 equals 14.

You can override the order of precedence of operators by putting the element you want calculated first in parentheses ( ). Parentheses are themselves considered an operator and have the highest precedence of all. In the preceding example, parentheses can be used to force the addition to be performed before the multiplication:

$(6 + 2) * 4$

This expression evaluates to 32. When you are performing a math calculation using variables and the calculation is not returning the expected result, it's smart to perform a test using simple numbers as in the example here, organizing the calculation in the same way as you are using your variables, to see if you get the expected result.

Nesting of parentheses also affects the way in which expressions are evaluated. The expression in the innermost parentheses is evaluated first, and the expression in the outermost is evaluated last. PHP makes short work of this problem:

```
$theAnswer = 5+((8*3+(44/11)+9)-9);
```

It works from the innermost parentheses (44/11) outward:

Innermost parentheses calculated first. 44/11=4	`$theAnswer = 5+((8*3+(44/11)+9)-9);`
24 + 13 = 37 — * performed before +	`$theAnswer = 5+((8*3+4+9) - 9);`
37 - 9 = 28	`$theAnswer = 5+(37 - 9);`

```
$theAnswer = 5+28;
```

```
$theAnswer = 33;
```

As your coding skills grow, you will find that often several lines of code can be packed into one by creatively nesting the expressions.

Strings

As the name implies, a string is just a string of text characters, like this:

```
"It's a lovely day in the neighborhood"
```

```
"The one after 9.09"
```

If you are writing code in a word processor (yes, some people do that), when you type quotation marks, ensure that the program is not "automagically" turning them into curly opening and closing quotation marks. In PHP and other programming languages, quoted strings must be enclosed in the basic, straight-up-and-down quotation mark, like this: ".

When you are working with text within your code, put it in quotation marks to turn it into a string. A string will be treated as is, and the PHP will not attempt to evaluate it:

```
print "Hello, Fred";
```

Outputs: Hello, Fred

```
print "1134+123";
```

Outputs: 1134+123

PHP can add two numbers together, but because the expression "1134+123" is a string, it was not evaluated, but simply displayed. However, remove the quotation marks, and PHP will add the numbers:

```
print 1134+123;
```

Outputs: 1257

Any part of your code not contained within string quotation marks is going to be processed by the PHP parser.

You can also use single quotation marks instead of double ones:

```
'This is also a string'
```

Note, however, that when you use PHP's convenient "variable in a string" format, there is a big difference between single and double quotation marks. In a string with double quotation marks, the variable is displayed as its value, whereas with single quotation marks, the variable remains simply text, as shown in these examples:

```
$heatComment = "very hot";
```

In double quotes, variables are evaluated

```
print "Today is $heatComment.";
```

Outputs: Today is very hot.

```
$heatComment = "not so warm";
```

In single quotes, variables are displayed as text

```
print 'Today is $heatComment.';
```

Outputs: Today is $heatComment.

Strings become more problematic when the string itself contains single or double quotation marks:

```
print "She turned, said "So long, then" and quietly closed
the door."
```

Outputs: Parse error: parse error, unexpected T_STRING in www-root/chapter1_PHP/double_single_quote_dif.php on line 18

In this case, the quotation mark after the word said closes the string prematurely, so what follows is not considered a string and is run through the processor. Because no part of So long, then" and quietly closed the door." makes any sense to PHP, an error message is displayed.

There are two simple fixes for this problem: Either use two different types of quotation marks, single and double, so PHP can see what's going on, or escape the problematic characters by preceding each one with a backslash. Escaping tells PHP to see the next character as is, not in its symbolic usage in the code, as shown here:

```
print 'She turned, said "So long, then" and quietly closed
the door.'
```

```
print "She turned, said \"So long, then\" and quietly closed
the door."
```

Both output: She turned, said "So long, then" and quietly closed the door.

You'll often escape some common characters, such as these:

\n	New line
\t	Tab
\$	Dollar sign

For instance, you'll often want to add the dollar sign to a number that represents currency before displaying it onscreen. Of course, in PHP the dollar sign indicates the start of a variable, so it's important to escape it when you really mean a dollar sign, as shown here:

Example of escaped $ symbol

```
$itemPrice = 19.99;

echo "Only \$$itemPrice!";
```

Outputs: Only $19.99!

There are a huge number of string-related functions that enable you to perform operations on strings, from stripping white space from the ends of strings, to determining where a particular character or substring appears and extracting it. All nonnumerical data with which you work, and most of the data that your scripts obtain from external sources such as files, is in the form of strings, so you need to become expert at getting strings into the formats that you need for your code.

Using \t (tab) and \n (new line) won't affect the formatting of XHTML as displayed to the viewer, but it will affect the layout of the generated code. If you are outputting a table with PHP, it can be helpful to format the code with /n line breaks after each </tr>; otherwise, the whole table is one very long line in your code source.

*Learn more about Magic Quotes
and SQL injection at http://www.
php.net/manual/en/security.
magicquotes.php.*

BEWARE MAGIC QUOTES

A "helpful" feature called Magic Quotes automatically escapes the single and double quotation marks of strings stored in variables, to prevent PHP newbies from creating forms that can accept malicious code that performs nasty operations such as SQL injections, which are an attempt by a hacker to read data from a database.

To see Magic Quotes in action, imagine that a user submits the inspiring comment shown in **Figure 1.2**.

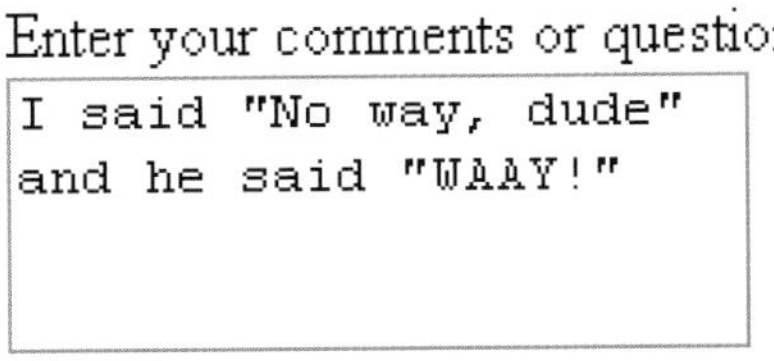

FIGURE 1.2 With Magic Quotes
active, if you enter this into the
form…

Enter your comments or questions.

```
I said "No way, dude"
and he said "WAAY!"
```

If you echo that data back to the form field, a technique we will explore in Chapter 2, you will see the slashes that Magic Quotes added (**Figure 1.3**).

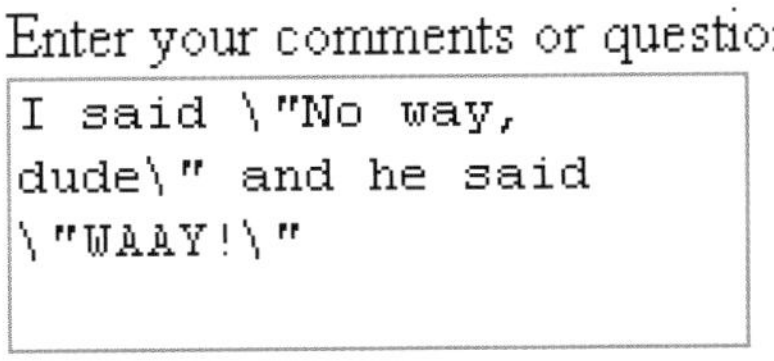

FIGURE 1.3 …if you echo the data
back to the form field, you will see
the escape characters that the Magic
Quotes feature added.

Enter your comments or questions.

```
I said \"No way,
dude\" and he said
\"WAAY!\"
```

To remove these Magic Quotes slashes, you need to apply the `stripslashes` function to the string:

```
$printable = stripslashes($userCommentString);
```

Most experienced programmers will tell you that Magic Quotes are evil, and that we should all go to the php.ini file (the file that sets up various PHP features), turn off Magic Quotes, and then use `add-Slashes()` (the opposite of `stripslashes()`) to selectively escape quotation marks only when we choose to and not give control of this task to the system. However, if you are using PHP from a hosting service, it's unlikely that you will have access to the php.ini file, and Magic Quotes is usually on.

You can check whether Magic Quotes is on before processing a form by entering the following code:

gpc stands for GET, POST, COOKIES

```
if (get_magic_quotes_gpc())  { echo "Magic Quotes are on"; }
```

(An expression like this will be easier to understand after we discuss functions later in this chapter.)

For an interesting take on escaping characters, read Harry Fueck's article at http://www.Webmasterstop.com/63.html.

If Magic Quotes is on, adjust your code accordingly, usually by stripping slashes immediately after the form is submitted and then using validation to limit what can be typed in the form. We'll discuss how to manage Magic Quotes issues further in Chapter 2.

Arrays

Numeric and string variables are scalar—that is, they hold a single piece of data: a number or string of text. Sometimes, however, we want to store several pieces of data together because those pieces of data make up a logical group of some kind. An *array* is a variable that can hold more than one piece of data. Arrays are great tools for organizing data sets. Each element of an array can be a number, a string, or even another array.

There are two types of arrays; indexed arrays, so called because we reference the elements of the array by an index number, and associative arrays, so called because we reference the elements by an associated name.

Indexed Arrays

Conceptually, an indexed array can be thought of as a number of values, such as:

```
24, 55, 99, 302, 6
```

or:

```
"Sarah", "John", "Mary", "Jim"
```

The format to create an array is:

```
$arrayName = array (value, 1, value 2,..value n)
```

Let's put three high scores from a game into an array:

```
$highScores= array (200,185,224);
```

One way to view the contents of an array is to use a foreach loop to traverse the array and write every item in it:

```
foreach ($highScore as $score) {

print "$score<br />";

}
```

Outputs:

200

185

224

We will look at loops in more detail later in the chapter.

To get a single item out of an array, put its location number in square brackets after the array name. Arrays are numbered from 0 not 1, so to get the second item out of this array, we write

```
print "Item 2 is $highScore[1]";
```

Outputs: Item 2 is 185

The process is very simple, if a little confusing at first.

To add another score to the end of our array, we would write

```
$highScores[242];
```

We can also sort the array from lowest to highest:

```
sort ($highScores);
```

> Write out the contents of the array using a foreach loop

```
foreach ($highScore as $score) {

print "$score<br />";

}
```

Outputs:

185

200

224

242

We can count the number of items in an array with the count function.

```
print count($highScores)."<br />";

print "There are ".(count($highScores))." scores in the
array.<br />";
```

Outputs:

There are 4 scores in the array.

Associative Arrays

Each element of a numerical array is a single value, but each element of an associative array is made up of two parts: a key (name) and a value. Conceptually, an associative array looks like this:

```
"San Francisco":"49ers", "Oakland":"Raiders",
"Miami":"Dolphins"
```

Here's how to create an associative array:

```
$teams = array ('San Francisco'=>'49ers',
'Oakland'=>'Raiders', 'Miami'=>'Dolphins');
```

You can write the key and value of each element of the array:

```
foreach ($teams as $name => $nickname) {

print "The nickname of the $name NFL team is the
$nickname.<br />";

}
```

Outputs:

The nickname of the San Francisco NFL team is the 49ers.
The nickname of the Oakland NFL team is the Raiders.
The nickname of the Miami NFL team is the Dolphins.

With an associative array, you can obtain a value by name:

```
print $teams['San Francisco']."<br />";
```

Outputs: 49ers.

Functions

A script is a simply a text file of code with the correct file extension: .html, .php, or .js, for example.

When you program, you will write scripts that each perform a specific task; for example, you might write one script to enable a user to register as a member, and another script to display the contents of a shopping cart.

As you start to write your scripts, you'll often discover that you are writing the same piece of code that you wrote earlier. For example, at an e-commerce site you may have to read product information from the database at many different times, and you can end up with many scripts containing duplicate code that lets you do that.

If you organize such code into a special code structure called a *function*, you need to write it only once and then let many scripts access, or *call*, the function. Furthermore, because a function that may be many lines long can be stored in a separate file and called by a single line within your script, moving repetitious code into functions makes scripts shorter and easier to read.

Functions are conceptually simple. Each one performs a specific function, or task, in your program, and has three properties:

- A function is a block of code that is executed when it is called.

- A function has its own variable space, so a variable defined in your main script that is not explicitly passed to your function will be unknown to your function.

- A function can return data to the calling script.

You call a function simply by stating its name and passing it any data it needs to do its job. Such data is known as the function's *arguments*, and arguments are contained in the brackets that follow the function's name.

For example, a function that returns product information needs to be passed data, such as a product SKU, to know which product to read from the database.

Calling a Function

The format for calling a function is

```
$myResult = $functionName($argument_1, argument 2,
...$argument_n)
```

In the case of our e-commerce site, we might use the following function call to get product information by passing a single argument, the product number 549833, to the function getProductInfo:

```
$myProductInfo = getProductInfo("549833");
```

This code will cause the variable $myProductInfo to be set to the result returned from the function (the left side is set to the result of the right side, remember). Such a function might return an array containing all the information about the product.

Writing a Function

The format for writing a function is

The code for the function goes here

$var1, $var2, etc. are set to the values of argument 1, argument 2, etc.

```
function $functionName ($var1, $var2, ...$varNth) {

    return $someData

}
```

To continue our e-commerce example, the function called by $myProductInfo = getProductInfo("549833"); might look like this:

```
function getProductInfo($productNum) {
```

Code that puts all the product's data into an array goes here

Return the array

```
    return $productDataArray;

}
```

It would set $myProductInfo in the calling script to the value of $productDataArray. Again, the left side is set by the right side—that is, the variable on the left is set to the value returned by the function.

Every programming language has lots of built-in functions. A simple example is the PHP `date()` function, which returns the current date. All we have to do is call it, using arguments to indicate the format in which we want the result:

| m = month as digits with preceding zero, d = day as digits with preceding zeros, y = year as two digits |

```
$todaysDate = date("m/d/y");

print "Today's date is $todaysDate.";
```

Outputs:

Today's date is 07/04/06

You can see all the arguments for the date function, which includes various formats for date and time, at http://www.w3schools.com/php/ func_date_date.asp.

The beauty of a function is that we simply pass the function the data it needs to do its work, and the result comes back—and as long as the function does its task in a useful and predictable way, who cares exactly how it is done?

We can also write our own functions. Suppose that we constantly have to add two large numbers together in our script. Rather than write the same piece of virtually identical code over and over again, we can create a function to do this job, like this:

| The function |

```
function addNumbers($firstNum, $secondNum) {

return $firstNum + $secondNum;

}
```

| Call the function |

```
$total = addNumbers(4, 7);

print $total;
```

Outputs: 11

This example shows how functions accept data, process that data, and return the result to you.

Let's break this process down a little.

The function itself is three lines (highlighted), the last line being simply a closing bracket. On the first line, we see that the function is called `addNumbers` and can accept two pieces of data, or two parameters. The single line of code that this function contains returns the total of the values of `firstNum` and `secondNum` to the calling code.

The calling code looks like this:

```
$total = addNumbers (4, 7);
```

The left side is a variable that will receive the result returned by the function. The right side calls the function and passes two arguments to its parameters. Once the function has been called, it's as if our calling line looks like this:

```
$total = 11;
```

The function `addNumbers(4, 7)` returns 11. Of course, you could do that calculation in your head, but PHP can also make short work of more challenging math:

```
$total = addNumbers(102462, 40043);
```

Outputs: 142505

In reality, we tend to use variables as arguments, rather than actual values, when calling a function, like this:

```
$total = addNumbers ($firstNum, $secondNum);
```

Typically, a function that we write ourselves would go near the start of the script in which we want to call it. Alternatively, if we wanted to call this function from many different scripts, we would put it in a separate script file, probably with other related functions, and use the PHP `include` command to include this script, and thereby the functions within it, in every page that will use it.

Code Structures

We've discussed the basics of variables, operators, and functions. We'll now move on to some coding structures that enable us to give your code decision-making powers.

Code structures enable processes to be run on your data, such as a conditional test to determine whether two pieces of data match (a submitted password and a stored password, for example) or loops that can run the same process on each element of an array.

The if-then-else Structure

The most common code structure you will write is `if-then-else`. It provides a basic decision-making capability and is known as a *conditional* test because it simply tests whether a certain condition is true and returns one of only two possible responses: TRUE or FALSE. The code then executes one of two pieces of code. Conceptually, it's a fork in the path of the code flow: TRUE takes us down one path, and FALSE takes us down another.

An `if` statement is structured like this:

if (this statement is true) *then* (do these things) *else* (do these different things)

You probably use this structure conversationally every day.

"If they have fresh bread, then buy a sourdough loaf, else get some bagels."

"If you love me, then marry me, else this whole romance is off!"

Well, maybe you don't use that second one every day, but you get the idea: if a certain thing is true, then we do one thing; if it's false, then we do something else (**Figure 1.4**).

FIGURE 1.4 An `if` statement executes one of two pieces of code depending on whether the test resolves to TRUE or FALSE.

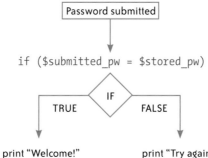

Here is how to write a conditional statement in PHP:

```
if(condition is true) {
    execute this code
} else {
    execute this other code
}
```

PHP doesn't actually use the word then *in an* `if-then-else` *statement—it's simply implied by the structure—but it does use the word* else, *as shown in the examples.*

Here's a simple `if-then-else` example:

```
if($temp > 72) {

    print "It's warm today!";

} else {

    print "Not so hot.";

}
```

You don't have to write the `else` piece of the structure if you don't need it, as shown here:

```
if($cartItemsCount == 0) {

  echo "Your cart is empty!";

}
```

This example also demonstrates the Boolean operator mentioned earlier; in comparisons, 1 is the same as TRUE, and 0 is the same as FALSE, and so these terms can be used interchangeably in your code. If you are just testing for any value, not specifically TRUE or 1, the code can be further simplified to just this:

```
if($memberID) {

  echo "Welcome, member!";

}
```

NULL is an explicit setting for nothing, as opposed to 0 which equates to FALSE. For example, if you are writing a file and a certain piece of data in a set isn't yet available, you can use NULL to indicate this.

As long as the value of $memberID is not FALSE, 0, NULL, or "" (an empty text string), then this code will evaluate to TRUE. This shorthand is useful, because you don't need to create a special variable containing a Boolean 1 or 0 to track whether a person is a member. You simply test for $memberID, which you can assume will be a unique number for each member and is probably needed for many other purposes, and as long as it's set to something, the person will be greeted. Effectively, this test is for whether a piece of data has a value.

To test for the presence of FALSE, 0, NULL, or "" (an empty string), you can use the not operator !, an exclamation point.

Evaluates to TRUE if $logIn = FALSE, 0, NULL, or "" or has not been set at all

```
if(!$logIn) {

  echo "Sorry, you must log in first.";

}
```

Interestingly, if the variable $logIn has never been mentioned in your code up to this point (so that it doesn't even exist), this statement will still resolve to TRUE, because the $logIn variable is not set. The test will not, as you might expect, generate an error message as a result of testing a nonexistent variable. It simply looks for the value and provides a response according to whether the variable is found.

PHP's Simple if-then-else Structure

PHP also has a shorthand version of if-then-else that is ideal for simple responses. Its structure is

```
condition to test ? true statement : false statement
```

For instance, you can enter this:

```
$comment = $livesLeft  > 0 ? "Play again!": "Game over";
print ($comment);
```

If the player has any lives left, the will screen display "Play again!"; otherwise, it will display "Game over." If you have more than one true or false statement, though, you'll need to use the full if-then-else structure.

However, in reality, if we were at this point in a game where the player had just lost a life, we might need to perform a number of steps (that is, execute a lot of lines of code) to either reset the game so the user can play again or, if the user is out of lives, clean up the current game and offer the user the chance to start a new game. We might write two functions, one called repeatLevel and another called startNewGame; each of these functions would contain all the code needed to perform the respective tasks. We won't write these two imaginary functions here; we'll just see how to call them.

In such a case, the shorthand if-then-else format is ideal:

```
$comment = $livesLeft  > 0 ? repeatLevel():startNewGame()
```

In this example, no parameters are being passed by the function calls— their parentheses are empty. These functions don't need to receive any additional data to perform their tasks. That's not uncommon.

Creating Functions

Being a smart programmer, you would have recognized, when scripting the two pieces of code that repeated levels and started games, that each is a self-contained piece of functionality that may be needed by many different scripts. Every level of our hypothetical game may need to call one or the other of these functions when a life is lost.

When you recognize a self-contained piece of functionality like this, it is logical to move this code into a function and call it from the main script.

During the preproduction phase of your site, it's important to determine the major functions that manage the basic operations of your site before you start scripting. Perhaps your site needs to read lots of files from disk, so it would make sense to write a function to do this. What information would that function need to perform this task? Simple: The name of the file and the folder it's located in.

So we would write a function called readFile (not illustrated here) that requires these two parameters to be passed to it. Such a function would be called with a script like this:

```
$fileFolder = "products"

$fileName = "hedgeclipper3_description.txt"

$fileText= readFile ($fileFolder, $fileName)
```

With the function behind the scenes doing the work, any time we need to read a text file, we just load our two variables with the folder name and file name and call the function (the highlighted line)—and pow!—we have that text from the file in the $fileText variable ready to use.

This kind of thinking allows you to develop your site in a considered manner. First, you write the functions that do the repetitive tasks, and then, after testing the functions with hard-coded variables, you write the scripts required for each task the site performs. Any script can then call, and pass parameters into, those functions—parameters that will change depending on the current state of the data when the function is called.

In this way, individual scripts provide high-level control of the functionality beneath, passing data to functions as required by the purpose of the script and using the returned results in the next steps of the process that the script performs.

Not all processes can, or should, be removed from the script's flow into a function, but if you catch yourself thinking "I've written this before," then it's probably time to backtrack and convert that chunk of code into a reusable function.

Typically, I run a separate folder of function files that I can link to each page of my site with a single line of code, so that I can call these functions at any time and have to maintain them in only one place.

The creation and use of functions in this way is extensively illustrated in the upcoming chapters.

The else-if Structure

A variation of `if-then-else`, called the `else-if` structure, allows us to perform several comparisons, rather than just one, on the data.

This is the format of the `else-if` structure:

```
if(some condition is true) {

  do this

} elseif(some other condition is true) {

  do this other thing

} elseif(some other condition is true) {

  do this other thing

} else {

  if none of the other conditions match, do this default
thing

}
```

You can have as many `else-if` statements as you want.

Suppose we want to give feedback to students about how well they did on a test by checking their scores against a maximum-possible score and then providing one of three responses, depending on their scores.

This example puts together almost everything we have looked at so far in this chapter. We are going to set two variables, do a little math on them, then do some comparing, and finally provide a result.

```
$maxScore = 100;

$yourScore = 78;

if($yourScore > $maxScore*0.66) {

    print "Great job - you are in the top third.";

} else if ($yourScore < $maxScore*0.33)  {

    print "You are in the bottom third. You must try
harder.";

} else {

    print "You are in the middle third. Good effort.";

}
```

There are two points to note here.

First, if the maximum test score were changed to 200, the script would give a score of over 133 (in the top third) the "Great job" response. By having the code calculate the passing score rather than hard-coding it, we make the script more flexible. Now we can use it to obtain a comment on an exam score no mater what the maximum score is.

Second, we made life easy for ourselves by first testing for the high score and then testing for the low score. If we tested for the middle score, we would need to test for two things: whether the score is less than two-thirds *and* whether it is greater than one-third. We avoid this double testing by first testing for each extreme result, which requires only one comparison; anything that doesn't fit those extreme tests must be in the middle—the `else` part of the code.

Note that each conditional test—for example, `if ($yourScore < $maxScore * 0.33)`—has both a `<` comparison operator and a `*` multiplication operator. Precedence dictates that the multiplication will be performed before the comparison, which is, of course, what we want.

Converting Part of a Script to a Function

Now let's turn this piece of code into a function, so that we can access its functionality from any script.

```
$examComment = examFeedback (300, 194);

print $examComment;

function examFeedback($maxScore, $yourScore) {

    if($yourScore > $maxScore*0.66) {

            return "Great job - you are in the top third.";

    } else if($yourScore < $maxScore*0.33)  {

            return "You are in the bottom third. You must try
    harder.";

    } else {

            return "You are in the middle third. Good effort.";

    }
}
```

Annotations (left margin):
- Call for function → `$examComment = examFeedback (300, 194);`
- Outputs returned result from function → `print $examComment;`
- Function starts → `function examFeedback($maxScore, $yourScore) {`
- If starts → `if($yourScore > $maxScore*0.66) {`
- Close if → `}`
- Close function → `}`

To make this function available to many pages, save the function in its own script. If you named that script exam_function.inc, *then you simply add include* "pathName/ exam_function.inc"; *to any other script, and that script will be able to call the function.*

As you can see, only three quick steps turn a piece of code in the flow of the script into a function:

- Add the word `function` and a name for the function.

- Change the variables to be tested into handlers for the arguments that will be passed by the calling code.

- Replace the `print` command with `return`, so that the variable in the calling line (`$examComment`) is set to whatever the result of the function's work might be.

To call this function we might write the following:

```
$examComment = examFeedback (300, 194)
```

In this case, we pass to the function the data that this student scored 194 out of a possible 300, and the function will return the text string "You are in the middle third. Good effort." and that string will be stored in the `$examComment` variable.

In reality, after creating a function and firing it some hard-coded data like 300 and 194 in the preceding example to be sure it works, you would then replace the hard-coded numbers with variables, like this:

```
$examComment = examFeedback($thisExamMaxScore,
$studentScore);
```

(These variables would have been set earlier, perhaps by a script that read the data, and they would change as each student's exam data is read and processed.) Now when the function is called by this line of code, the current values of `$thisExamMaxScore` and `$studentScore` get passed to the function, and `$examComment` is set to the appropriate text string. Now we have created a truly dynamic piece of code that can respond according to the current status of two variables and takes up only one line in our code flow.

Loops

Loops are code structures that let you rapidly perform the same task on each item or set of data—a process known as iteration. Finding a match in a list of items is a typical example of the use of loops to iterate through a data set.

Like `if-then-else` structures, loops have a conditional part to them: the looping continues as long as a stated condition is true.

The while Loop

CODE 1.6: Part of loops1.php

The `while` loop structure requires one piece of data: a counter.

```
while (something is true) {
```

Do some things repeatedly

```

}
```

Here's a simple example:

```
$i= 1;
while ($i<10) {
```

Print i and then add 1 to it

```
  print $i++;
}
```

Outputs: 123456789

As long as i is less than 10, this `while` loop keeps going. Each time it repeats, the single line of code inside the loop prints the value of i and then adds 1 to it. After nine repeats, i becomes equal to 10, the test condition evaluates to FALSE, and the looping stops.

Be careful when coding `while` loops to ensure that the test condition will eventually evaluate to FALSE; otherwise, you create an infinite loop, where the computer may never return control to the user, effectively freezing the machine.

The for Loop: The Iterator

The `for` loop structure requires three pieces of data, like this:

```
for (start condition; termination condition; increment/
decrement)
```

Here's an example:

```
for ($i=20; $i<=25; $i++) {

 print $i."<br />\n";

}
```

Outputs:

20

21

22

23

24

We initialize (set the start condition of) the variable i to the value 20, ($i=20; $i<25; $i++), and we tell the loop to continue looping as long as i is less than 25 ($i=20; $i<25; $i++). Each time the loop repeats, we increment i by 1, using the ++ increment operator ($i=20; $i<25; $i++).

So in this example, the second time the loop runs, i will equal 21. The code within the loop (print $i."
\n";) simply writes the current value of i at each repetition, along with a <br /> tag to add line breaks to the XHTML and a \n element to add line breaks to the source code.

Note also the arrangement of the { }—the curly brackets, or braces. The braces go around the lines of code that will run each time the loop repeats. When the looping ends, PHP will move to the line after the closing brace and continue execution of the rest of the script.

If we use <= (less than or equal to) in this example, we print all the way up to the value in the termination condition, 25.

```
for ($i=20; $i<25; $i++) {

   print $i."<br />\n";

   }
```

Outputs:

20

21

22

23

24

25

The power of `for` appears when you use `i`, our incrementing counter, to iterate (sequentially access) the elements of an array of data. Inside the loop, the code references the current location in the array as `i`. Then, each time the loop repeats, our code processes the next item in the array, because `i` is now one more than last time. Let's see this in action.

CODE 1.7: Part of loops_
interation_on arrays.php

Build an array of records

```
$emailRecords = array ("john@abc.com","sue@def.com","jim@ghi.
com", "annie@jkl.com");
```

Set a target name to find in the array

```
$nameToVerify = "jim@ghi.com";
```

Default comment to print later

```
$comment = "No match.";
```

First location in an array is 0, so start counter at 0

```
for ($i=0; $i < count($emailRecords); $i++) {
```

If TRUE, change comment

If a match, change comment

```
    if ($emailRecords[$i] == $nameToVerify) {

        $comment = "Yes, $emailRecords[$i] is a valid email.";
```

Exit loop—no point continuing once we have found a match

```
        break;
```

End of if loop

```
    }
```

End of for loop

```
}
```

```
print $comment;
```

Outputs: "Yes, jim@ghi.com is a valid email."

What is interesting about this script is that it is dynamic—that is, the `for` loop repeats as many times as there are elements in the array. This repetition occurs because the condition `$i < count($emailRecords)` states that `i` must be less than the `count` value of the array (the number of elements that the array contains), rather than some fixed value. No matter how many more elements are added to the array—as more members join, for example—the loop will always run exactly the right number of times to process them all, because our code counts the number of elements and uses that value, whatever it happens to be at that time. Once you start to use this kind of dynamic code rather than fixed values, you are on your way to becoming a good programmer.

Array Numbering

Because the stated test condition operator is less than (and not less than or equal to, as you might expect), the looping stops as soon as $i = 4$. If you think this might cause the fourth and last element of the array not to be processed, you'll be wrong. Array numbering starts from 0, so the four array elements are numbered 0, 1, 2, and 3. The expression `count($emailRecords)` resolves to 4 (the array contains four elements), so therefore we want to stop when $i = 4$ and not run the loop, because we are past the last element of the array, numbered 3. Now you start to see the logic behind numbering arrays starting from 0, not 1.

The foreach Loop

Using a counter in a `for` loop is useful in a variety of situations, such as when you want to extract only up to a certain number of elements from an array. The `for` structure provides very tight control over the conditions under which a loop runs, as it allows us set a starting value other than 1 if we wish, and it also allows us to state how much gets added to (or subtracted from) the iterator each time the loop runs. For example, we could use `i+2` instead of `i++` if we wanted to look at every second item for some reason.

However, when we just want to run through the entire array sequentially from first to last, we can use the simpler `foreach` construct.

The format of the `foreach` loop is

```
foreach ($thisArrayName as $thisArrayItem) {
```

Do something with $thisArrayItem in here

```
}
```

The `foreach` loop doesn't use a counter; it automatically runs as many times as there are elements in the array. Each time it loops, *$thisArrayItem* (or whatever descriptive name you might use for this variable) is set to the next item in the array so that you can perform some test on it.

CODE 1.8: Part of loops_
interation_on arrays.php

Build an array of e-mail address records

Set a target name to find in the array

Default comment to print later

Let's modify the preceding example to create a `foreach` loop:

```php
$emailRecords = array ("john@abc.com","sue@def.com","jim@ghi.
com", "annie@jkl.com");

$emailToVerify = "jim@ghi.com";

$comment = "No match.";

foreach ($emailRecords as $thisEmail)

    if ($thisEmail == $emailToVerify) {

        $comment = "Yes, indeed, $thisEmail is a valid email.";

        break;

    }

}
```

If a match, change comment

No point continuing once we have found a match

End of if loop

End of foreach loop

```php
print $comment;
```

Outputs: Yes, indeed, jim@ghi.com is a valid email.

Associative arrays, where each element is made up of a key (a name) and a value, can also be processed with a `foreach` loop. With an associative array, the format of the `foreach` loop is as follows:

```php
foreach ($arrayName as $thisArrayKey => $thisArrayItem) {
```

Do something with $thisArrayKey and $thisArrayItem in here

```php
}
```

Each time the loop executes, *$thisArrayKey* and *$thisArrayItem* (and again, you can name these two variables whatever makes sense to you) are set to the next element's key and value.

CODE 1.9: Part of loops_
interation_on arrays.php

Create an associative array

Let's modify our array of e-mail addresses to create an associative array, where each key is the user name and the value is the e-mail address.

```php
$emailRecords= array (

    "John Jones" => "john@abc.com",

    "Suzie Q" => "sue@def.com",

    "Jim James" => "jim@ghi.com",

    "Ann Kerchan" => "annie@jkl.com");
```

Set a target name to find in the array

```php
$emailToVerify = "jim@ghi.com";
```

Default comment to print later

```php
$comment = "No match.";

foreach ($emailRecords as $thisName => $thisEmail) {
```

If a match, change comment

```php
  if ($thisEmail == $emailToVerify) {

      $comment = "Yes, indeed, $thisName is a member.";
```

No point continuing once we have found a match

```php
      break;
```

End of if loop

```php
    }
```

End foreach loop

```php
}

print $comment;
```

Outputs: Yes, indeed, Jim James is a member.

This code performs a common operation on an associative array: searching by value and returning the corresponding key, or vice versa.

CODE 1.10: loops_foreaxh_send_email.php

As a final example, let's send each person in our array a personalized e-mail:

Use an associative array to send e-mail

```php
$emailRecords= array (

    "John Jones" => "john@abc.com",

    "Suzie Q" => "sue@def.com",

    "Jim James" => "jim@ghi.com",

    "Ann Kerchan" => "annie@jkl.com");


foreach ($emailRecords as $thisName => $thisEmail) {

  $emailAddress = $thisEmail;

  $messageBody = "Hi, $thisName, we are glad you are a
member!";

  $subjectLine = "Greetings from the Codin' site";
```

Send the e-mail using the PHP mail function

```php
  mail ($emailAddress, $subjectLine, $messageBody);

  print "The message \"$messageBody\" was sent to
$thisName.<br />";

}
```

Outputs:

The message "Hi, John Jones, we are glad you are a member!" was sent to John Jones.

The message "Hi, Suzie Q, we are glad you are a member!" was sent to Suzie Q.

The message "Hi, Jim James, we are glad you are a member!" was sent to Jim James.

The message "Hi, Ann Kerchan, we are glad you are a member!" was sent to Ann Kerchan.

The `mail()` function does actually send e-mail if your server is set up to do this, and we will look at this capability in more depth in the next chapter. During testing, you may want to comment out the `mail()` function (by preceding it with double slashes), or perhaps use only your own e-mail address in the array, lest you send lots of unwanted e-mail to the same person. Note also that using this script for spamming can cause plagues of frogs to descend upon you.

Objects

Object-oriented programming is beyond the scope of this book, but you should at least know what it is. You will eventually want to get there with your coding, as you will see after reading this overview of its concepts.

Objects are made up of properties (object variables) and methods (object functions). An object is used as a cookie cutter to make numerous instances, or copies, of the object, each with its own values for the properties .

For example, a Spaceship object in a video game might enable the creation of numerous instances of spaceships, and each spaceship could have its own set of values for properties such as speed, weapon power, and fuel level. However, as the spaceships are all derived from the same object, they can share methods (capabilities) such as `takeOff()` and `hyperDrive()`.

Each time you create a new instance of an object, you can pass the object the values for the properties of the new instance. So one spaceship might be slow and heavy and have massive firepower, while another might be fast and light but less well armed. The result depends on the values you use for the object's property variables when you instantiate (create) that instance.

Each time an instance is created, the object returns a pointer to that instance. You can think of the pointer as the object's handle—a means of locating its data in memory. An instance pointer is usually stored in an array along with the other instances of this object.

When we call a method (function) of an object, the only parameter we need to pass is the instance pointer—all the instance's data is already associated with it; we are then running the method on this particular instance of the object's data.

With all the instances accessible from the pointer array, we can perform iteration on the array with high frequency, calling the `moveSpaceship()` method for each spaceship instance, which moves each spaceship a different amount, depending on its speed, weight, and weapons. To the game player, the spaceships move around apparently entirely independently of each other, yet they are all powered by the same underlying code, because they are all instances of the same Spaceship object.

Object-oriented programming isn't useful only in writing games, although games are a great application for it. This concept can be applied to such data sets as these:

- Customer list (all customers have a name, physical address, e-mail address, and so on).

- Seats in a theater-booking system (all seats have a price, section and row number, distance from the stage, and so on).

- E-commerce site (all items have an SKU, product name, description, price, and so on).

Perhaps the most important feature of OOP is code encapsulation: an object is an isolated island of code with its own internal methods (functions) and properties (variables). Programming that is performed on other parts of the code does not affect the internal workings of an object. This behavior is especially useful when more than one programmer is working on the same project; because each object is its own island of code, all that a programmer needs to be know about other objects with which his or her code interacts is how to call the other objects' methods. How they do what they do doesn't matter.

OOP also offers inheritance: an object can inherit the methods and properties of other objects. For example, if we want our theater seat booking application to also allow the theater-goer to book a limousine, the objects that make up limousine booking functionality can inherit all the payment and address information methods from the theater booking objects.

Object-oriented programming is best learned after you have some skill with the procedural style of programming shown in this book. Perhaps one day I'll write *OOPin'...*

Summary

This chapter has discussed the basic PHP programming concepts and techniques. The simplest way to learn more about almost any PHP topic is to type **php** followed by whatever you want to know about (**php associative arrays**, for example) in Google. Also, there are excellent examples for every feature of PHP at http://w3schools.com/php, and if you really want details, go to http://www.php.net and enter a function name in the search field. Professional programmers post comments on their experiences with each function there, so if you run into difficulties or just want to see how the pros do it, this is a great place to look.

This chapter serves as only a superficial look at the capabilities of PHP and programming languages in general, but it's enough to get us started. Armed with these programming fundamentals, it's now time to start building some practical examples and put this knowledge into action.

CHAPTER 2

Processing Forms

ENSURE THAT FORM DATA IS IN THE RIGHT FORMAT FOR YOUR NEEDS AND PROTECT YOUR SITE FROM ATTACKS

Display informative error messages

Problem: First Name field contains punctuation

Problem: Last ame field is empty

Problem: Email address has no @

Problem: A crude effort to hack the site by injecting code through the form

---

Codin' - Form processing - Mozilla Firefox

File   Edit   View   Go   Bookmarks   Tools   Help

Go   G

Disable▾   Cookies▾   CSS▾   Forms▾   Images▾   Information▾   Miscellaneous▾

Send me a message!

- First Name must be letters and numbers, spaces, dashes and ' only.
- Last Name must be letters and numbers, spaces, dashes and ' only.
- Email must be a valid format (e.g. john@yahoo.com).
- Message can only contain letters, numbers and basic punctuation " ' - ? !

First Name*

`Joe!`

Last Name*

Email*

`joe2bbd.com`

Enter your comments or questions.

```
print ($password);
```

Go

Done

The first PHP programming skill that any Web programmer needs is the ability to manage the data submitted from forms filled out by the user, as forms are the primary way that users communicate with you. Without forms, your site is a one-way street.

The most common type of form is a signup process of some kind; the form might require simply an e-mail address to send the visitor a newsletter, or it might require extensive information such as name, address, e-mail address, and credit card data for a store checkout. For a classified ad site or a dating site, there may be pages and pages of user information to gather and store.

About User-Supplied Data and the Need for Validation

The most important point to keep in mind when gathering data from forms is to distrust the data. Because forms enable a transfer of data from any visitor's browser to the server, they can be an open door to useless garbage, malicious code, and even unwanted files. Fortunately, by running some tests on the data when it first arrives on the server, you can reject data that does not meet the test criteria you define.

By asking—and helping—the user to make corrections to such rejected data until it passes those tests, you can insist that form data be correctly structured and deter all but the most determined hacker. This process of testing the data to see if it meets certain criteria is called *validation*.

Unless you validate incoming data, people can type anything into a form: from nonsense that is tiresome to find and delete, such as invalid e-mail addresses, to malicious code that can compromise the site in some way. Then there are simply the inevitable user errors and typos, such as an e-mail address with 2 instead of @ or a comma instead of a dot—the kinds of mistakes that many visitors make. If you let such errors in, the users may think they have provided accurate information and expect you to e-mail them, but if you can't because their information is incorrect, it's bad for business.

Also, bad data can cause your code to generate errors. Particularly problematic are text strings containing characters that also have meaning within the code, such as " and ' , which can cause PHP to close a text string before the end is reached; PHP will then try to evaluate the remainder of the string as code, and errors will result. As we saw in Chapter 1, such characters can be escaped, so that PHP realizes their purpose.

The bottom line on validation is that the vast majority of your visitors want the information they submit to be accurate—we want Granny to get her Mother's Day gift—so the primary purpose of validation is to help the user, and the secondary, though also very important, is to protect your site from hackers. How much you validate form data is up to you and should be based on the effects of bad data on your business and your code, the amount of security your site warrants, and your site's perceived exposure to willful action. If in doubt, seek professional help from a Web security expert. But take this advice: No validation is not enough.

Validation is a circular process, in which the user submits the form, and then your code checks the submitted data against the validation criteria. If there are problems, the code reloads the form page along with a list of the errors. The user can then make changes and submit the form again. This round-and-round continues until the form passes validation, at which point the data is stored or used in some process (**Figure 2.1**).

FIGURE 2.1 Flowchart for form validation. When the form is first loaded, it is not processed (left path). Once the form is submitted (right path), the data is validated and is either redisplayed for corrections or passed to other processes.

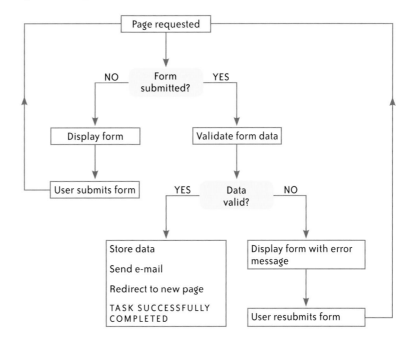

Here are some steps you can take to validate the submitted data.

Is There Any Data at All?

First, you might check that data was actually entered in each field of the form—any data. You can test for an empty text string; if that's what you find, the field is still blank. Fields where user-entered data must be present are said to be *required*.

```
if (first_name=="") {

  $error[] = "Please enter your first name"

}
```

Check for a Specific Character or Word

Next, you might check that a field contains a specific character: Does the e-mail address have an @ symbol in it, for example? Functions to perform a variety of tests on strings are built into PHP. For example, strstr checks whether one string contains text defined in a second string.

```
$submittedEmail = "kate@bbd.com";

$string = "@";

$result = strstr($submittedEmail, $string);

if ($result) {print "@ is present!";}
```

prints "@ is present"

The $result function will test TRUE if the text in $submittedEmail contains the text of $string—in other words, if an @ is present.

Check for Patterns in the Data

While checking for an individual character can be an improvement over simply testing for any text in the fields, for the best chance of getting worthwhile, safe data, we need to check for patterns: the presence of certain types of characters in the data, and even the order in which characters appear.

For example, mailing addresses don't start with the " character, but a bit of unwanted code might, so you might decide that you will reject a street address that starts with " and require the user to change it. Using a special code structure known as a *regular expression* made up of symbols that represent certain data elements, you can test

Here we are adding a text element to an array called $error in which we can store numerous descriptions of errors that might be associated with the form. We'll discuss later in this chapter how to set up such an array and display the accumulated errors to the user.

each piece of form data for a specific pattern of characters and for positions of characters within the string. You might check that a street address contains letters and numbers, but does not contain (or), a typical calling card of a hacker who is looking for weaknesses in your site by passing in code through the form.

Regular expressions can test an e-mail address to ensure that it is at least structurally correct. It can't determine whether the e-mail address is genuine or not, but it can at least tell you that the e-mail address is correctly constructed, as in abc@def.com.

By using regular expressions, for example, to ensure that the user's name information can hold only letters and numbers (and perhaps dashes and periods), you can reject characters such as ;, [, and {, making it more difficult for a hacker to inject malicious code.

Regular expressions are the best way to ensure that you are getting well-formed data. They are rather complex to write, but thankfully there are lots of them out on the Web ready to be used (after testing) as is.

Requiring an E-mail Address to Confirm Membership

Because e-mails are your primary connection with your constituents, it can be worth requiring users to respond to an e-mail that you send them at the address they entered before providing the password, download, or pages for which they signed up.

If you want users to confirm by e-mail that they want to be members (and thereby confirm that they have an accessible e-mail address), create a Boolean field in your database called `confirm_flag` or something similar. (Once someone confirms, you'll set the flag to 1.) After a user submits the form, you record the person's data in the database and set `confirm_flag` to a random number generated by PHP. This person is now in your records.

Then send an e-mail to the provided address. This e-mail should contain a link that the user must click or paste into a browser and submit. The random number is in the query string of the URL. When the user clicks the link in the e-mail, the confirmation PHP page that is requested reads the random number in the query part of the link's URL string, looks up the users' record in the database, and changes that record's confirmation flag from the random number to 1. Then the confirmation script e-mails the requested newsletter or displays a link to whatever the member is now entitled to obtain.

It's a bit of work to set up an e-mail address confirmation system like this, but the value of having a confirmed e-mail address for a visitor to your site is not to be underestimated; once you have a visitor's e-mail address, you can start to build a long-term relationship with that person.

Creating the Form

We'll return to validation later. Now we'll turn to writing the code for forms.

Creating the XHTML for a Form

We'll start with some simple XHTML for the form.

CODE 2.1: forms1.php4

```
<!DOCTYPE html PUBLIC "-//W3C//DTD XHTML 1.0 Transitional//
EN" "http://www.w3.org/TR/xhtml1/DTD/xhtml1-transitional.
dtd">

<html xmlns="http://www.w3.org/1999/xhtml">

<head>

<meta http-equiv="Content-Type" content="text/html;
charset=iso-8859-1" />

<title>Codin' - Form processing</title>

<link type="text/css" media="screen" href="css/codin_styles.
css" />

</head>

<body>

  <div id="content">

  <form action="<?php $_SERVER['PHP_SELF'] ?>" method="POST">

      <h3>Send me a message!</h3>

  <label for="first_name">First Name*</label><br />

      <input name="first_name" type="text" size="20"
id="first_name" /><br />

    <label for="last_name">Last Name*</label><br />

      <input name="last_name" type="text" size="20" id="last_
name" /><br />

      <label for="email">Email*</label><br />

      <input name= "email" type="text" size="20" id="email"
/><br />
```

```
    <label for="message">Enter your comments or questions.</
label><br />

    <textarea name="message" rows="3" cols="20"
id="message"></textarea><br />

    <p>Your information will not be sold or shared with
others.</p>

        <input type="submit" name="submitted" value="Go" />

    </form>

  </div>

</body>

</html>
```

The submit button passes the value submitted (highlighted). **Figure 2.2** shows the results in the browser.

You will notice, if you fill in the form and click the Go button to submit it, that everything you entered disappears. We'll fix this annoying default behavior later.

Creating a Self-Requesting Page

When a visitor submits a form by clicking the Go button, the form data is passed to the page stated in the form element's Action attribute. Typically, this page is the same page as the form itself. It may seem strange to request a page from itself, but by placing the PHP that processes the form before the form's XHTML code and having the page request itself every time the form is submitted, we can test the submitted data and easily redisplay the form to the user in the event of errors, along with helpful PHP-generated directions to correct them. Only when the submitted data passes validation do we record that data and move on to another page of the site.

This self-requesting process is represented by the thin lines with arrows on the flowchart in Figure 2.1. When the form is submitted, the page reloads. The difference is that any data the user has entered is now available to PHP.

Let's set up the page reloading mechanism. You may be used to seeing a form with an action URL like this:

```
<form action="http://www.somesite.com/index.htm"
method="POST">
```

The page referenced in this URL is requested when the submit button of the form is clicked. To make the form self-requesting, we replace the URL with the following PHP:

```
<? php $_SERVER['PHP_SELF'] ?>
```

The form element then looks like this:

CODE 2.2: Part of forms2.php

```
<body>

  <div id="content">

  <form action="<? php $_SERVER['PHP_SELF'] ?>"
method="POST">

      <h3>Send me a message!</h3>

  <label for="first_name">First Name*</label><br />
```

See the sidebar "Super-global Arrays" later in this chapter for more information about these arrays.

This code returns the URL of the current page from PHP's $_SERVER super-global array, which contains all kinds of interesting information about the Web server.

This approach is better than using the page's actual URL, because by letting the page reference itself in this way, you can ensure that the page always reloads itself when the form is submitted, even if the name of the page later changes.

Next, we'll add some PHP at the top of the page, before the <DOCTYPE> declaration. This code lets us distinguish between a normal page load, such as when the page first loads, and a page load that occurs because the form has been submitted, causing the page to request itself.

We do this by testing the super-global $_POST array, which holds form data that was submitted from a form that uses POST as its method attribute in the form element.

CODE 2.3: Part of forms2.php4

```php
<?php

if ($_POST['submitted']) {

  echo "Form submitted!";

  }

?>


<!DOCTYPE html PUBLIC "-//W3C//DTD XHTML 1.0 Transitional//
EN" "http://www.w3.org/TR/xhtml1/DTD/xhtml1-transitional.
dtd">

<html xmlns="http://www.w3.org/1999/xhtml">

<head>

<!--some code not shown here -->

  <div id="content">

  <form action="<?php $_SERVER['PHP_SELF'] ?>" method="POST">

      <h3>Send me a message!</h3>

  <label for="first_name" >First Name*</label><br />

      <input name="first_name" type="text" size="20"
id="first_name" /><br />

<!--etc-->
```

When we load the page, we see the form as in Figure 2.2, but if we click Go to submit the form, PHP outputs the "Form submitted!" message (**Figure 2.3**).

FIGURE 2.3 Click Go to submit the form; the "Form submitted!" message appears.

You may want to bookmark the page at this point, as you will want to clear the POST array between tests. Closing the browser window ends the PHP session (more on sessions later) and clears the POST array. Select the bookmark to load the page again. Alternatively, if you set the current page you are working on as the browser's home page and select it to load in a New Page window (see your browser Preferences), then you can just click the window shut and press Control-N to open a new window and load the page. Then you don't even need a bookmark.

By testing for the submitted data from the submit button's name attribute, we can tell whether the page is loading as a result of the submission of the form, and if it is, we can process the form data. If submitted is not set, the PHP code to process the form (just a simple message at this point in our form's development) is skipped, and the page simply displays the form; this behavior always occurs when the page first loads.

So in this example, if you load the page by typing its URL, the message does not appear, but if you click the submit button of the form, the message "Form submitted!" will appear. This behavior occurs because when the page is first loaded, there are no POST values set, but when the form is submitted, all of the inputs return their values —even the button. Because there is now a value assigned to the submitted input (in this case, Go), the if statement evaluates to TRUE (1), and the code inside the test runs. In theory, you could check against any of the fields in the form, but the check will fail if a field is blank so this is not the best idea. Later, we will exchange the line echo "Form Submitted!" for code that actually processes the form.

Super-Global Arrays

Super-global arrays are so called because the data they contain is available at any time from any page. PHP has eight of these arrays:

$_POST: Contains data from forms submitted using the POST method.

$_GET: Contains data from forms submitted using the GET method.

$_COOKIES: Contains cookie data.

$_SERVER: Contains a variety of information about the server.

$_SESSION: Contains information about the server.

$_REQUEST: Contains a combination of the $_POST, $_GET, and $_COOKIES arrays in one mega-array.

$_ENV: Contains environment variables related to the script's shell.

$_GLOBAL: Contains all the global variables associated with the script.

To learn more about the POST and GET methods of submitting a form, see "Fundamentals of PHP Superglobals" at php-builder.com: http://www.phpbuilder.com/columns/ian_gilfillan20050801.php3.

Using the $_POST Super-Global Array

PHP has several super-global arrays, including $_SERVER, $_GET, and $_POST. They are known as super-global arrays because they have unlimited scope within PHP, and you can access their values from anywhere within any script.

PHP's super-global $_POST array receives all form data when the form is submitted using the POST method. Specifically, this array contains the name and the associated value of each form element, that value being the data that the user entered in the element. For example, if I submitted this form, the $_POST array might contain the following:

```
first_name="Charles";

last_name="Wyke-Smith";

email="charles@bbd.com";

message="Write code and prosper!"

submitted="Go";
```

For example, the data

```
echo ($_POST['first_name'])
```

would output "Charles".

Once the form is submitted, we copy the form data from the $_POST array into local PHP variables with short but clear names, so the user doesn't have to write all that $_POST data every time he or she wants to access the data. Then we can move on to clean-up and validation and not have to go back to the $_POST array again once the data in the new variables has been validated.

We will modify the code above the XHTML code to look like this:

CODE 2.4: forms3.php

```php
<?php
if ($_POST['submitted']) {
    $first_name = ($_POST['first_name']);
    $last_name = ($_POST['last_name']);
    $email = ($_POST['email']);
    $msg = ($_POST['message']);


echo $first_name;
echo $last_name;
echo $email;
echo $msg;
}
?>
```

This approach is fine for this example, but in a live site you should never write unvalidated variables to the screen as doing so leaves your site exposed to a cross-site scripting attack. We will takes steps to prevent this problem when we validate this form later in the chapter.

End of if POST submitted

It is more economical to work with the form data in an array than as four variables, but for clarity's sake, we use four separate variables in these examples.

Figure 2.4 shows the results.

Here we move the POST array contents into four variables and then, as a quick test to make sure our code is correct, write them to the screen.

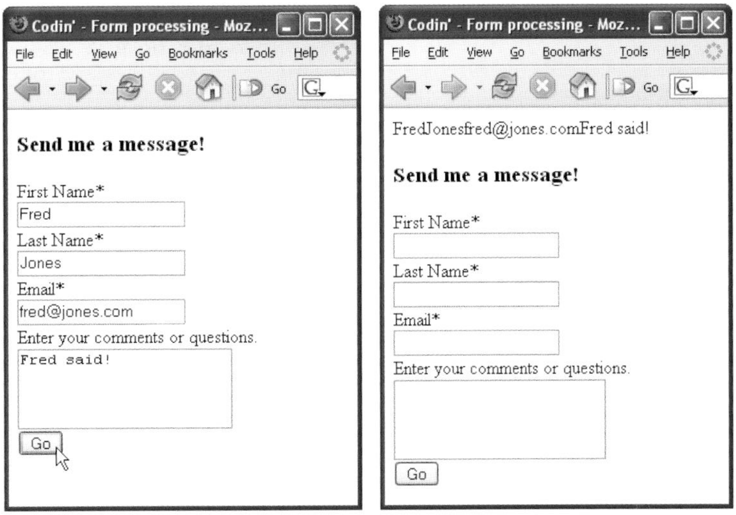

FIGURE 2.4 We enter the data and submit the form, and PHP displays the variables set from the $_POST array at the top of the form.

PHP needs to be able to communicate with an SMTP mail server running on the same server to e-mail the form. If this step doesn't work, contact your server administrator. You may want to e-mail the administrator the URL http://www.php.net/mail along with your request.

Although this example doesn't use headers, you can also optionally send header information, such as reply-to, from, cc, and bcc, and even send attachments. Learn about this at the PHP Resource Index, at http://php.resourceindex.com/ Documentation/Examples_and_ Tutorials/E_Mail/.

Sending E-mail to Yourself with PHP

You can now e-mail the unvalidated form data to yourself, the site's administrator (remember that you won't usually be the one filling out the form), by using PHP's mail function.

It is quite simple to send e-mail from a PHP script. The basic format of PHP's e-mail function is

```
mail(emailaddress, subject, message, [headers])
```

so you can e-mail the form data to yourself like this:

```php
<?php
if ($_POST['submitted']) {

    $first_name = ($_POST['first_name']);

    $last_name = ($_POST['last_name']);

    $email = ($_POST['email']);

    $msg = ($_POST['message']);
```

CODE 2.5: forms4.php4

| Set up variables for use in the mail function |
| Assemble the e-mail body text in a variable |
| Remove once the text looks right onscreen |

```php
$destination_email="charles@bbd.com";

$email_subject="My PHP form info";

$email_body = "$first_name\n$last_name\n$msg\n$email";

echo $email_body;
```

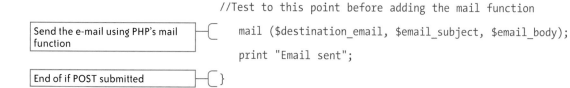

```
                                             //Test to this point before adding the mail function
```

Send the e-mail using PHP's mail function

```
                                                 mail ($destination_email, $email_subject, $email_body);

                                                 print "Email sent";
```

End of if POST submitted

```
                                             }
```

```
?>
```

Figure 2.5 shows the result.

FIGURE 2.5 A simple message confirms that our e-mail was sent to the mail server —although PHP cannot verify that your e-mail server actually sent the e-mail.

E-mail headers can be used by hackers to send spam (AKA e-mail injection attacks). To help protect yourself from such attacks, read the sidebar "Preventing E-mail Injection Attacks"

You can comment out the e-mail sending code at this point, as it gets tedious receiving an e-mail every time you submit the form. We'll uncomment the code later when the form is ready for final testing.

In this example, we create three new variables and populate them with information before using them as arguments in the `mail` function.

When the form is submitted, if you set `$destination_email` to your own e-mail address, you will start receiving data from the form at the site—a simple capability that opens interesting worlds of communication and site monitoring.

Again, remember that the data you get from this form is not validated and is potentially garbage or dangerous—security comes first.

Now that you have experienced the undeniable thrill of receiving an e-mail from a PHP script you wrote yourself, let's continue on our quest to obtain useful and untainted data. The first step toward getting this kind of data from the visitor is to make completing the form as easy as possible.

> ### Preventing E-mail Injection Attacks
>
> Using PHP, it's easy to send e-mail to users who submit their e-mail addresses via a form on your site. However, if you do not take steps to protect your site, you are opening yourself up to e-mail injection attacks, where a spammer adds long lists of e-mail addresses and messages to your form, even in fields that receive information other than e-mail addresses, and thereby causes your e-mail servers to send lots of spam with your server name as the source—a great way to have your ISP cut off your service! Here are a couple of URLs that describe how these attacks work and how to protect yourself from them:
>
> *   http://www.bl0g.co.uk/index.php?dt=060214
>
> *   http://www.nyphp.org/phundamentals/email_header_injection.php
>
> The basic validation techniques shown in this chapter go a long way toward protecting you from such attacks.
>
> One other important bit of advice: If you set e-mail headers—so that your e-mail shows a From: address, for example—don't use user-provided information in the headers unless you sanitize that data first, as this is a classic method for piggy-backing large amounts of e-mail to the e-mail server.

Creating Sticky Stay-Filled Forms

Have you ever filled out a long form and submitted it and then been told that you made a mistake and been presented with the whole blank form to fill out again? Some users will give up immediately when this happens, and this is definitely not a way to endear your site to users..

In a user-friendly site, if the form is re-presented, it is filled out exactly as it was submitted, so the user can quickly correct errors. Forms that use this approach are said to be *sticky*. Stickiness is not the normal behavior of a form, so let's see how to make our forms sticky.

When a page loads, fields are either blank or display default data that is defined in each element's value attribute. Anything we enter is replaced by one of these states each time the page loads. If we want the user-entered data to persist from page load to page load (between submissions of the form), we must make it do that by adding the form data variables to the markup of the form. If those variables have values after the form is first submitted, they will be displayed in the form fields.

Here's the process. You may already know that if we supply the optional value attribute for a text field, as shown here, then that attribute's value is displayed in the form field.

```
<input type="text" name="email" value="Enter your email">
```

Figure 2.6 shows the results.

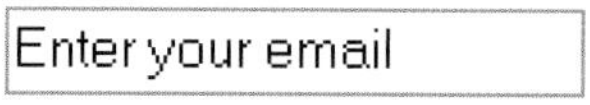

FIGURE 2.6 Field text generated by the value attribute.

```
Enter your email
```

So we will replace (or add) each element's value attribute with the corresponding PHP variable. We switch from XHTML to PHP just to write the single variable, and then we revert to XHTML:

```
<input type="text" name="email" value="<?php echo $email ?>">
```

Now the value of the variable (the data submitted by the user) is displayed in the field when the pages reload, and our field is sticky.

Let's use this technique to modify our form so that any text the visitor enters remains in the fields, even if the page is reloaded by the user or is redisplayed to the visitor because of validation errors (**Figure 2.7**).

```
<form action="<?php $_SERVER['PHP_SELF'] ?>" method="POST">
        <h3>Send me a message!</h3>
    <label for="first_name">First Name*</label><br />
        <input name="first_name" type="text" size="20"
id="first_name" value="<?php echo $first_name ?>" /><br />
        <label for="last_name">Last Name*</label><br />
        <input name="last_name" type="text" size="20" id="last_
name" value="<?php echo $last_name ?>" /><br />
        <label for="email">Email*</label><br />
        <input name= "email" type="text" size="20" id="email"
value="<?php echo $email ?>" /><br />
        <label for="message">Enter your comments or questions.</
label><br />
        <textarea name="message" rows="3" cols="20"
id="message"><?php echo $msg ?></textarea><br />
        <p>Your information will not be sold or shared with
others.</p>
```

The Value of Value

It can be confusing, after learning that each attribute has a name and value, to discover that there is also an attribute named value. Like all attributes, the value attribute has a value, which is the text string that appears in the field. As if this stuff isn't difficult enough...

CODE 2.6: forms5.php4

```
<input type="hidden" name="submitted" value="1" />
    <input type="submit" value="Go" />
</form>
```

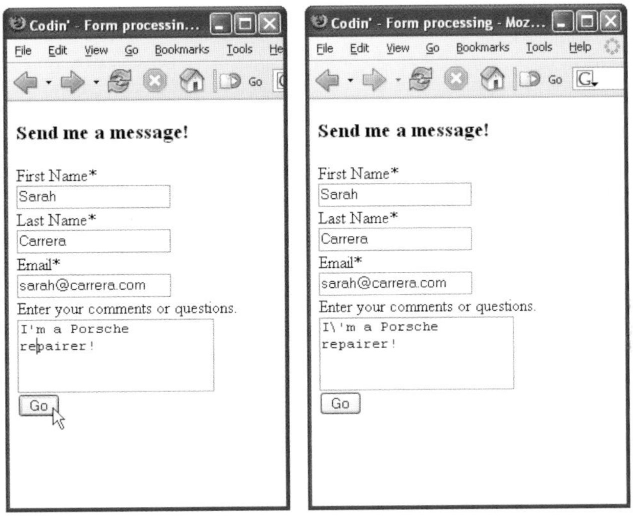

FIGURE 2.7 Now the form retains the data entered in it after it is submitted. Note that because Magic Quotes (see Chapter 1) escapes the $_POST data, a slash appears in front of the single quotation mark.

With the PHP tags in the form code, when the form data variables are loaded from the $_POST array after the form is submitted, the form's input values are set to the variables' values, and our form is now sticky.

However, we also see the work of Magic Quotes. The form data displayed in the right screen in Figure 2.7 has been through the $_POST array, and so Magic Quotes has escaped the single quotation mark in the comment field.

Combating Magic Quotes

In Chapter 1, we briefly discussed Magic Quotes, a feature that "automagically" adds \ backslashes in front of ' and " characters in the form's $_POST, $_GET, and $_COOKIES data. We'll now look at this feature in more detail. **Figure 2.8,** which we first saw in Chapter 1, shows text that has had Magic Quotes applied to it.

Magic Quotes was originally added to PHP to help prevent code from being entered into forms and spoofed cookies—for example, to prevent SQL injections on poorly protected forms, where malicious database code is submitted through them. Hackers know that, on many sites, the form information will be passed unchecked to

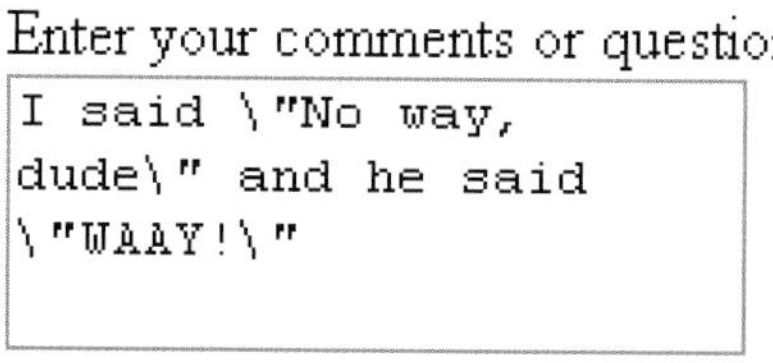

FIGURE 2.8 Magic Quotes adds escaping slashes in front of quotation marks (double and single) in form and cookie data.

For a primer on SQL injection attacks and how to avoid them, read Chris Shiflett at http://shiflett.org/articles/security-corner-apr2004. He also has a good Webcast about assessing code for vulnerabilities: see http://brainbulb.com/php-security-audit-howto.mov.

The two steps here—first putting the POST data into variables and then stripping slashes—can be done in one step, but the line of code is more complex:

```
$first_name = stripslashes
(@$_POST['first_name']);
```

—and so on for each variable

The examples that follow show the process as two steps because we can then check them against get_magic_quotes_gpc(). However, you can use whichever method you prefer.

CODE 2.7: forms5_combat_magic_quotes.php4

the query string that adds the data to the database for storage; if they (not you) are lucky, their code may modify the database query enough to return passwords or credit card information.

Enter your comments or questions.

```
I said \"No way,
dude\" and he said
\"WAAY!\"
```

Although escaping slashes added by Magic Quotes can help cause such code to fail, a competent programmer who is on top of security issues will find it inconvenient to have to keep track of which strings have had Magic Quotes run on them and to have to run `strips-lashes()` functions on such strings every time they are displayed onscreen. Also, if you accidentally run `stripslashes()` on text that you think has had Magic Quotes applied to it but hasn't, you will strip out any slashes that might actually be part of the string.

Because in this chapter we are only e-mailing the data we collect from the form, we don't need to escape the problem characters such as " and '. However, these characters do need to be escaped if we are going to put text in our database; we will discuss how to do this in Chapter 3.

So because we *are* going to validate the data to help protect against evil code injection, we want to remove the effects of automated Magic Quotes by using the `stripslashes()` function; then later we can use the `addslashes()` and `stripslashes()` functions to escape and unescape strings respectively, as needed.

All you need to do to combat Magic Quotes is to run the `strips-lashes()` function on each piece of data after you have moved it into variables, like this:

```
if ($_POST['submitted']) {
  $first_name = $_POST['first_name'];
    $last_name = $_POST['last_name'];
    $email = $_POST['email'];
    $msg = $_POST['message'];
```

If Magic Quotes is on, remove Magic Quotes effect
No argument needed—returns 1 if Magic Quotes is on; else 0

For testing only

```
if ( get_magic_quotes_gpc() ) {

   //Print "magic quotes is on";

   $first_name = stripslashes($first_name);

   $last_name = stripslashes($last_name);

   $email = stripslashes($email);

   $msg = stripslashes($msg);

}
```

Magic Quotes is on by default, but if you are running your own Web server, you can go into the php.ini file and turn Magic Quotes off. Then the code we are discussing here is unnecessary; it won't have any effect if Magic Quotes is turned off.

Here we use the `get_magic_quotes_gpc()` function to check whether Magic Quotes is on and, if it is, run the `stripslashes()` function on each variable. This process just removes the slashes added by Magic Quotes and has no other effect on the data. If the server has Magic Quotes turned off, the data is left unchanged.

Validating Your Forms

We can now redisplay the filled form without any Magic Quote–affected data. The next step in the process is to validate the data.

Although validation significantly reduces the chances that someone will hack your site, it is highly recommended that you get professional advice if your site is going to accept and store sensitive information such as credit card numbers or medical information.

To see the options available in action, in the following sections we'll validate this form in three increasingly precise ways. First, we'll look for *any* data in the fields; second, we'll test for the presence or absence of certain characters in the fields; and finally, we will use regular expressions, which let us look for patterns in the data and so give us a means to ensure, where needed, that the data is entered in formats that our code can process, and that our code repels most code attacks.

Some of this chapter, particularly the part on writing regular expressions, can be daunting to the beginner, but remember that the code is available for download from the Codin' Web site, and you don't have to understand how it works to use it, so don't be put off. You can skim the parts that seem difficult and simply use the code shown here in your forms.

Checking for Empty Fields

Let's begin by testing the First Name field only. We will simply determine whether the field is empty and prompt the user to fill it if it is (**Figure 2.9**).

CODE 2.8: forms6.php4

| Initialize variable | `$error_msg=0;` |

| Test for empty text string | `if ($first_name=="") {` |

```
        $error_msg="Please enter your first name";

    }
```

| Display error only if error variable is not 0 | `if ($error_msg) {` |

```
        echo ($error_msg);

    }
```

FIGURE 2.9 If the field is empty, the error message is displayed; otherwise, nothing is displayed.

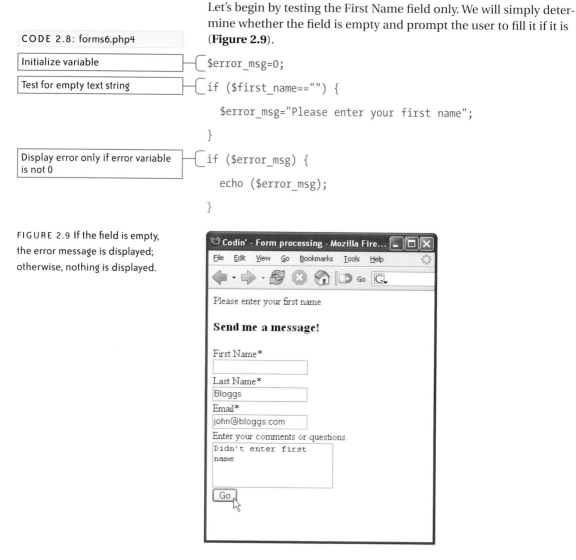

In a Boolean TRUE/FALSE test like the one we just added, anything other than 0, FALSE, NULL, or an empty text string evaluates to TRUE, so our error message text string replaces the initial value of 0, which causes the test to evaluate to TRUE and the error message to be displayed.

Validating Multiple Fields

Managing error messages becomes more complex when we test multiple fields. If we put every error message in its own variable, we then have to test each one separately to see if it contains an error, requiring tedious code writing and creating a lot of code in a large form. Also, writing responses to the errors as we encounter them is going to cause the error messages to appear *before* our page layout, rather than *on* the page at a location of our choosing. So we now are going to set up a method for accumulating the error messages as we test the fields and then writing these messages on the page directly above the first form field after we have them all.

Building an Error Message Array

We'll start by accumulating the error messages in an array (**Figure 2.10**).

CODE 2.9: forms7.php4

Intialize array	`$error_msg=array();`
Test for empty text string	`if ($first_name=="") {`
Add to the array	`$error_msg[] ="Please enter your first name";`
	`}`
Test for empty text string	`if ($last_name=="") {`
Add to the array	`$error_msg[] ="Please enter your last name";`
	`}`
Test for empty text string	`if ($email=="") {`
Add to the array	`$error_msg[] ="Please enter your email";`
	`}`
	`if ($msg=="") {`
Test for empty text string	`$error_msg[]="Don't forget to write your message!"; /`
Add to the array	`}`
Temporary code to write out the error messages	`foreach ($error_msg as $err) {`
	`  echo ("$err  ");`
	`}`

FIGURE 2.10 The error messages are written from the array, before the start of the XHTML page.

> **Codin' - Form processing - Mozilla Firefox**
>
> File Edit View Go Bookmarks Tools Help
>
> Please enter your first name
> Please enter your last name
> Please enter your email
> Don't forget to write your message!
>
> **Send me a message!**
>
> First Name*
>
> Last Name*
>
> Email*
>
> Enter your comments or questions.
>
> Go

Note the construction $error_msg[]= *something*. This code causes *something* to be added as the next item in the array—so each error message becomes an array item that we can output later.

Try submitting the form with various combinations of blank and filled fields, to see the error checking in action.

Creating an XHTML List of the Error Messages

Once we can be sure we are gathering the error messages correctly, we can write them as part of the XHTML page, right above the form (**Figure 2.11**).

CODE 2.10: forms8.php4

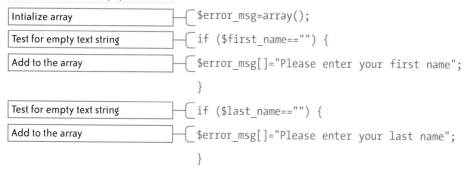

Intialize array
```
$error_msg=array();
```

Test for empty text string
```
if ($first_name=="") {
```

Add to the array
```
$error_msg[]="Please enter your first name";
}
```

Test for empty text string
```
if ($last_name=="") {
```

Add to the array
```
$error_msg[]="Please enter your last name";
}
```

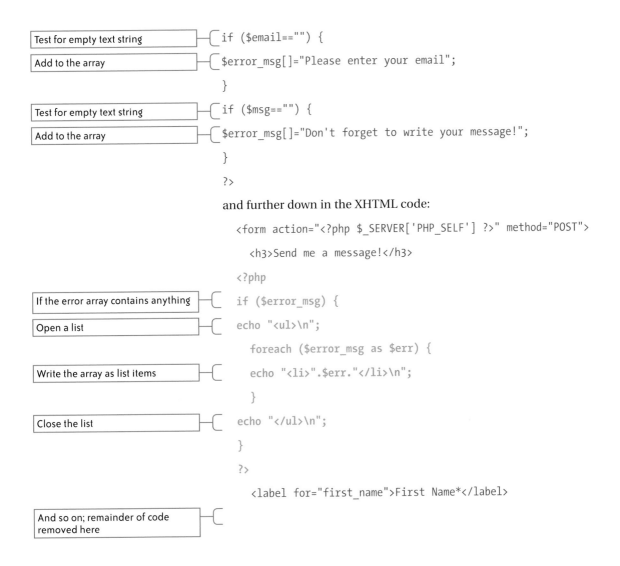

Test for empty text string	`if ($email=="") {`
Add to the array	`$error_msg[]="Please enter your email";`
	`}`
Test for empty text string	`if ($msg=="") {`
Add to the array	`$error_msg[]="Don't forget to write your message!";`
	`}`
	`?>`

and further down in the XHTML code:

```
<form action="<?php $_SERVER['PHP_SELF'] ?>" method="POST">
    <h3>Send me a message!</h3>
<?php
```

If the error array contains anything	`if ($error_msg) {`
Open a list	`echo "<ul>\n";`
	`    foreach ($error_msg as $err) {`
Write the array as list items	`    echo "<li>".$err."</li>\n";`
	`    }`
Close the list	`echo "</ul>\n";`
	`}`
	`?>`
	`    <label for="first_name">First Name*</label>`
And so on; remainder of code removed here	

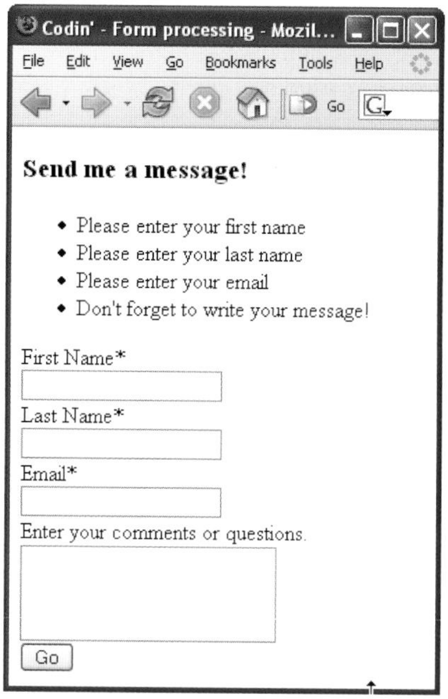

FIGURE 2.11 By accumulating the error messages in an array and writing them out later, we can add them at a location of our own choosing within the XHTML.

This is the XHTML output of the list created by the preceding highlighted code, assuming that we enter nothing in the form.

```
<ul>

<li>Please enter your first name</li>

<li>Please enter your last name</li>

<li>Please enter your email</li>

<li>Don't forget to write your message!</li>

</ul>
```

Here's how this code works. If we have a list of error messages to display, we open the list with `<ul>`. We also add \n after each `ul` and `li` as formatting (line breaks) for the source code so we don't see the list as one long line of code when we view it. XHTML ignores \n, by the way; it affects only the formatting of the code itself. Then for each item in the array, we open a list item `<li>`, write the next error message, and close the list item. After the loop has finished, we close the list. This is a nice little example of PHP's ability to output XHTML dynamically: in this case, a number of list items based on the number of error messages in the array.

Assuming that this is all the validation we want to do, once the user has entered information that does not generate errors, we can

In the downloadable example, the user is redirected to a simple page, called form_confirm.php4, after successfully filling out the form. The total content of this page is one line of text that says "Thanks for submitting the form," so we won't waste space showing its code here.

CODE 2.11: Part of forms9.php4

e-mail the form information and then redirect the browser to a different page, where we can tell the user that the form was successfully filled and, in the real world, provide whatever the user signed up for (**Figure 2.12**).

Here's the PHP code so far, with one additional line to redirect the browser.

```php
<?php
if (@$_POST['submitted']) {
   $first_name = @$_POST['first_name'];
      $last_name = @$_POST['last_name'];
      $email = @$_POST['email'];
      $msg = @$_POST['message'];
   if (get_magic_quotes_gpc() ) {
      $first_name = stripslashes($first_name);
      $last_name = stripslashes($last_name);
      $email = stripslashes($email);
      $msg = stripslashes($msg);
   }
   $error_msg=array();
if ($first_name=="") {
$error_msg[]="Please enter your first name";
}
if ($last_name=="") {
$error_msg[]="Please enter your last name";
}
if ($email=="") {
$error_msg[]="Please enter your email";
}
if ($msg=="") {
$error_msg[]="Don't forget to write your message!";
}
```

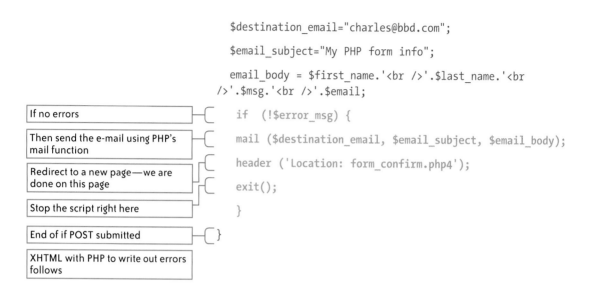

```
$destination_email="charles@bbd.com";

$email_subject="My PHP form info";

email_body = $first_name.'<br />'.$last_name.'<br
/>'.$msg.'<br />'.$email;

if  (!$error_msg) {

mail ($destination_email, $email_subject, $email_body);

header ('Location: form_confirm.php4');

exit();

}
```

If no errors	
Then send the e-mail using PHP's mail function	
Redirect to a new page—we are done on this page	
Stop the script right here	
End of if POST submitted	`}`
XHTML with PHP to write out errors follows	

FIGURE 2.12 After being submitted blank the first time (hence the displayed error messages), the form is now correctly filled. When this correctly filled form is submitted, the form passes validation, the form data is sent by e-mail, and the browser loads a new page, form_confirm.php4.

You must send any header *information to the browser before anything —even a white space—is output to the browser, or PHP will generate an error message. You can read more about this issue in Chapter 6.*

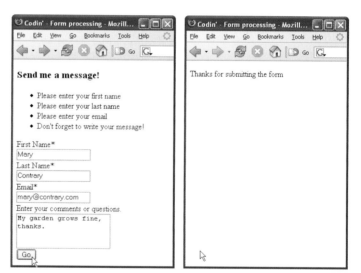

Note the use of the header function to forward the browser to a new page once the form passes validation—it might be to a thank-you page or a members' area.

Checking for Specific Characters

Let's improve on the "no blank fields" rule of this form and look for specific required characters in the fields. We can look for a specific character using the `strrpos` string function. This function enables us to specify a string and a character (and a start offset from the beginning of the string if we need it) and test whether the character appears in the string. This is the function's format:

```
strrpos (string, character, offset)
```

The function returns 0 if the character is not in the string; it returns the character's numeric location in the string if it is. We will use this function to check whether the e-mail address contains an @ symbol, like this:

```
if (!strrpos($email,"@"))
```

Note that we need double parentheses because the `strrpos` function uses the inner ones to enclose its arguments, and the `if` statement uses the outer ones to enclose the function—the item being tested. Also, because we want to check whether the @ symbol is *not* present, we use the "not" exclamation point at the start of the `if` statement—we are testing for the absence of the @ symbol, rather than its presence. Here is this function in our script, replacing the previous `if` statement:

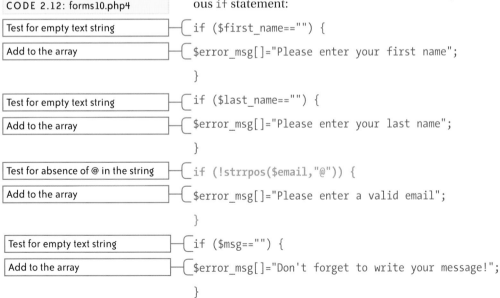

CODE 2.12: forms10.php4

Test for empty text string
```
if ($first_name=="") {
```
Add to the array
```
$error_msg[]="Please enter your first name";
```
```
}
```

Test for empty text string
```
if ($last_name=="") {
```
Add to the array
```
$error_msg[]="Please enter your last name";
```
```
}
```

Test for absence of @ in the string
```
if (!strrpos($email,"@")) {
```
Add to the array
```
$error_msg[]="Please enter a valid email";
```
```
}
```

Test for empty text string
```
if ($msg=="") {
```
Add to the array
```
$error_msg[]="Don't forget to write your message!";
```
```
}
```

Figure 2.13 shows the results.

FIGURE 2.13 Now, the e-mail field
no longer accepts just any string of
text; it must contain the @ symbol.

Here's another example of this kind of testing: If we want to check
that a zip code entry contains at least five characters, we can use the
`srtlen` string length function, which takes just one argument—the
string to be counted—and returns the numeric character count of
the string.

It's too short to be a ZIP code! ──┤ ─⌐ `if (strlen($zip)<5) { etc...`

Validating with Regular Expressions

The best way to validate forms—which goes beyond looking for
characters, counting strings, and performing other string testing
with the PHP string functions—is to use regular expressions. With
regular expressions, we can be much more specific about what it
takes to validate the form. We can use a regular expression (or regex)
to look for patterns of characters in the data.

The functions `ereg` and `eregi` compare a string with a pattern
defined by a regular expression. (Unlike `ereg`, `eregi` does not differentiate between uppercase and lowercase characters.) These functions have this format:

TRUE if string matches pattern ──┤ ─⌐ `eregi` *(pattern, string)*

The simplest way to write a regular expression is to use one of the character classes, such as [[:alpha:]], which on its own checks for any letter of the alphabet, or [[:digit:]], which checks for the presence of any number.

Using Some Simple Regular Expressions

Let's digress from our form for a moment to check out some simple regular expressions.

If we have a form that requires a phone number, we can check for the presence of at least one number in the phone number field.

```
$phoneString= "555-1234";

if (eregi('[[:digit:]]', $phoneString)) {

    echo ("There is a digit in this string.");

}
```

Prints "There is a digit in this string."

We can also check that the entire string consists of numbers, by using the ^ (start of the string) and $ (end of the string) regex metacharacters (for more information, see the sidebar "Metacharacters in Regular Expressions").

Metacharacters in Regular Expressions

Certain characters, known as metacharacters, are used as code symbols in regular expressions. The metacharacters are as follows:

[	Opening square bracket	.	Period (or dot)
\	Backslash	|	Vertical bar (or pipe symbol)
^	Caret	?	Question mark
$	Dollar sign	*	Asterisk (or star)

+	Plus sign
(	Opening parenthesis
)	Closing parenthesis

If we want to use any of these characters within our regular expression as a character that we want to test for, we must escape the character—in the case of the dollar sign, like this: \$.

We can also use the + metacharacter, which indicates one or more occurrence. Combining these elements, we can create the following validation script. Note that in this example, the dash has been removed from the phone number.

```
$phoneString= "5551234";

if (eregi('^[[:digit:]]+$', $phoneString)) {

    echo ("Entire string is digits.");

}
```

| Prints "Entire string is digits." |

This expression means "From the start ^ to the end $ of the string, there can be any number + of digits (and therefore no letters or symbols)."

By using the ! negation symbol on the `if` expression, we can make this same code reject anything that is not digits. Now we put the dash back into the phone number.

```
$phoneString= "555-1234";

if (!eregi('^[[:digit:]]+$', $phoneString)) {

    echo ("Non-digits present.");

}
```

| Prints "Non-digits present." |

In the real world, it would make sense to allow the user to enter spaces or dashes between the groups of numbers that make up the phone number. We can accomplish this by using the | (or) metacharacter, better known as the pipe symbol (press Shift-\). The character that follows each pipe symbol can appear in our string—in this case, we're including a space and a dash.

```
$phoneString= "415 555-1234";

if (eregi('^([[:digit:]]| |-)+$', $phoneString)) {

    echo ("OK - only numbers, spaces and dashes present<br />");

}
```

| Prints "OK - only numbers, spaces and dashes present
" |

You can download this example, with the four regexes (I think that's a word), from the Codin' Web site.

Validating an E-mail Address Pattern

A more complicated pattern to validate is that of an e-mail address, where the pattern to be checked may be some combination of letters, numbers, underscores, and dashes; followed by @; followed by more letters, numbers, underscores, and dashes; then a period; and then two to four letters. For instance, **john_smith23@abc.com** matches this description, but **& xyz ! @ .coomm** does not.

Here is a regular expression to validate the format of an e-mail address:

```
eregi("^([[:alnum:]]|_|\.|-)+@([[:alnum:]]|\.|-)+(\.)([a-z]{2,4})$", $email)
```

This code may look daunting, but if you use the + signs to divide it into three pieces, you will see that no piece is much more complex than the ones we have already discussed.

The highlighted parts of this code are elements we haven't seen yet. Note that each of the three occurrences of . (period) has a backslash in front of it to escape it. This coding ensures that the character will be literally interpreted as a period and prevents it being seen in its functional role in a regular expression, where it means "one character." Note also that the last of the three pieces (highlighted) uses the quantity curly brackets—{2-4}—ensuring that only two to four characters can follow the final period. We associate the [a-z] class (lowercase letters only) with this quantifier by enclosing them in plain brackets.

For our form, we need a regex to validate the text fields as well as the e-mail field. Look at this expression:

```
eregi ("^([[:alnum:]]|-|\.| |')+$", $testString)
```

This function returns TRUE if the string contains any combination of letters, numbers, dashes, periods, spaces, and single quotation marks.

Using include to Add the Regular Expressions

Now let's create some functions based on these regular expressions. We'll put them in a separate PHP script and use the include function to add them to our form script. Then we can not only use the functions as if they were actually in the form script, but we can also share them with other form pages. Here are four functions, each returning 1 or 0 (TRUE or FALSE), based on the testing of a passed string against a regular expression.

Simple form validation functions:

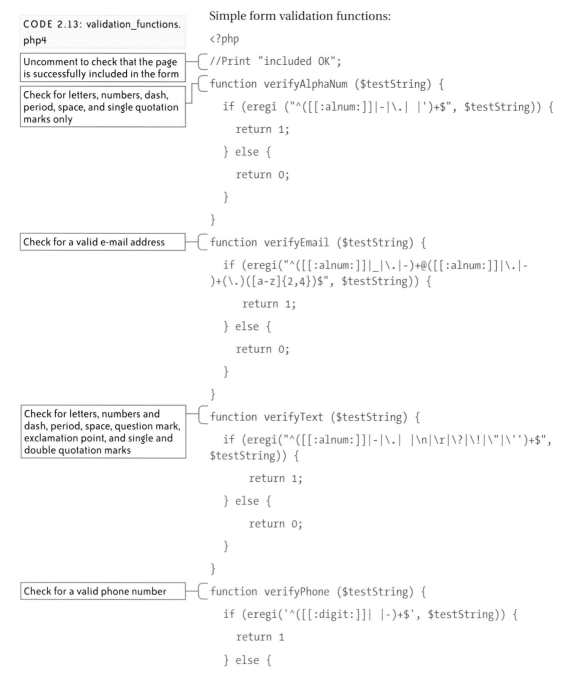

CODE 2.13: validation_functions. php4

Uncomment to check that the page is successfully included in the form

Check for letters, numbers, dash, period, space, and single quotation marks only

Check for a valid e-mail address

Check for letters, numbers and dash, period, space, question mark, exclamation point, and single and double quotation marks

Check for a valid phone number

```php
<?php
//Print "included OK";
function verifyAlphaNum ($testString) {
    if (eregi ("^([[:alnum:]]|-|\.| |')+$", $testString)) {
        return 1;
    } else {
        return 0;
    }
}
function verifyEmail ($testString) {
    if (eregi("^([[:alnum:]]|_|\.|-)+@([[:alnum:]]|\.|-
)+(\.)([a-z]{2,4})$", $testString)) {
        return 1;
    } else {
        return 0;
    }
}
function verifyText ($testString) {
    if (eregi("^([[:alnum:]]|-|\.| |\n|\r|\?|\!|\"|\'')+$",
$testString)) {
        return 1;
    } else {
        return 0;
    }
}
function verifyPhone ($testString) {
    if (eregi('^([[:digit:]]| |-)+$', $testString)) {
        return 1
    } else {
```

```
        return 0;

    }

}

?>
```

Save this page as **form_validation.php4** in the same folder as the form. (In practice, you might have a special folder for included functions.)

Now use the include function to include the validation script in the form script. Right at the start of the form file add the following:

```
<?php

include ("validation_functions.php4");

if (@$_POST['submitted']) {

    $first_name = @$_POST['first_name'];

    $last_name = @$_POST['last_name'];

    $email = @$_POST['email'];

    $msg = @$_POST['message'];
```

CODE 2.14: forms11.php4

Now we modify our four tests on the field data to look like this:

Test for valid first name

```
$valid = verifyAlphaNum ($first_name);

if (!$valid){

$error_msg[]="First Name must be letters and numbers, spaces,
dashes and ' only.";

}
```

Test for valid last name

```
$valid = verifyAlphaNum ($last_name);

if (!$valid){

$error_msg[]="Last Name must be letters and numbers, spaces,
dashes and ' only.";

}
```

Test for valid e-mail address

```
$valid = verifyEmail ($email);

if (!$valid){

$error_msg[]="Email must be a valid format (e.g. john@yahoo.
com).";

}
```

Test for valid message text

```
$valid = verifyText ($msg);

if (!$valid){

$error_msg[]="Message can only contain letters, numbers and
basic punctuation \" ' - ? ! ";

}
```

Figure 2.14 shows the form with invalid data in each field; **Figure 2.15** shows the form correctly filled in.

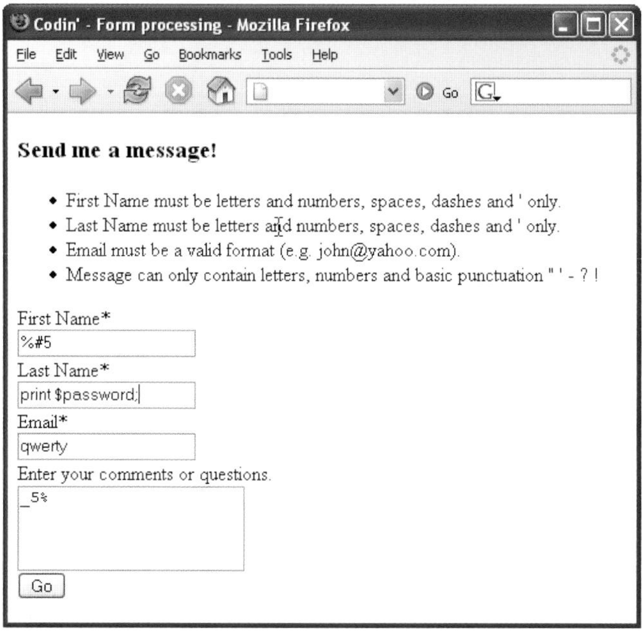

FIGURE 2.14 Form with invalid data in each field.

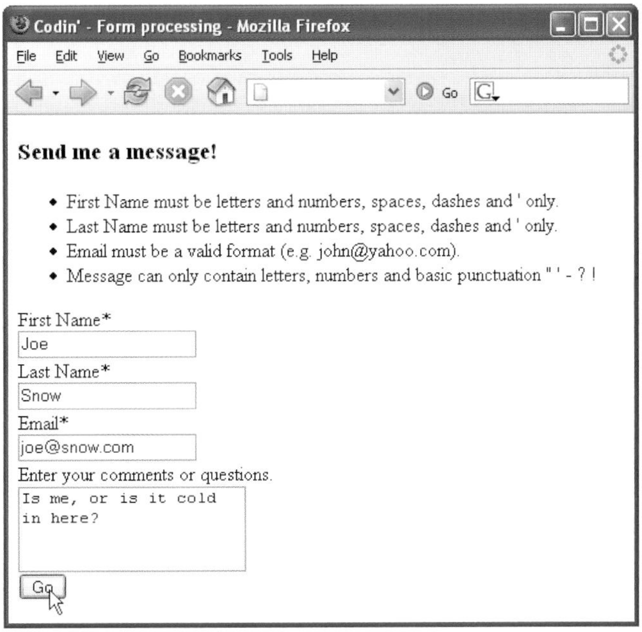

FIGURE 2.15 Form with valid data in each field. When this data is submitted, the form will validate successfully..

For each of the four pieces of data, if the test result returned from the included functions is 0, FALSE, then an error message is added to the error array.

Now we have a good way to test the form. We help keep the user from making some basic mistakes, we reject the worst garbage, and we prevent malicious use of code symbols such as (,), {, and }.

Regular expressions can be a pain to write (the coding in this section has reminded me), but there are lots of them already written and available if you search around, so if you can just understand enough to make minor modifications to achieve whatever validation you specifically need, you can easily harness the power of regular expressions to take control of the data that enters the system.

Storing Form Data in Flat Files

With our form now delivering validated data, its work is done, so the next question is what to do with that data? Let's now see how to store the data we collect from our forms in text data files, known in programming parlance as flat files.

Programmers use the term *flat file* to differentiate data files used by the code from database files. The files are flat because they typically store data in two dimensions: rows and columns.

Because most PHP-based sites use a database to store data, flat files are primarily used as a means of importing and exporting data between sources such as Microsoft Excel spreadsheets and the database. However, if you develop a Web site where the only dynamic element is a form such as the one we created earlier in the chapter, you may decide that the site doesn't require a database. Perhaps all you want to do is record the form data somewhere so you have a record of it. In that case, a simple flat file may be all the storage you need.

We are now going to learn the techniques we need to record the form data (using the form we created) in a flat file on the server. We will accumulate all the data from form submissions in this one file, which we can later read back into PHP or open in programs such as Microsoft Word or Excel.

Recording all the form data in a log file like this is useful even if you use a database to manage the data. Database information can change over time—users update their records, for example—and a log file lets you preserve the original data of every form submission.

In the remainder of the chapter, we'll examine the process of writing data in a file and look at a working example.

Working with Flat Files

The file we will create for recording the form data will be tab-delimited; the values from the form variables will be stored with tabs between them like this:

Jim*TAB*Dalton*TAB*jim@xyz.com*TAB*More code, please!*LINE BREAK*

Each time the form is successfully submitted, we will create a new line of text in the file, with each piece of data separated from the next by a tab. At the end of each record, we will insert a new-line entity (**Figure 2.16**).

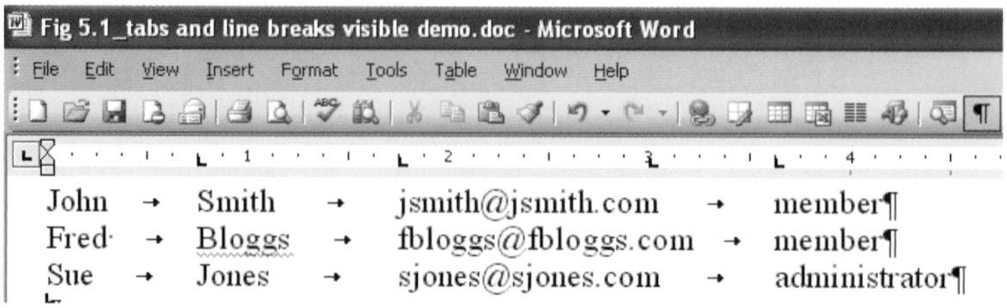

FIGURE 2.16 Records displayed in Word with tabs and line breaks visible. Each value of the record is separated with a tab, and each record ends with a new line. Note that the Hidden Characters ¶ option is selected.

I usually use tabs rather than commas as delimiters in flat files, because tabs are widely used for export from Excel and other programs that handle data, and also because commas often appear within the data and can incorrectly end a string.

There is no explicit command to create a file with PHP; you simply attempt to open a file of a given name. If the file exists, PHP opens it, and if the file doesn't exist, PHP will first create it and then open it.

To open a file (or create and open it), you use the fopen() function, whose format is as follows:

```
fopen (filename, access type)
```

Here's an example:

```
$filePointer = fopen ("data/my_data.txt", "a+");
```

In this simple example, the file is in the same folder as the page, within the Web site folders. This is not a very secure place to store it, as anyone who can guess the URL can access it. We will address this issue later in this chapter.

All subsequent operations on the file are referenced through the $myPointer variable. For example, to close the file, we use the following:

```
fclose($filePointer);
```

If the file open operation fails, then $filePointer will be set to 0.

Choosing the Read/Write Mode

The access type of the file, which determines what we can do with the file once it is open, can be one of six options, as shown in **Table 2.2**.

TABLE 2.2 File Access Modes

ACCESS MODE	READ/WRITE	FILE POINTER POSITION (NEW DATA IS WRITTEN HERE)	CREATE FILE IF IT DOESN'T EXIST?
r	Read only	Start	No
r+	Read/write	Start	No
w	Write only	Start	Yes
w+	Read/write	Start	Yes
a	Write only	End	Yes
a+	Read/write	End	Yes

Generally, I use r if I just want to read from the beginning of the file, and a+ if I want to write, because I usually add more data after whatever is already there. Usually I don't read and write in the same operation and close the file between those steps. Note that a file is automatically closed at the end of a script, but I always like to close a file explicitly as soon I am done with it. That's just good practice—files are more subject to corruption when they are open.

Storing Flat Files above the Root Folder

The flat file that we are about to create has to live somewhere on the Web server. Because this file will ultimately contain user data submitted from a form, security concerns dictate that we don't want it in the same folders as our Web pages because the file could then be viewed by simply typing its URL. Because only files within the root folder are part of the Web site, the best place for this file is above the root folder of the site, where it can't be accessed over the Web (that is, it can't be displayed in a browser or downloaded through a URL using HTTP).

We first need to create a folder called files to store the flat file. We'll create this folder in the same folder that contains the wwwroot folder, which is the root folder of the Web site. The root contains all the folders and files that make up the Web site. Our new files folder is at the same level as the root folder and not within the root folder.

The root folder of my development site is four folder levels up from the folder where my script will reside, so to achieve an extra level of security, the relative path from my script to the `files` folder I just made is as follows:

`../../../../files/`

Each `../` means "Up one folder," so the preceding path means "Up four folders and into a folder called files." (This path will be different for each site, depending on the location of the script relative to the root folder.)

Unfortunately the `../` file reference may not work on servers running Windows. If the `../` syntax doesn't work for you, try the native Windows syntax, which is a little different: instead of using forward slashes to differentiate directories, use backslashes. This approach creates problems, however, because in PHP the backslash is the escape character. Therefore, for a similar file structure in Windows, this would be the code:

`$myFilePath ="..\\..\\..\\..\\files\\";`

Creating a Flat File

Our first step in creating and writing to the file is to define where we want it created and what we want to name it by constructing variables for the file path and the file name, like this:

Up four folder levels and into a folder called files

```
$myFilePath = "../../../../files/";
```

The file name

```
$myFileName = "form_data_file.txt";
```

Together, these two variables will provide a relative URL for the file.

Now we can open the file, automatically creating it first if it doesn't already exist, like this:

```
$myPointer = fopen($myfilePath.$myfileName, "a+");
```

The dot operator between the two variables combines them into:

```
"../../../../files/form_data_file.txt";
```

This is the relative URL of our file with respect to the script that we are writing.

Usually, you will find that your Web server is set up so you cannot create files below the root level folder (that is, within the folders of the site) for security reasons. However, you usually can write to the level above the root folder, which is not accessible over HTTP, and most ISPs give you access as the site owner to one level above the root. This approach helps ensure that malicious files cannot be written into folders within the structure of your Web site and later executed. You may need to contact your ISP's technical support staff, or the system administrator if you are on a corporate server, to determine the best location and appropriate permissions for flat files.

For Adobe Dreamweaver Users

Typically, when you set up a site in Dreamweaver, you set the root folder as the top level of the Remote View window and a corresponding root folder of the site on your local machine as your local view. To work with files above the root level, you must reset the top-level folders of *both* views one level higher. If you set only the Remote view one level higher, Dreamweaver will not automatically upload to the right location. In other words, the views must be balanced; if the Remote view is set to one level above wwwroot, then you must do the same for the Local view.

Writing to a File

Once the file is open and the $filePointer variable is created, we can use the fputs() function to write something in that file. The fputs() function's format is as follows:

```
fputs(filePointer, data)
```

If we have a variable with some data, such as

```
$data = "A test string of data!"
```

then we can write it in our opened file like this:

```
fputs($myPointer, $data)
```

Then we close it, like this:

```
fclose($myPointer);
```

The file will then contain the string "A test string of data!"

Creating a File: Code Example

To see the file creation process in action, we'll attempt to open, and thereby create, a file on disk.

CODE 2.15: write_to_a_flat_ file1.php4

The first step is to simply try to create the file and output a response to the screen if we can. We start by creating variables for the file path and file name.

The path to a folder above the root level of the server

Opens the file, or creates the file if it does not exist

```
$myFilePath = "../../../../files/";

$myFileName = "form_data_file.txt";

$myPointer = fopen($myFilePath.$myFileName, "a+");

if ($myPointer) {

  print ("File opened");

}

}
```

Outputs: File opened

A test on the $myPointer variable will return TRUE if the file was successfully created and opened. Use your FTP client to look in the files folder you created; if the path to the folder is correct, the newly created file form_data_file.txt will be in there. If you get an error message when you run the script, the file path likely is incorrect.

In the next step, we create some dummy data variables so we can test that we are successfully assembling all the data we want to write in the file before we attempt to write data from the form.

CODE 2.16: write_to_a_flat_file2.php

Create some dummy data variables

```php
$first_name = "Charles";

$last_name = "Wyke-Smith";

$email = "charles@bbd.com";

$msg = "PHP is sooooo very easy!";
```

Assemble all the form data and delimiters in a variable

Put tabs between record elements and a new line at the end

```php
$form_data = $first_name . "\t" . $last_name . "\t" . $email
. "\t" . $msg . "\n";
```

Open the file; a+ sets the file position indicator to end-of-file

```php
$myPointer = fopen($myFileName, "a+");
```

Append the data to the file

```php
fputs ($myPointer, $form_data);
```

Close the file

```php
fclose($myPointer);
```

In the four highlighted lines in the preceding code, we assemble the variables into a tab-delimited string with a line break at the end, and then we open the file, put the data in the file, and close the file.

Once you have this code working, try reloading the page a few times. Every time you reload the page, the script will run again, and a new line will be added at the end of the file.

After doing this four times myself, I downloaded the file (**Figure 2.17**).

FIGURE 2.17 The flat file displayed in Microsoft Word.

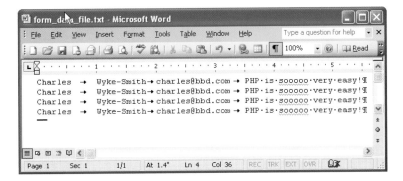

Although you can view the file in Notepad on the PC (Programs > Accessories > Notepad) or in TextEdit on the Mac, a better approach is to open it in Microsoft Word, as shown in Figure 2.17. In Word, you can turn on the Show Hidden characters feature in the toolbar (highlighted in the figure) to see the tabs, indicated as arrows, and the line breaks, indicated as ¶ (and, incidentally, the spaces, indicated as dots), so that you can confirm that the data is structured the way you intended.

Importing a Tab-Delimited File into Excel

Microsoft Excel makes it easy to import tab-delimited files. Simply open the file with Excel; you will need to select All Files to be able to see it in the Open window (**Figure 2.18**).

FIGURE 2.18 Select the All Files choice to see the .txt file in Excel's Open window.

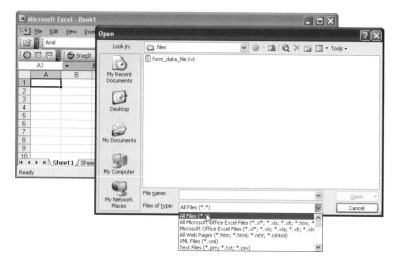

Excel will display the following screens. Note that Excel immediately recognizes that the file is a tab-delimited file. Notice the import options for the file formats in **Figures 2.19**, **2.20**, and **2.21**. For our example, we don't need to change anything—simply click Next each time.

FIGURE 2.19 Excel Import Wizard Step 1: Delimiters or spaces in the file?

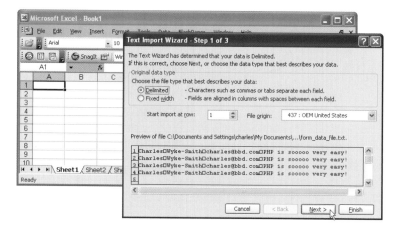

Click Next.

FIGURE 2.20 Excel Import Wizard
Step 2: Delimiter type?

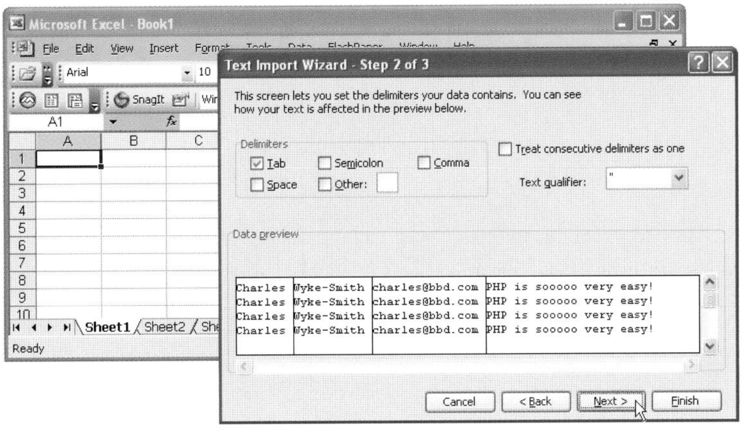

Click Next.

FIGURE 2.21 Excel Import Wizard
Step 3: Data format of columns?

*Not all files come in straightforward
formats, but you can use Excel's
powerful filtering capabilities
to open almost any kind of data
file that has been organized with
delimiters and then save it from
Excel as a tab-delimited file ready for
use in your program.*

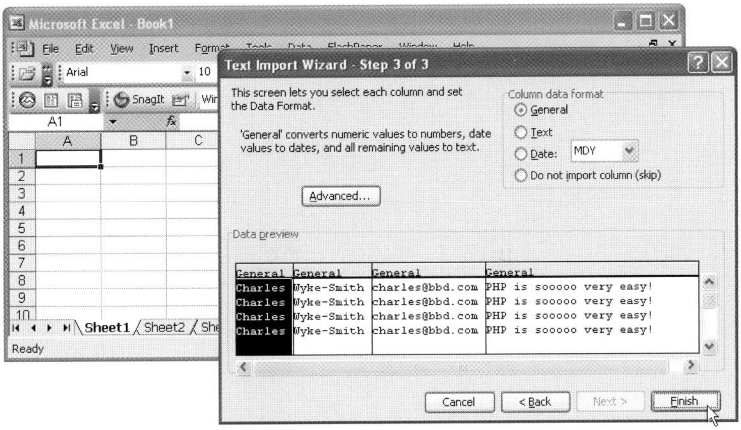

Click Finish, and the imported file is displayed in Excel (**Figure 2.22**).

FIGURE 2.22 Viewing the imported
file in Excel confirms that is correctly
formatted.

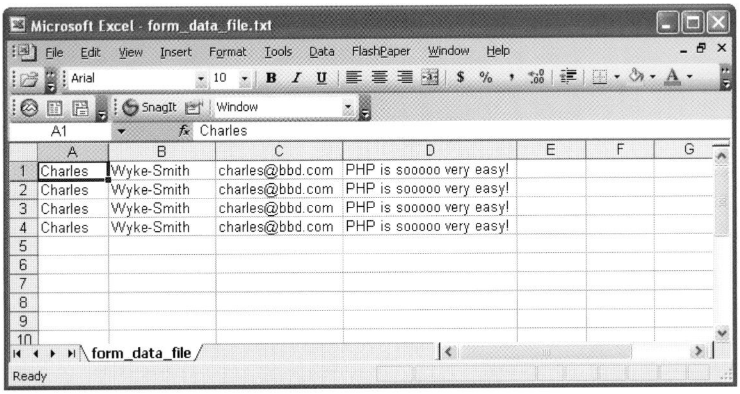

With our code successfully writing these temporary data variables to the file, as opening the file proves, we can now refine the code to write the real form data to the file.

Creating a Write-to-File Function

Now we can put this knowledge to work to record to a flat file the data from the form we created earlier in the chapter. We'll create a function from our file-writing code so we can pass the form data variables to it as parameters. All we need to do is change our variable names to function parameters, like this:

```
$first_name = "Charles";

$last_name = "Wyke-Smith";

$email = "charles@bbd.com";

$msg = "PHP is sooooo very easy!";

function writeToFile ($first_name, $last_name, $email, $msg) {
```

Create a variable for the file name — `$myFileName = "form_data_file.txt";`

Assemble all the form data and delimiters in a variable — `$form_data = $first_name. "\t" . $last_name . "\t" . $email . "\t" . $msg . "\n";`

Open the file for writing at the end of any existing data — `$myPointer = fopen($myFileName, "a+");`

Append the data to the file — `fputs ($myPointer, $form_data);`

Close the file — `fclose($myPointer);`

```
}
```

Now we'll save this function in its own file, which we'll name flat_files3.php4. To enable the form page to use this function, we need to include it in the form's script, just as we did with the validation functions, so we'll go back to our registration form and add the include clause at the top of the file:

```
<?php

require_once ("validation_functions.php4");

require_once ("write_to_a_flat_file4.php4");
```

And so on — `if (@$_POST['submitted']) {`

CODE 2.17: forms12_flat_file_
write.php4

If no error messages, then send the
e-mail using PHP's mail function

Write data to a flat file

Redirect to a new page—we are
done on this page

Stop the script right here

Further down in the script—after the validation functions, so we
know we are working with nice, clean data—we add the following:

```
if (!$error_msg) {

mail ($destination_email, $email_subject, $email_body);

writeToFile ($first_name, $last_name, $email, $msg);

    header ('Location: http://www.bbd.com');

    exit();

}
```

Now when the form is successfully filled out, three things happen:
the data is sent in an e-mail message, the data is written to a flat file,
and the user is redirected to another page. Even though we are not
using a database, we are now able to record the submitted data.

Figure 2.23 shows how our log file looks in Dreamweaver after three
users have signed up.

*The file created here exists only on the server, not in your source files, so
you have to download the file to view it. You can do this in Dreamweaver
by simply double-clicking the file in the Remote view. The file will instantly
download to the corresponding location in your Local view and open in
Dreamweaver.*

FIGURE 2.23 Dreamweaver's Code
view does not support tabbed
layouts, so the columns don't align.

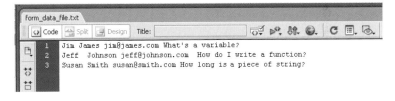

Figure 2.24 shows how the log file data looks when we import it
into Excel.

FIGURE 2.24 Data entered in
the form is read from the flat file
into Excel.

Reading a Flat File with PHP

So far, we have only opened the file our code has created with other applications, but let's now read the data from the file using PHP and write a report of the data in a table. The function we use is fgets() whose format is as follows:

$fgets(*filepointer, maxReadLength*)

The file will be read until the number of characters defined by maxReadLength is reached, a line break is encountered, or the end of the file is reached—whichever happens first.

If a line break stops the reading process, the next time fgets is called the read process will start from the beginning of the next line. This enables us to use a loop to call fgets repeatedly and so read and output the file element by element, line by line.

Reading a File Line by Line

The process of reading is similar to writing: we open the file, read each line from it, and close the file. In this first step, we use a while loop (highlighted in the following code) to simply write each line.

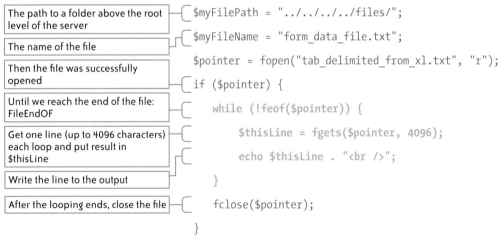

CODE 2.18 read_flat_file1.php4

The path to a folder above the root level of the server	`$myFilePath = "../../../../files/";`
The name of the file	`$myFileName = "form_data_file.txt";`
	`$pointer = fopen("tab_delimited_from_xl.txt", "r");`
Then the file was successfully opened	`if ($pointer) {`
Until we reach the end of the file: FileEndOF	`    while (!feof($pointer)) {`
Get one line (up to 4096 characters) each loop and put result in $thisLine	`        $thisLine = fgets($pointer, 4096);`
Write the line to the output	`        echo $thisLine . " ";`
	`    }`
After the looping ends, close the file	`    fclose($pointer);`
	`}`

Figure 2.25 shows the results.

FIGURE 2.25 As a first test, we simply read the file and output each line, with no formatting.

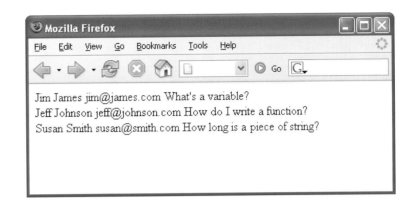

Jim James jim@james.com What's a variable?
Jeff Johnson jeff@johnson.com How do I write a function?
Susan Smith susan@smith.com How long is a piece of string?

Extracting Each Element of the Record

Now let's try accessing each value in each line. We will use the explode function to convert the string of text that makes up each record into an array of elements as we read the string from the file. The explode function breaks our string apart by allowing us to define the delimiter that is used to divide the string into the array elements—in our case, the tab. Then each element of the array can be written.

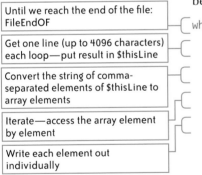

Until we reach the end of the file: FileEndOF

Get one line (up to 4096 characters) each loop—put result in $thisLine

Convert the string of comma-separated elements of $thisLine to array elements

Iterate—access the array element by element

Write each element out individually

```php
while (!feof($pointer)) {

    $thisLine = fgets($pointer, 4096);

    $lineArray = explode("\t", $thisLine);

    foreach($lineArray as $item) {

    echo $item."<br />";

    }

}
```

Figure 2.26 shows each element of the array written to its own line.

FIGURE 2.26 By converting each flat file from a string into an array of values, we can write each value on its own line in the browser.

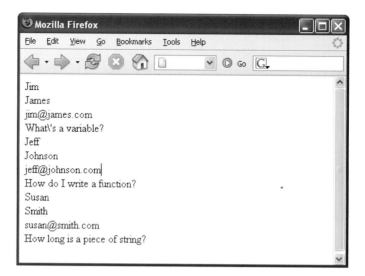

Displaying the File in a Table

To create a useful report from our delimited file, we need to organize it into neat columns. In XHTML, the right way to lay out rows and columns of data like this is with a table. The following code shows how to create the table.

CODE 2.19: Part of read_from_a_file3.php4

Start a table	`print '<table border="1">';`
As long as we have not found the end of the file, repeatedly...	`while (!feof($pointer)) {`
Open a table row	`print '<tr>';`
Get the next line of the file, up to 4096 characters	`$thisLine = fgets($pointer, 4096);`
Move the tab-delimited elements of the line into array elements	`$lineArray = explode("\t", $thisLine);`
Here comes a foreach loop within the while loop; for each element in the array...	`foreach ($lineArray as $item) {`
...open a table cell, write the data, and close the cell	`echo '<td>' . $item . '</td>' ;`
Close the foreach loop	`}`
Then close the table row	`print '</tr>';`
Close the while loop	`}`
After while loop ends (no more rows), close the table	`print '</table>';`

Figure 2.27 shows the table.

FIGURE 2.27 In this last step, we write the records with each value in a table cell.

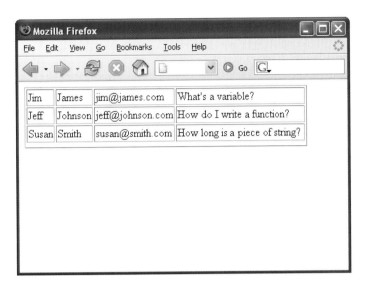

Jim	James	jim@james.com	What's a variable?
Jeff	Johnson	jeff@johnson.com	How do I write a function?
Susan	Smith	susan@smith.com	How long is a piece of string?

Note that the outer `while` loop extracts each line and then the inner `foreach` loop writes each element of that line. This code will write as many lines with as many elements as the file happens to have. It's totally dynamic, and the number of times each of the two loops run is totally dependent on the data that the loops process.

Summary

That covers the basics of creating forms and reading and writing files.

If your data storage needs are simple, flat files may be all you need, but as soon as you have more than one data set, it's usually best to work with a database. So let's now move on and learn how to set up a database, add tables to hold the data, and read and write data between our PHP scripts and the database.

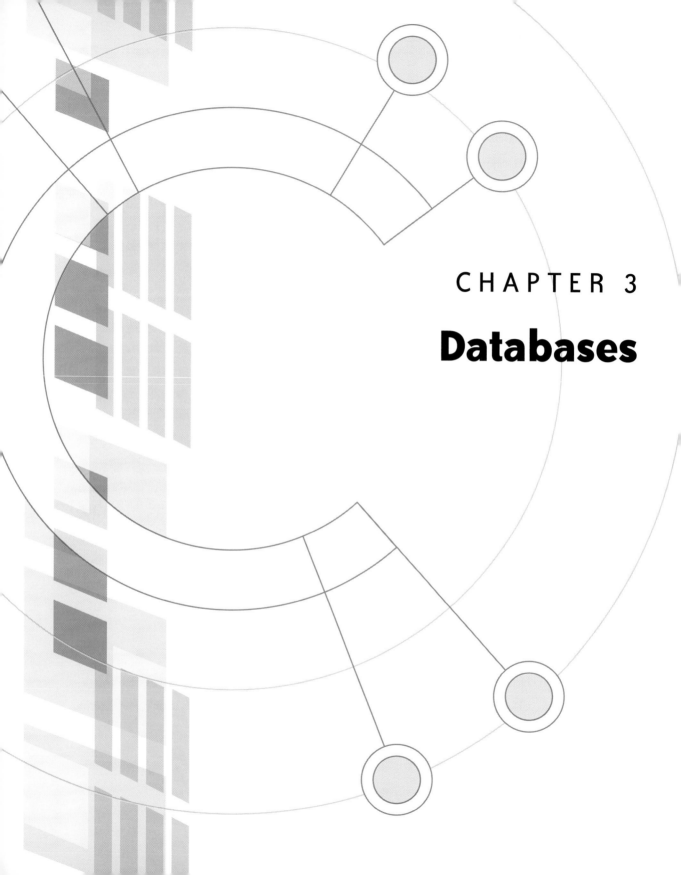

CHAPTER 3

Databases

DEVELOP DATABASES

Create a database and then start adding tables to it

Define the type of data that the table will hold

Start adding records to the table

Display the records in a Web browser

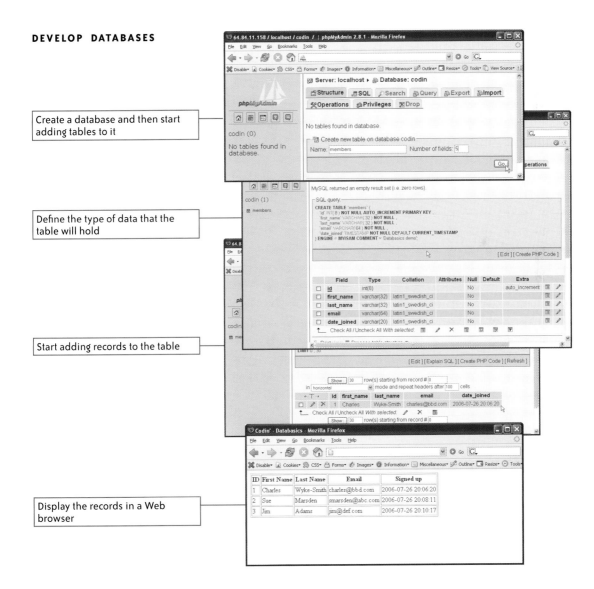

Learn about database concepts in Chapter A, which can be downloaded from the Codin' *Web site.*

Only in the simplest sites is it practical to store the associated data in flat text files. A site of any complexity will have typically have numerous sets of data, and such data is best stored in a database. Databases are made up of tables with a Microsoft Excel spreadsheet-like layout. Each table holds a different set of data relating to our site, such as member information, product specifications, and file names—whatever the functionality of the site requires.

A table is a grid layout, made of columns and rows. Each row represents a *record*: a single instance of the data that the table holds, such as a particular member's information (**Figure 3.1**). Each column holds a type of data element contained in the records. The individual data elements are known as *values*. The box that contains the value is referred to as a *field*.

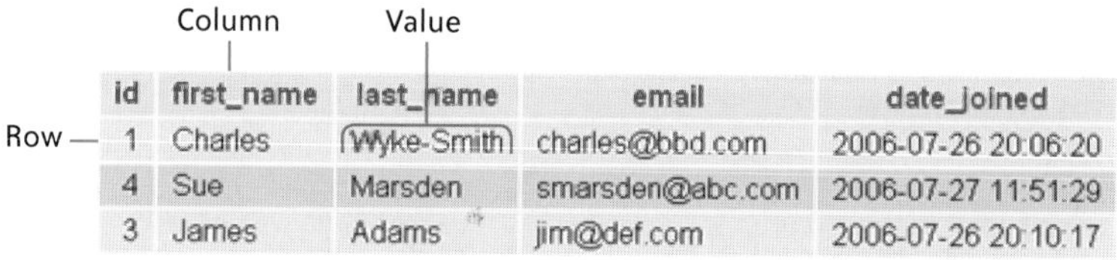

FIGURE 3.1 Anatomy of a SQL table.

Column		Value			
id	first_name	last_name	email	date_joined
1	Charles	Wyke-Smith	charles@bbd.com	2006-07-26 20:06:20
4	Sue	Marsden	smarsden@abc.com	2006-07-27 11:51:29
3	James	Adams	jim@def.com	2006-07-26 20:10:17

Row —

Database tables are managed using SQL. We can send SQL instructions to the database, to initially create and occasionally edit the structure of the tables. For most sites, such tasks are primarily performed during the site's initial development. More frequently, we use SQL to query—that is, read, write, modify, and delete—the data within the tables during the operation of the site.

Database management is greatly simplified with a tool like phpMyAdmin, the confusingly named database tool for the open-source mySQL database.

Before you can store any data in a database, you have to create the tables that will hold the data. In this chapter, we will use a single table to store our site's member names and e-mail information—data similar to that in the form we have worked with in the previous chapter. Before we create this table and put data in it, let's consider the various types of data that a database can hold.

Data Types and Lengths

Each column of a database table has an associated data type setting; all fields (the boxes that contain the individual data items) in a column are therefore of the same data type. When creating a table, we can define the type of data each column's fields will hold, such as integers (whole numbers), floats (decimal numbers), or variable characters (strings of varying lengths), so that the database knows what type of data it is managing in that column. There are more than 25 different data types that can be assigned to fields in your database. **Table 3.1** lists the ones you will use most.

TABLE 3.1 Common MySQL Data Types

TYPE	SIZE (AMOUNT OF DATA USED)	DESCRIPTION (RANGE INDICATES HIGHEST AND LOWEST PERMISSIBLE VALUES)
CHAR[Length]	Length bytes	A fixed-length field from 0 to 255 characters long.
VARCHAR(Length)	String length + 1 bytes	A fixed-length field from 0 to 255 characters long.
TINYTEXT	String length + 1 bytes	A string with a maximum length of 255 characters.
TEXT	String length + 2 bytes	A string with a maximum length of 65,535 characters.
MEDIUMTEXT	String length + 3 bytes	A string with a maximum length of 16,777,215 characters.
LONGTEXT	String length + 4 bytes	A string with a maximum length of 4,294,967,295 characters.
TINYINT[Length]	1 byte	Range of −128 to 127, or 0 to 255 unsigned.
SMALLINT[Length]	2 bytes	Range of −32,768 to 32,767, or 0 to 65535 unsigned.
MEDIUMINT[Length]	3 bytes	Range of −8,388,608 to 8,388,607, or 0 to 16,777,215 unsigned.
INT[Length]	4 bytes	Range of −2,147,483,648 to 2,147,483,647, or 0 to 4,294,967,295 unsigned.
BIGINT[Length]	8 bytes	Range of −9,223,372,036,854,775,808 to 9,223,372,036,854,775,807, or 0 to 18,446,744,073,709,551,615 unsigned.
FLOAT	4 bytes	A small number with a floating decimal point.
DOUBLE[Length, Decimals]	8 bytes	A large number with a floating decimal point.
DECIMAL[Length, Decimals]	Length + 1 or Length + 2 bytes	A DOUBLE stored as a string, allowing for a fixed decimal point.
DATE	3 bytes	In the format of YYYY-MM-DD.
DATETIME	8 bytes	In the format of YYYY-MM-DD HH:MM:SS.
TIMESTAMP	4 bytes	In the format of YYYYMMDDHHMMSS; acceptable range ends in the year 2037.
TIME	3 bytes	In the format of HH:MM:SS
ENUM	1 or 2 bytes	Short for enumeration, which means that each column can have one of several possible values.
SET	1, 2, 3, 4, or 8 bytes	Like ENUM except that each column can have more than one of several possible values.

As you can see, many of these data types have an optional length attribute (maximum number of characters) for a field. The size in bytes of memory used by each field becomes important only as you build large databases, so it's of somewhat academic interest at this stage; however, you should set the length for field data where you can. The idea is to assign the largest value (that is, the greatest number of characters) that you may need to store, but no more, so that the database does not overassign memory to that field. If in doubt, however, be generous.

Let's look at our form's data and see how to assign data types and lengths to the fields.

Each data record will consist of the following fields, shown here with their field types and the length of the data each field can hold.

FIELD	TYPE	LENGTH OR VALUE	OTHER SETTINGS
id	int	20	auto-increment, primary key
first_name	varchar	100	
last_name	varchar	100	
email	varchar	64	
signup_date	timestamp		

The id field will hold the primary key (unique identifier) for each record for this table; this will be an integer, and we will have SQL generate that number for us. The signup_date field will hold a timestamp: the date and time at which the record was created. Like the ID, this value will be generated by SQL. Its format is fixed so there is no need to assign a length to it.

Creating the Database and Tables

Log in to phpMyAdmin with the user name and password created for you by the system administrator. If you are commercially hosted, your ISP will provide this information.

An instance (installed version) of mySQL can hold multiple databases, each with its own login username and password. Often you will find that a database was already created for you by the administrator or ISP who installed mySQL on the server.

If no database has been created, as the left panel of the phpMyAdmin interface shows in **Figure 3.2**, you need to create one.

FIGURE 3.2 The left panel of the main phpMyAdmin screen shows that no databases have been created.

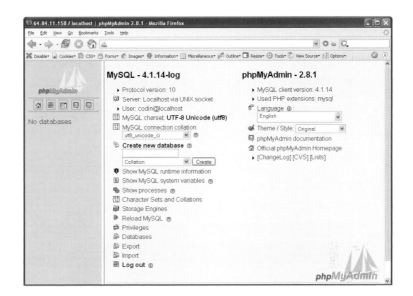

Creating a Database

To create a database, follow these steps:

1. Type the name of the database you want to create in the Create New Database field, located in the first column of the main phpMyAdmin panel.

    We'll name the database **codin**.

2. Leave the drop-down menu set to Collation (unless you are going to use SQL to compare text strings in Cyrillic or some other non-Latin character set, which you're not).

    Your screen should look like **Figure 3.3**.

FIGURE 3.3 Getting ready to create your database.

3.   Click Create.

The database is created (**Figure 3.4**). You can see the confirmation that the database has been created, and the SQL used to generate it:

```
CREATE DATABASE `codin` ;
```

Additionally, you can see that no tables exist yet in this database; that is what we will create next.

FIGURE 3.4 Our database is created. Note that the SQL query used to generate the database is displayed.

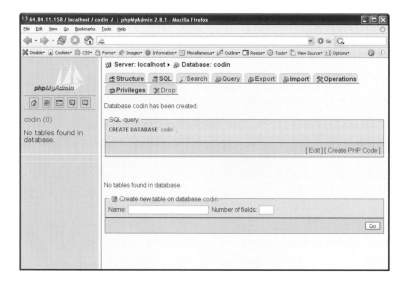

Creating a Table

We'll now add a table to the mySQL database.

1.   Click the Structure tab at the top of the main phpMyAdmin panel. (Note that when adding a subsequent table, you will first need to click the Database: *databasename* link above the tabs.)

2.   In the form that appears, enter the table name and the number of fields (**Figure 3.5**).

We'll name our table **members** and enter **5** as the number of fields.

FIGURE 3.5 The Structure tab shows the structure of your tables. No tables exist yet, but we are about to create one.

In Figure 3.5, the Drop tab is highlighted in red not because it is the current selection, but as a warning—Drop enables you to delete a database and all its tables.

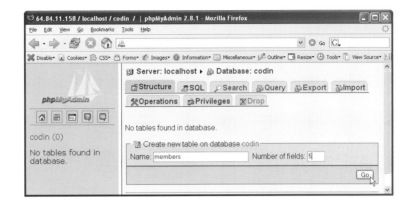

3. Click Go.

You will now set the attributes for your table. The screen you are working with here is very wide and may require horizontal scrolling to see all of the attributes that can be set for each field.

4. On the left side of the screen, assign the field name, data type, and length or value to each of the five fields, according to the type of data the field will hold (**Figure 3.6**).

FIGURE 3.6 Setting up the database fields, data types, and length or values: the left side of the screen.

You can change a field's data type later, so if in doubt, make a best guess and do some tests to see if the field data type allows you to add the data you want to add. For example, you will not be able to write text in an INT (integer) field, but as soon as you switch the type to TEXT, you can. See W3 School's overview of data types at http://www.w3schools. com/php/php_mysql_create.asp. For detailed information, see the mySQL site: http://dev.mysql.com/ doc/refman/5.0/en/data-types.html.

5. Scroll to the right side of the screen and set the Extra attribute of the id field to auto_increment.

With this attribute set, the first record created will automatically be assigned the value 1, the next record will be assigned the value 2, and so on. If a record is deleted, its ID will never be reused in the table.

We'll also use the id field as the table's primary key.

6. Click the primary key radio button for the `id` field to select the field that will be the table's primary key (**Figure 3.7**).

FIGURE 3.7 Click the radio button to indicate which field is the primary key.

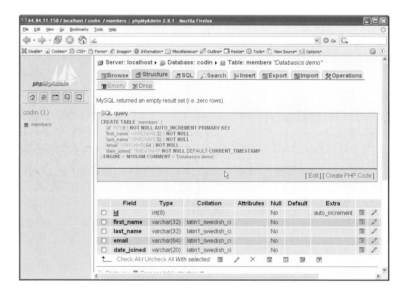

7. When you are done, click Save (visible in Figure 3.6).

The new table is created (**Figure 3.8**). Note the SQL query.

FIGURE 3.8 The new table is created. Because mySQL was developed in Sweden, the Collation (character set) setting defaults to latin1_swedish, but this works flawlessly under all conditions I have encountered and will not affect the performance of our table.

You may want to copy the text of the SQL query and paste it into a text file for safekeeping. If you need to create the table again, perhaps after doing some tests and deleting it, you can instantly re-create it by clicking the SQL tab, pasting the query into the SQL Query field, and clicking Go.

Connecting with Your Database

With our tables constructed in phpMyAdmin, we can now start to use our PHP scripts to query the table's data.

Any SQL that acts upon the data in a database is known generically as a query. Almost every query you write will be one of these types:

- SELECT: Retrieves data

- INSERT: Adds data

- UPDATE: Changes data

- DELETE: Deletes data

Before issuing a SQL query from PHP, you first open a connection and then select a database; remember that a single mySQL installation can contain multiple databases, so you need to not only connect with the server running mySQL, but also indicate which database you want to query.

Opening a connection

To open a connection, we use this format:

```
mysql_connect(host server, user name, password)
```

We make a connection with the `mysql_connect` function. This function's first argument is the address of the server where the database is hosted; this can be an IP address or a mySQLserver's domain name, or if the database and Web server are running on the same computer (as is typically the case), the term `localhost` works as a shorthand reference. The `mysql_connect` function's other two arguments are the user name and password that were assigned to the database when it was created.

Typically, these three credentials are stored in variables, often in an include file above the root folder, but it's fairly safe to include them in PHP files below the root level since only the output of PHP files is ever displayed in a Web page.

CODE 3.1: 1_connect.php4

```php
$hostUrl="localhost";

$userName="codin";

$password="codin1234";

$connectID = mysql_connect($hostUrl, $userName, $password)

  or die ("Sorry, can't connect to database");

print $connectID . "<br />";
```

Temporary display of connect status = Resource id #2 or similar if okay

If the connection is successful, $connectID, or whatever you call this variable, is set to a pointer to the connection. If you actually run this bit of code, you will see the pointer variable printed (**Figure 3.9**).

FIGURE 3.9 We have successfully connected with the database; the connection pointer is set.

As you can see, the value of the $connectID pointer is not very informative, but as long as it's set, we don't need to know more. As you will see, all subsequent interaction with the database uses the $connectID variable as a reference.

Note also the use of the die function, which is called if the connection fails to be established. It is aptly named, because your script will stop running if this error is triggered; in this case, die outputs a text string if the connection is not made. However, die is also a useful tool for creative and user-friendly handling of database error messages, as you can replace the text string with a call to a function that does whatever you want to have happen if a connection fails, such as redirecting to a page where the user can read your groveling apology for the problem and perhaps be offered some way to report it.

Selecting a Database

Once the connection is established, we can select the database, using PHP's `mysql_select_db` function.

The format is:

```
mysql_select_db (database name, connection pointer)
```

To connect to our database, we use the following:

```
mysql_select_db("codin", $connectID)

  or die ("Unable to select database");
```

The only problem you might encounter at this fairly simple step is a typing error, such as the wrong database name, so for this example, we'll combine this step with the next: adding a record to the database.

Using INSERT to Add Data to a Table

With the connection established and a database selected, we can query—or perform an operation on data in—the database.

There are no records in our members table yet, so let's add one. To add a new record to a database, we use a SQL INSERT statement. The format is:

```
INSERT INTO (field1, field2, field3,…) VALUES (value1, value
2, value 3,…)
```

Here's an example of a SQL INSERT statement:

```
INSERT INTO members (first_name, last_name, email) VALUES
("Charles", "Wyke-Smith", "charles@bbd.com")
```

To send this SQL statement from our PHP script to the mySQL database, we use it as an argument in PHP's `mysql_query` function.

The format of the `mysql_query` function is:

```
mysql_query (SQL query, connection pointer)
```

So a query that would add a record with my first name, last name, and e-mail would look like this:

```
mysql_query ('INSERT into members (first_name, last_name,
email) VALUES ("Charles", "Wyke-Smith", "charles@bbd.com")',
$connectID)

  or die ("Unable to insert record into database");
```

In this example, the entire query is enclosed in single quotation marks, and elements within the query are enclosed in double quotation marks. Depending on what is in the query string (PHP variables, for example), you may need to switch this arrangement around, as you will see in a later chapter.

Closing the Connection

Finally, although PHP will automatically close a connection at the end of a script, it is always good practice to do this explicitly, using the mysql_close function, once you have finished your interaction with the database. The mysql_close function takes one argument—the connection pointer:

```
mysql_close($connectID);
```

INSERT: An Example

The following example shows everything we have seen so far. This script will add a record to our new database table.

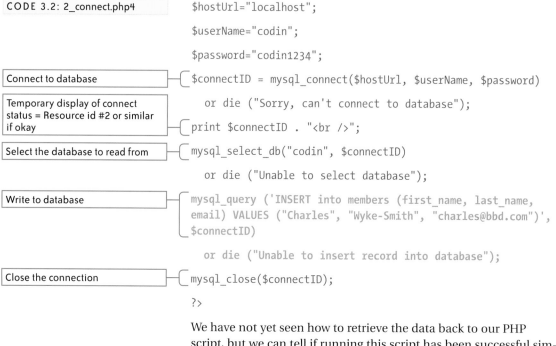

CODE 3.2: 2_connect.php4

```
$hostUrl="localhost";

$userName="codin";

$password="codin1234";
```

Connect to database

```
$connectID = mysql_connect($hostUrl, $userName, $password)

    or die ("Sorry, can't connect to database");
```

Temporary display of connect status = Resource id #2 or similar if okay

```
print $connectID . "<br />";
```

Select the database to read from

```
mysql_select_db("codin", $connectID)

    or die ("Unable to select database");
```

Write to database

```
mysql_query ('INSERT into members (first_name, last_name,
email) VALUES ("Charles", "Wyke-Smith", "charles@bbd.com")',
$connectID)

    or die ("Unable to insert record into database");
```

Close the connection

```
mysql_close($connectID);

?>
```

We have not yet seen how to retrieve the data back to our PHP script, but we can tell if running this script has been successful simply by selecting our table in phpMyAdmin and clicking the Browse tab (**Figure 3.10**).

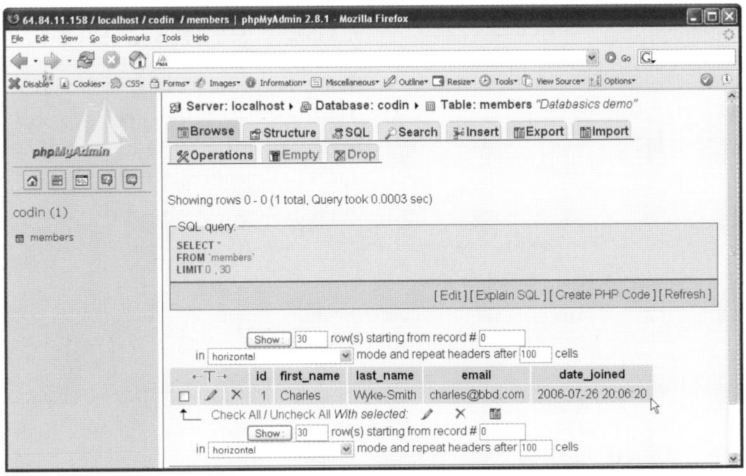

FIGURE 3.10 A record added to the members table (highlighted in green).

The SQL query shown in Figure 3.10 is the one that phpMyAdmin ran when the Browse button was clicked to select the records from the database for display in this screen.

You can see that the new record has automatically been assigned ID 1 because of the auto-increment setting for the id field. Note that the date and time have also been automatically added because of the timestamp settings on the date_joined field. For now, every time you load this page, a new record with a unique ID and a timestamp will be created.

Using SELECT to Read Data from the Database

To read from the database, we need to execute a SELECT query, which looks like this:

```
SELECT field1, field2,… FROM tablename WHERE fieldN=some value
```

As you will see next, we will use this query in PHP's sql_query func-tion in the same way as we did the INSERT query.

We will first see how to select *all* the records in a table, so we will use SELECT like this, without the optional WHERE clause:

```
SELECT * FROM members
```

The * (Shift-8) means "everything," so this code will select all the data from the members table. Once selected, it is available to PHP.

Accessing database results with PHP can seem complicated until you get the hang of it. Each result (record) returned, often consisting of several fields—five in our example—is held in what is known as a row. A row in the context of a query result is an associative array of the names and values of the returned database fields. After running a SELECT query, we can access the rows of the result one by one by using the `mysql_fetch_row` function in a `while` loop, like this:

```
while ($row = mysql_fetch_row($myDataID)) {
```

Do something to the fields of this row

```
}
```

The `while` loop repeats as many times as there are rows returned, so whatever code goes inside the loop will act on each row in turn.

Unfortunately, if you try to directly access the `$row` variable containing the array—for example, using `print $row;`—the code just returns the word `Array`; rather than outputting the row's fields, which is not very helpful. If you use the `print_r $row;` command, PHP will print the array's fields, but the output is formatted only in the source code, so it's sometimes useful to wrap `print_r` output with `<pre></pre>` tags; however, I prefer to use a `foreach` loop, which allows formatting tags to be added easily to the output. Within the `while` loop, which accesses each row, we use a `foreach` loop that lets us individually access the fields of each row.

Repeats times the number of rows

Repeats times the number of fields in the row

```
while ($row = mysql_fetch_row($myDataID)) {
    foreach ($row as $field) {
        print $field;
    }
    print "<br />";
}
```

This code will print each field of each row to the screen, with a line break after each row.

CODE 3.3: 3_connect_insert_
select.php4

Let's add this code to the previous INSERT example code, right after the INSERT query.

Connection and database selection code omitted here—see previous code

Write to database

```php
mysql_query ('INSERT into members (first_name, last_name,
email) VALUES ("Sue", "Marsden", "smarsden@abc.com")',
$connectID)

   or die ("Unable to insert record into database");
```

Read from database

```php
$myDataID = mysql_query("SELECT * from members", $connectID);

while ($row = mysql_fetch_row($myDataID)) {

foreach ($row as $field) {

   print $field;

   }

   print "<br />";

}
```

Close the connection

```php
mysql_close($connectID);
```

Now each time we write a new record to the database, we immediately write all the records, including the new one, to the browser (**Figure 3.11**).

FIGURE 3.11 The only two records in our database table are output. The formatting could be improved, though.

I changed the name and e-mail values in the hard-coded test variables at this step so that we don't get the same data in every record.

As you can see, each row is simply written as a long string without spacing between the values. By adding some XHTML to our code, we can improve the onscreen layout by writing the data in an XHTML table (**Figure 3.12**).

CODE 3.4: 4_connect_insert_
select_table.php4

```php
$myDataID = mysql_query("SELECT * from members", $connectID);
```

Open the table and write out the headings

```php
print "<table border=\"1\">\n";

print '<tr style="font-weight:bold; text-align:
center;"><td>ID</td><td>First Name</td><td>Last Name</
td><td>Email</td><td>Signed up</td></tr>';

while ($row = mysql_fetch_row($myDataID)) {
```

Open a table row
```php
    print '<tr>';
```
For each field
```php
    foreach ($row as $field) {
```
Write the value in a cell
```php
        print '<td>'.$field.'</td>';
    }
```
Close the row
```php
    print "</tr>\n";
}
```
Close the table
```php
print '</table>';
```

FIGURE 3.12 Adding some XHTML writes the results as a table.

Again, I changed the hard-coded name variables before running the code.

It takes a little practice to determine where to add the XHTML elements of the table in the PHP. View the source code in your browser to ensure that your table elements are nested correctly in the XHTML output.

The table opens and writes a table row with the headings before the `while` loop starts. Each time the `while` loop starts, a new table row is opened, and before the loop finishes, the row is closed. Each time the `foreach` loops runs, a table cell is opened, the data is written to it, and then the cell is closed. After the `while` loop runs for the last time, the table is closed.

Now that you see how to display all the data in a table, you can modify this procedure to get the returned data into whatever format or variables you want. Let's now be more selective, both with our SQL queries and with the elements of the query results that we select with PHP.

Specifying Fields to Retrieve

So far we have used * (all) as the argument for our SELECT statements, and so we have retrieved all the fields of the returned records. Let's now be a little more specific. We'll modify our previous query, replacing the * with the names of two fields.

CODE 3.5: Part of 5_select_by_ field.php4

```
$myDataID = mysql_query("SELECT first_name, email FROM
members", $connectID);
```

Except for modifying the hard-coded column headings, no other changes are needed (**Figure 3.13**).

FIGURE 3.13 Our query retrieves only the first name and e-mail address of each record.

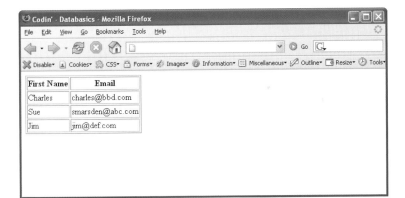

Matching with WHERE in SELECT Statements

If we want to retrieve some information from a specific member's record, we might have that person submit his or her e-mail address and then use that address to find the person's record and retrieve the fields we want. Let's modify the query code to look like this:

CODE 3.6: Part of 6_select_by_ value.php4

```
$targetEmail="jim@def.com";

$myDataID = mysql_query("SELECT first_name, last_name, email
from members WHERE email = '$targetEmail'", $connectID);
```

Only one person matches this query (**Figure 3.14**).

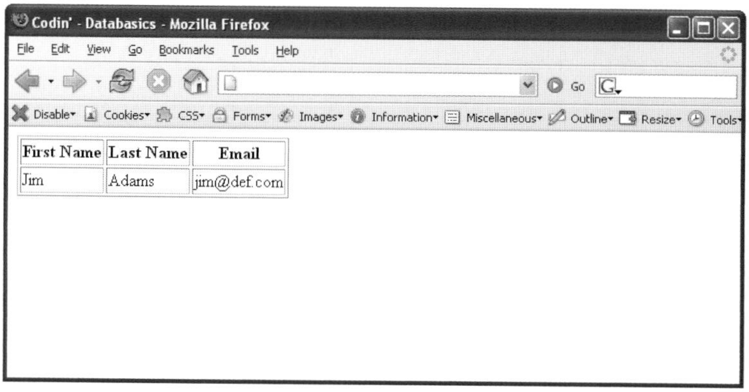

FIGURE 3.14 Using the e-mail address in the WHERE clause of the SELECT statement, we can find the name of the person with that e-mail address.

First Name	Last Name	Email
Jim	Adams	jim@def.com

Using UPDATE to Modify Values in a Record

When a value in a record is replaced by another value, that's an update. Such modifications are made using the UPDATE statement. The format is:

```
UPDATE tablename SET field1 = value1, field2 = value2,… WHERE fieldN = valueN
```

Let's say that Jim wants to change his first name from Jim to James. We'll call the UPDATE statement to do this before we call the SELECT statement, so we can see the effect of the UPDATE statement in the browser (**Figure 3.15**).

CODE 3.7: Part of 7_modify_by_value.php4

```
$targetEmail="jim@def.com";

$name_update = "James"
```

Modify a record

```
$myDataID = mysql_query("UPDATE members SET first_name = '$name_update' WHERE email = '$targetEmail'", $connectID);
```

Read from database

```
$myDataID = mysql_query("SELECT first_name, last_name, email from members WHERE email = '$targetEmail'", $connectID);
```

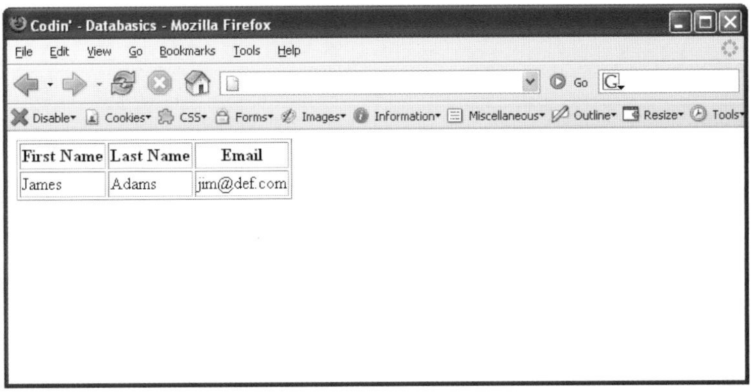

FIGURE 3.15 The UPDATE statement enables us to change the values of fields in a record. Here the user's first name is modified (compare to Figure 3.14).

Using DELETE to Remove a Record from a Table

Inevitably, at some point we will want to delete records from our database. The format of the DELETE statement is:

```
DELETE FROM table name WHERE field name = value
```

At the moment, our database contains three member records: for Charles, Sue, and Jim. Sue has quit, so her record is going to be deleted. Here, we delete Sue's record and then write all the records that remain in the table (**Figure 3.16**).

CODE 3.8: Part of 8_delete_by_value.php4

Delete a record

```
$myDataID = mysql_query("DELETE FROM members WHERE first_name = 'Sue'", $connectID);
```

Read from database

```
$myDataID = mysql_query("SELECT * from members", $connectID);
```

FIGURE 3.16 Sue's record, ID 2, has been deleted from the table.

> ### A Warning about DELETE
>
> Be sure to specify a WHERE clause when issuing a DELETE query. The query `DELETE FROM members` will instantly and permanently delete *all* the records from the members table. Don't say I didn't warn you.

Summary

Blending SQL statements into the arguments of the PHP functions that relate to SQL can be challenging at first. Hopefully, the examples in this chapter will serve as templates for your specific needs.

We have not yet looked at JOIN statements, which are queries that access data across more than one table, but we will see these in action later.

Armed with these basic PHP and SQL techniques, we can now undertake some more challenging real-world projects.

CHAPTER 4

Content Management

**CREATE A SIMPLE CONTENT
MANAGEMENT SYSTEM TO
MANAGE A LIST OF LINKS
AND ASSOCIATED DATA**

Use a form to create records in the
database

Display listings at your site and...

...manage listings from an
administration page...

...by using JOINs to access data
across database tables

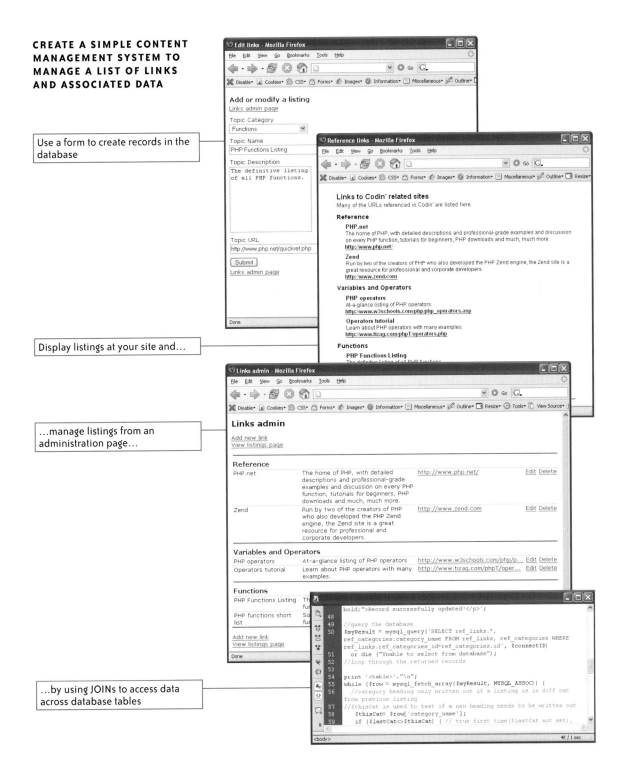

In this chapter, we look at how middleware and a database can help you manage the content on your site. One of the key functions of a content management system, or CMS, is to separate the content from the code so that nontechnical members of the site team can add content without touching the code. Some sites allow visitors to add content as well as view it—Wikipedia (www.wikipedia.com), for example—but in our case, we will assume that visitors will see only the content in its published form, and that only the site's administrators can add or delete content.

For the project in this chapter, we will create two kinds of pages: public pages that display the content and can be viewed by visitors; and administration pages used to add, modify, and delete content that can be accessed only by you, the site administrator.

The Web site created for this book includes a page of links to other sites that provide additional information related to the topics that the book covers, and the code for this page contains a number of interesting features. We will use the development of this page to explore content management here.

Public Pages and Administration Pages: Overview

In creating my page of links, I first decided that each link would not only have an associated title and some descriptive information relating to it, but also would be assignable to a category, so I could sort and display the links grouped by these categories. As you will see, implementing that decision required quite a bit of coding.

The information about each link consists of four pieces of data:

- Link category
- Link name
- Link description
- Link URL

Figure 4.1 shows the links on the Reference Links page, which is the page that is displayed to the visitor.

FIGURE 4.1 The Reference Links page. Each listing has four pieces of data associated with it: the category, heading, description, and URL.

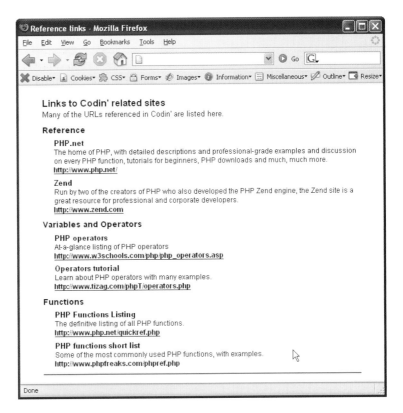

A category heading (for instance, Functions) is displayed only once for each group of related links, even though a category is assigned to every listing in the database; the code we will write will organize the links and present them under their common heading. Only a few categories and links have been added at this point, but it's easy to add more using the administration pages.

The other two pages we will create are administration pages, which will not be viewable by visitors to the site: the Links Admin page (**Figure 4.2**), where the administrator can view all listings, and delete a listing or select it for editing, and the Edit Links page (**Figure 4.3**), where the administrator can use a form to add and modify (edit) listings.

FIGURE 4.2 The Links Admin page lets the administrator view the information about the links, select a link for editing, and delete a link.

Long URLs are displayed truncated, because it's impossible to make them wrap to a second line in Firefox and other standards-compliant browsers, and so they would otherwise force the table to be very wide. The actual href *reference to which the link points is full length (and therefore fully functional), as shown in the status bar at the bottom of the screen. You will see how this truncation of the displayed URL was achieved later in this chapter.*

FIGURE 4.3 The Edit Links page. This form with this content (including the correct setting of the drop-down menu) was loaded by clicking the PHP Functions Listing Edit link on the Links Admin page. You would click Add New Link on the Links Admin page to display this form empty, to add a new listing.

The coding of the Edit Links page is complex because the code has to determine, when the page loads, which task it needs to do:

- If Add New Link is clicked, the Edit Links form is displayed empty.

- If an Edit link is clicked (on the listing display page), the Edit Links form is loaded with the data for that listing.

- If the Submit button is clicked, the code must then determine whether the listing is new or already exists. If it is new, a new record is created in the database.

- If the listing exists and is therefore being edited, the corresponding record is updated in the database.

You will see shortly how we use an `else-if` conditional structure to run the appropriate code for each of these four possibilities.

Creating the Database Tables

See the section on database design in Chapter A at the Codin' *Web site for a quick overview of primary and foreign keys, normalization, and how to work with multiple database tables.*

Unlike the other database examples that we have seen so far, our listings require two database tables: a listings table and a categories table. We need two tables because each category name can relate to many listings, and if we simply store the category name with each listing record, each category name will be duplicated many times; if we ever need to edit a category name, we would then have to do this in numerous places.

So we will keep the category names in a separate categories table in our database, and as we add each link record to the listings table, we will also add a foreign key (a number) that references the primary key for the category for each link. This approach increases the complexity of the SQL queries we will need to write, but the reality is that most database-driven sites require multiple tables, and therefore SQL queries across them, if the data is to be stored in a normalized way.

To manually enter listing records in the database using phpMyAdmin, select the ref_links *table in phpMyAdmin and click Insert. Then enter the text for each field—but leave the* id *field blank because the database will use the auto-increment feature to insert the correct value for that field.*

Some of the quotation marks in the code are the ` *symbol (the top-left key on the keyboard)--a common feature when you use phpMyAdmin to help generate a query string. Click the SQL tab in phpMyAdmin to generate sql queries.*

FIGURE 4.4 The left side of the newly created listings table displayed in phpMyAdmin.

Creating the Listings Table

The table that contains the data relating to each listing, which we'll call ref_links, will have the following fields:

- id: The record's auto-incrementing primary key.

- ref_categories_id: A foreign key that is the primary key of the record's category in the category table.

- topic_name: The listing title.

- topic_desc: The listing description.

- topic_url: The listing URL.

Here is the query to create the listings table:

```
CREATE TABLE `databaseName`.`reflinks` (
`id` int( 10 ) NOT NULL AUTO_INCREMENT ,
`ref_categories_id` int( 3 ) NOT NULL default '0',
`topic_name` varchar( 100 ) NOT NULL default '',
`topic_desc` text NOT NULL ,
`topic_url` varchar( 100 ) NOT NULL default '',
PRIMARY KEY ( `id` )
) ENGINE = MYISAM DEFAULT CHARSET = latin1 COMMENT = 'ref_
links_joins_with_ref_categories';
```

Figure 4.4 shows the created listings table in phpMyAdmin.

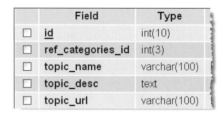

Field	Type
☐ **id**	int(10)
☐ **ref_categories_id**	int(3)
☐ **topic_name**	varchar(100)
☐ **topic_desc**	text
☐ **topic_url**	varchar(100)

We are going to manually add three link records in this table using phpMyAdmin, so that we can write the code to read records from the database. Later, you will see how to add and modify records directly from the Edit Links form.

Creating the Categories Table

The categories table, which holds the names of the categories with which the listings can be associated, has just two fields:

- `id`: The category's primary key.
- `category_name`: The category name.

As you saw in Chapter 3, phpMyAdmin can generate the SQL to create tables for you, so refer to that chapter if you need to jog your memory. Here is the query that phpMyAdmin generated to create the categories table. Note the difference between the ` and ' marks in SQL. The ' means that a value is contained within, whereas the ` denotes the name of a table, database, or field.

```
CREATE TABLE `databaseName`.`ref_categories` (
`id` int( 4 ) NOT NULL AUTO_INCREMENT ,
`category_name` varchar( 100 ) NOT NULL default '',
PRIMARY KEY ( `id` )
) ENGINE = MYISAM DEFAULT CHARSET = latin1 COMMENT =
'categories for ref_links table';
```

Figure 4.5 shows the created categories table in phpMyAdmin

Once I have set up the categories, I will change them only occasionally, so I decided to add and delete category names manually as needed using phpMyAdmin, rather than create a form and an associated PHP script to manage it. (Listings, on the other hand, will be added and edited frequently, so it is worth the time invested to write an administration system to manage them.)

FIGURE 4.5 The left side of the Categories table displayed in phpMyAdmin.

	Field	Type
☐	**id**	int(4)
☐	**category_name**	varchar(100)

To get us started developing and testing the listings management system, which is the focus of this chapter, I have added three category names to the categories table using phpMyAdmin (**Figure 4.6**).

FIGURE 4.6 Three category names added to the categories table.

←T→			id	category_name
☐	✎	✕	1	Reference
☐	✎	✕	2	Variables and Operators
☐	✎	✕	3	Functions

Creating the Edit Links Form

To remain focused on the task at hand, we will not add validation code to this form, so its fields are open to malicious code. If you use this form on a public page of your site, you should add validation code to check the form fields, as described in Chapter 2, to close the "hacker holes."

CODE 4.1: links_form_step1.php4

Display:block allows margins on inline elements

The next step is to create a form that we will use to add listings to the database and also to modify listings when we need to update them.

To keep us focused on the task at hand, we will set up the Edit Links form in a single step, so we are ready to add the PHP scripts. The form is similar to the form in Chapter 2.

Here is the code for the XHTML and the CSS styles (highlighted) for the Edit Links form:

```
<!DOCTYPE html PUBLIC "-//W3C//DTD XHTML 1.0 Transitional//
EN" "http://www.w3.org/TR/xhtml1/DTD/xhtml1-transitional.
dtd">

<html xmlns="http://www.w3.org/1999/xhtml">

<head>

<meta http-equiv="Content-Type" content="text/html;
charset=iso-8859-1" />

<title>Edit Links</title>

<style type="text/css">

body {font-family:verdana, arial, sans-serif; font-size:80%}

h3 {padding:10px 0 0 0; margin:0;}

label {display:block; margin:8px 0 2px 0;}

a {display:block; color:#066; margin:3px 0 10px;}

a:hover {color:#000; text-decoration:none;}

input[type="submit"] {display:block; margin-top:8px;}

</style>

</head>
```

```
<body>

<h3>Add or modify a listing</h3>

<a href="#">Test Link</a>

<form method="post" action="<?php $_SERVER['PHP_SELF'] ?>">

<label for="category">Topic Category</label>


<select name="category" size="1">

<option name="none">Select a Category</option>

<option name="1">A Menu Choice</option>>

</select>


<!--topic_name-->

<label for="topic_name">Topic Name</label>

<input name="topic_name" type="text" size="30" id="topic_
name" value="" />

<!--topic_description-->

<label for="topic_description">Topic Description</label>

<textarea name="topic_description"></textarea>

<!--topic_url-->

<label for="topic_url">Topic URL</label>

<input name="topic_url" type="text" size="30" id="topic_url"
value="" />

<input type="submit" value="Submit" name="submitted" />

</form>

</form>

</body>

</html>
```

Figure 4.7 shows the results.

FIGURE 4.7 The Edit Links form with
some simple CSS styles applied.

There are some important things to note about this code. First, the Topic Category (`select name`) drop-down menu currently has only two `option name` tags (which generate the menu choices). These tags are just placeholders, and later we will write code to automatically populate this menu with the category names from the `ref_catego-ries` table in the database each time the page loads.

Next, as indicated with highlighting, the form `input name` elements both have blank (empty string) value attributes, and there is no text (which would, if present, appear in the field) between the opening and closing tags of the `textarea` field. We will add variables in these

The Edit Links Form CSS

Observe that the Edit Links form layout requires no `<br />` line breaks to get everything to stack nicely down the page, even though form-related XHTML elements such `label` and `input` as are in fact `inline` elements that normally sit next to each other if there is room to do so. This change in their behavior is achieved by setting the `display` property of the `label` elements to `block`, which causes these elements to stack in the same way as `block` elements such as paragraphs and headings do by default.

A bonus of this approach is that, while `inline` elements don't accept margins and padding, now that these elements are transformed to `block` elements, we can apply some small vertical margin settings to them, so they neither touch nor have too much space between themselves and the input elements. Remove the `display:block` declarations from the `input` and `label` elements to see the difference. If you want to learn more about these aspects of CSS, see my book *Stylin' with CSS*, also published by New Riders.

locations later to display the data from the database in the form fields when we need to modify an existing record.

Setting Up the Database Connection

Because the Edit Links page will eventually contain more than one database query, it makes sense to establish the connection with the database at the start of the page and to close the connection at the bottom of the page. Then in between, in our code, we just need to issue the one-line SQL queries and don't have to open and close the connection for each one. At the first line of the code for the page, insert the following:

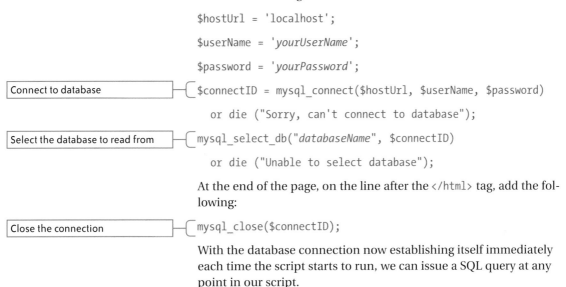

```
$hostUrl = 'localhost';

$userName = 'yourUserName';

$password = 'yourPassword';
```

Connect to database

```
$connectID = mysql_connect($hostUrl, $userName, $password)
    or die ("Sorry, can't connect to database");
```

Select the database to read from

```
mysql_select_db("databaseName", $connectID)
    or die ("Unable to select database");
```

At the end of the page, on the line after the `</html>` tag, add the following:

Close the connection

```
mysql_close($connectID);
```

With the database connection now establishing itself immediately each time the script starts to run, we can issue a SQL query at any point in our script.

You could put this connection code in an include *structure so you would have to maintain it in only one place for all the scripts that use the database. For clarity here, I have added the code to every page.*

CODE 4.2: All code in this section is in links_form_step2.php4

Displaying the Categories in the Topic Category Drop-Down Menu

The first database query we write will read all of the category names and their corresponding IDs (primary keys) from the `ref_catego-ries` table, so that we can populate the category menu.

The drop-down menu must display all the category names so the user can select from them, and it also must pass a value that indicates the selected choice when the form is submitted. Here's how the output should look:

```
<select name="category">

<option value="none">Select a Category</option>

<option value="1">Reference</option>

<option value="2">Variables and Operators</option>

<option value="3">Functions</option>

</select>
```

In this example, if the user selects Reference from the menu, then the name-value pair `category=1` will be passed to the page to which the form is submitted (in this case, itself). So for each category and ID returned by the database, we will write an option element, and as we do so, we will write the category's ID as the value, and we will write the category name between the opening and closing tags of the option.

First, we write the first two lines of the existing code because they won't change.

```
print '<select name="category">'."\n";

print '<option value="none">Select a Catagory</option>'."\n";
```

Next, we need to query the database. We have seen similar queries before. We simply read all the data in the table and thereby return the ID and category name for each record; the table contains only these two fields.

```
$Categories = mysql_query('SELECT * FROM ref_categories', $connectID);
```

Then, to create our drop-down menu, we need to loop through the retrieved records, writing an `option name` element containing the data from each record. To do this, we need the query to behave as an associative array (see Chapter 1), where each field of the record

Although we use single quotation marks to open and close the printed strings, so we can include double quotation marks in the output, we also have to concatanate \n (which adds a line break in the output code for readability) for each line. Using single quotation marks on the \n actually prints \n to the screen instead of breaking the line in the output, so for the \n, we need to use double quotation marks—another of those tedious details that we have to attend to to get nicely formatted XHTML.

can be referenced by name, so we use the `mysql_ fetch_array` function. The format is as follows:

```
mysql_fetch_array (record ref, array type)
```

In the preceding query, the record reference is `$Categories`, and the array type can be either `MYSQL_ASSOC`, to access the results by field name, or `MYSQL_INT`, to access the results by their numerical position in the array based on the order in which the results were returned. We will use `MYSQL_ASSOC` so that we can use the field names. Here is how we write the rest of the menu:

```
while ($Category = mysql_fetch_array($Categories, MYSQL_
ASSOC)){

print  '<option value="'.$Category['id'].'">'.
$Category['category_name']."</option>\n";

}

print '</select>'."\n";
```

Here we use the variable `$Category` to hold the subarray of the data of each record as the records are sequentially read from the mother array-of-arrays `$Categories` variable, which is the complete query result. Each record is structured—for example, `id="3"`, `category_name="Functions"`.

Here's how all this code looks:

Remember that single quotation marks open and close the strings, but the double quotation marks are part of the output XHTML code. Once you understand this, the code is much easier to read.

CODE 4.3: Part of links_form_step3.php4

| Open the select (drop-down menu) |
| Add the default selection |
| Get the categories (ID and name for each) |
| Write the result in an associative array |
| Write the ID and name in each select |
| Close the select |

```
print '<select name="category">'."\n";

print '<option value="none">Select a Catagory</option>'."\n";

$Categories = mysql_query('SELECT * FROM ref_categories',
$connectID);

while ($Category = mysql_fetch_array($Categories, MYSQL_
ASSOC)){

echo "$RefLinks[cat_id]==$Category[id]<br>\n";

print  '<option value="'.$Category['id'].'">'.$Category['cate
gory_name']."</option>\n";

}

print '</select>'."<br />\n";
```

Now when the page is loaded, the menu is automatically populated (**Figure 4.8**).

FIGURE 4.8 The categories names stored in the database now populate the drop-down menu.

Adding Content to the Database Using the Edit Links Form

CODE 4.4: All code in this section is in links_form_step3.php4

Validate this data if you are allowing visitors to access this form. Refer to Chapter 2 to see how to validate form data.

The next step is to write the code to enable the Edit Links form to add a record to the `ref_links` table when the form is submitted. First, we need to determine whether the form has been submitted (posted to itself) and, if so, put the `$_POST` array values from the form into regular variables.

```
if ($_POST['submitted'])  {

    $category=($_POST['category']);

    $topic_name=($_POST['topic_name']);

    $topic_description=($_POST['topic_description']);

    $topic_url=($_POST['topic_url']);
```

Next, we need a SQL query that will add the information in the variables to the database.

The respective database fields for the variables are `ref_categories_id`, `topic_name`, `topic_desc`, and `topic_url`, so our query looks like this:

```
INSERT into ref_links (ref_categories_id, topic_name, topic_
desc, topic_url) VALUES ('$category', '$topic_name', '$topic_
description', '$topic_url')
```

Putting this into a `sql_query` function gives us the following:

```php
<?php
if ($_POST['submitted'])  {
  $category=($_POST['category']);
  $topic_name=($_POST['topic_name']);
  $topic_description=($_POST['topic_description']);
  $topic_url=($_POST['topic_url']);
```

Write to database

```php
  mysql_query ("INSERT into ref_links (ref_categories_id,
topic_name, topic_desc, topic_url) VALUES ('$category',
'$topic_name', '$topic_description', '$topic_url')",
$connectID)
  or die ("Unable to insert record into database");
  print "Record successfully added";
```

If we add this code after the database connection code at the start of our page and load the page, we can test that the Edit Links form data can be written to the database. Click Submit (**Figure 4.9**); if the record has been added, the message shown in **Figure 4.10** appears.

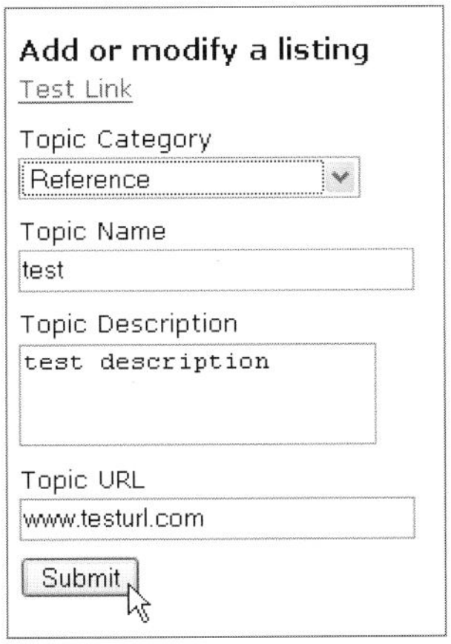

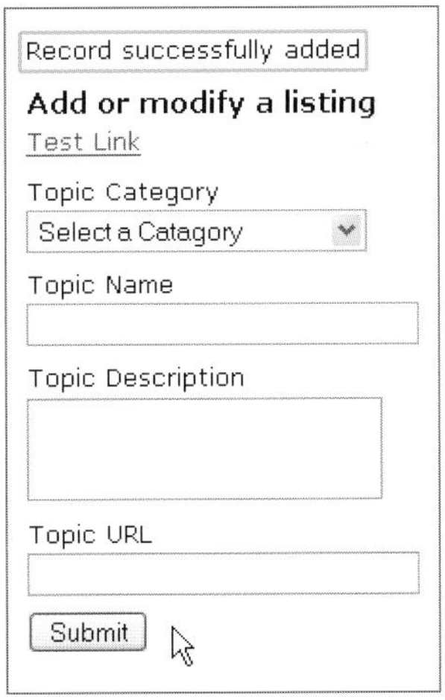

FIGURE 4.9 (Left) Click Submit to test whether the form data is added to the database.

FIGURE 4.10 (Right) The Record Successfully Added message indicates that the record was written to the database.

Although the Edit Links form is not yet sticky, so the form data is not redisplayed after the form is submitted, the Record Successfully Added message indicates that the data was written to the database. A quick check in phpMyAdmin confirms that the record is in the database (**Figure 4.11**).

FIGURE 4.11 The test record is in the database.

←T→	id	ref_categories_id	topic_name	topic_desc	topic_url
☐ ✎ ✗	17	1	test	test description	www.testurl.com

The record ID is 17 in Figure 4.11 because I have either deleted or temporarily hidden the previous 16 records, which I created during earlier testing. Your record ID will almost certainly be different.

The 1 in the `ref_categories_id` field is the ID of the category in the `ref_category` table whose name I selected from the drop-down menu. This is the value passed from the form's value attribute for that choice. Later, when we display the listings in the `ref_listings` table, our query will use this ID to extract the correct category name for each listing from the `ref_category` table.

We will return to this form later, as we will also use it to display records we wish to modify, but now it's time to create the other page needed to administer the records: the Links Admin page.

Creating the Links Admin Page

The main purpose of the Links Admin page is to display the records and to select a record for editing or deletion.

We'll start by writing all the records to an HTML table using a one-table SQL query. Then we will backtrack and convert that query to a JOIN query that also extracts the corresponding category names from the `ref_categories` table so that we can display the listings sorted by category.

I have quite a few records in my listings table; if you are following along, you may want to use the form we just created, or phpMyAdmin, to add three or four records—any placeholder text will do at this point—to your database so you have some records to display. Don't forget to select a category for each record from the drop-down menu as you go, so you can later display these records sorted by category.

Displaying the Listings Records from the Database

The objective of this exercise is to use PHP to write a table with the data from the `ref_listings` table. The basic structure of a table consists of three tags—`<table>`, `<tr>`, and `<td>`—which start a table, open a table row, and open a table cell (the location for the table **d**ata)—and their corresponding closing tags:

CODE 4.6: table_basics.htm

```
<table width="200" border="1">

  <tr>

    <td>Codin'</td>
```

The framework of code for this page will start by opening the connection to the database, then open a basic XHTML code template, and then end by closing the database connection. You can find this template file, basic_xhtml_db_connect.php4, in the download code for this chapter; simply add the code that follows as each step is covered.

FIGURE 4.12 A simple table. (New Riders is an imprint of Peachpit Press.)

```
    <td>for the</td>

    <td>Web</td>

  </tr>

  <tr>

    <td>from</td>

    <td>Peachpit</td>

    <td>Press</td>

  </tr>

</table>
```

The results onscreen look like **Figure 4.12**.

Codin'	for the	Web
from	Peachpit	Press

We'll start creating this table for our listing data by querying the database.

You are probably getting the hang of these queries by now, so we'll get straight to the finished code. After the query, we'll add the same while loop structure that we used earlier in the form to extract the records (the rows of the database table) as an associative array. Within the while loop, we'll temporarily add a foreach loop (highlighted) that simply dumps each row of data onto the page so we can test whether our query is getting the data we want.

CODE 4.7: Part of links_admin_step1.php4

Query the database

Loop through the returned records

Temporary foreach loop to test for the right data

Add a blank line between each record

```php
<?php

$myResult = mysql_query("SELECT * FROM ref_links",
$connectID)

  or die ("Unable to select item by ID from database");

while ($row = mysql_fetch_array($myResult, MYSQL_ASSOC)) {

  foreach ($row as $key => $value) {

    print "$key => $value<br />";

  }

  print '<br /><br />';

}

?>
```

Figure 4.13 shows the results.

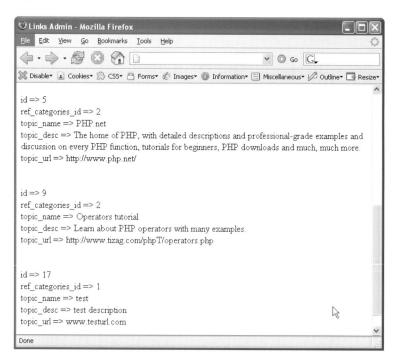

Writing the Listings Records in a Table

Now that we can access the records we want, we can easily write them in a table. Delete the `foreach` loop and the line with the two `<br />` tags that follow it, highlighted in the preceding code, and replace that code with the highlighted code shown here.

CODE 4.8: links_admin_step2.php4

Query the database

Loop through the returned records

```php
<?php

$myResult = mysql_query("SELECT * FROM ref_links",
$connectID)

    or die ("Unable to select item by ID from database");

print '<table border="1">'."\n";

while ($row = mysql_fetch_array($myResult, MYSQL_ASSOC)) {

    print '<tr>'."\n";

    print '<td>'.$row['topic_name'].'</td>'."\n";

    print '<td class="description">'.$row['topic_desc'].'</
td>'."\n";
```

```
    print '<td><a href="'.$row['topic_url'].'"    target="_
blank">'.$row['topic_url'];

    print'</a></td>';

    print '</tr>'."\n";

}

print '</table>'."\n";

?>
```

Now, after running the query, we open a table and then loop through the results, writing a row of the table with each loop. Imagine each

```
'.$row['data_name'].'
```

in the preceding code replaced with the corresponding bit of data from the database to more easily see what's going on in this code.

Once we have written all the rows, we close the table. **Figure 4.14** shows the onscreen result.

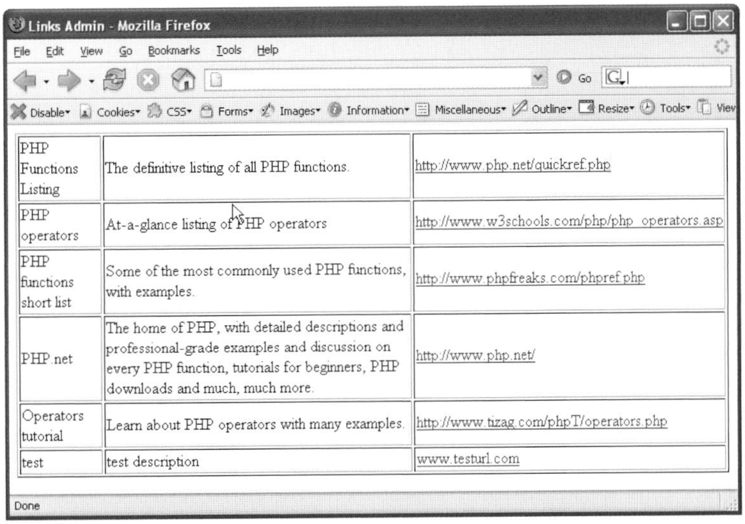

FIGURE 4.14 The listings records displayed as a table.

![Links Admin browser window]

The `target="_blank"` *attribute will not pass validation if you are using a STRICT DOCTYPE, as* `target` *is now a deprecated tag. In this situation, JavaScript whiz Jeremy Keith recommends using the following code to open a linked page in a new window:*

```
<a href="http://www.example.
com" onclick="window.
open(this.href); return
false">link text</a>
```

Because we wrote the URL into the `href` as well as displaying it (by writing it between the opening and closing `<a>` tags), the URL is active and takes us to the named page on the third-party site. Adding the attribute `target="_blank"` causes the linked page to open in a new window.

Because we added ."\n" (a line break) after each element in the table, our XHTML code output is nicely formatted and easy to check for accuracy; without line breaks, the entire code for the table would be one continuous line, requiring much horizontal scrolling to review. The browser ignores these \n line breaks when determining how to display the XHTML onscreen output, so their presence affects only the layout of the source code.

Here are a couple of records from the page source code to show you that each element is now on its own line, making the code much easier to understand.

CODE 4.9: Output of links_
admin_step2.php4

```
<table border="1">

<tr>

<td>PHP Functions Listing</td>

<td class="description">The definitive listing of all PHP
functions.</td>

<td><a href="http://www.php.net/quickref.php" target="_
blank">http://www.php.net/quickref.php</a></td>

</tr>

<!--records removed here-->

<tr>

<td>test</td>

<td class="description">test description</td>

<td><a href="www.testurl.com" target="_blank">www.testurl.
com</a></td>

</tr>

</table>
```

Displaying the Links Table Organized by Category

Now it's time to use both our database tables to display the records sorted by category. Figure 4.2 shows what we are shooting for; there, some CSS was used to make the table more stylish, but the underlying table structure is the same.

This next step is probably the most complex example in the entire book, so we will proceed step by step.

The Plan

We will first read both the listings table and the categories tables with a single SQL query called a JOIN, which joins data from multiple tables into a single data set.

As we write the table using these combined results, we will store the category ID of each listing after we write that listing into its table row; then, when we start to write the next listing, we will check whether it has the same category ID as the previous one. If the category ID has changed, we know that we have found the first record of the next category, so before writing it, we will write that new category name into a table heading. If this explanation is a little hard to understand, just read on, and everything will become clear.

Writing a SQL JOIN Query

The first step of our plan is to read both the listings table and the categories tables with a JOIN query that returns the required data from both tables in a single data set.

There are two ways of expressing a JOIN in SQL: explicitly, or using shorthand syntax that many programmers find easier to use.

The syntax for an explicit JOIN query is

```
SELECT fields_of_table1, fields_of_table2 FROM table_1 JOIN table2 ON foreign_key_of_table1=primary_key_of_table2
```

You can also use this shorthand:

```
SELECT fields_of_table1, fields_of_table2 FROM table_1, table2 WHERE foreign_key_of_table1=primary_key_of_table2
```

Here's the query we need, written in shorthand:

```
SELECT ref_links.*, ref_categories.category_name FROM ref_
links, ref_categories WHERE ref_links.ref_categories_id=ref_
categories.id
```

This query states that for each record selected, select all (*) fields from the links table and the category name from the categories table, in every case where the category ID in the listings record matches the category ID in the categories tables. If for some reason the record in the links table did not have a category specified, it would not be selected.

It so happens that this query returns the rows grouped by category, just the way we want them. If this were not the case, we could explicitly state how we want the query results organized, by using ORDER, like this:

```
$myResult = mysql_query('SELECT ref_links.*, ref_categories.
category_name FROM ref_links, ref_categories WHERE ref_links.
ref_categories_id=ref_categories.id ORDER BY ref_categories.
id,  ref_links.topic_name
```

We now replace the query in the previous code with our JOIN query. Again, we can use a temporary foreach loop to check the results that this new query returns. The new query and the temporary loop are highlighted here:

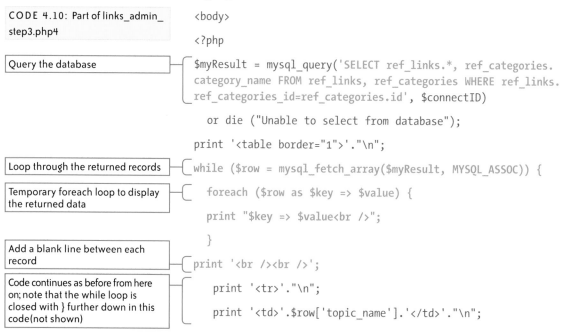

CODE 4.10: Part of links_admin_
step3.php4

```
<body>

<?php
```

Query the database

```
$myResult = mysql_query('SELECT ref_links.*, ref_categories.
category_name FROM ref_links, ref_categories WHERE ref_links.
ref_categories_id=ref_categories.id', $connectID)

   or die ("Unable to select from database");

print '<table border="1">'."\n";
```

Loop through the returned records

```
while ($row = mysql_fetch_array($myResult, MYSQL_ASSOC)) {
```

Temporary foreach loop to display the returned data

```
   foreach ($row as $key => $value) {

   print "$key => $value<br />";

   }
```

Add a blank line between each record

```
print '<br /><br />';
```

Code continues as before from here on; note that the while loop is closed with } further down in this code(not shown)

```
      print '<tr>'."\n";

      print '<td>'.$row['topic_name'].'</td>'."\n";
```

Figure 4.15 shows the results in the browser.

FIGURE 4.15 The JOIN query displays data from both tables. Most of the data displayed here is from the listings table, but the last item in each record is the name of the category from the categories tables. Our JOIN query was successful.

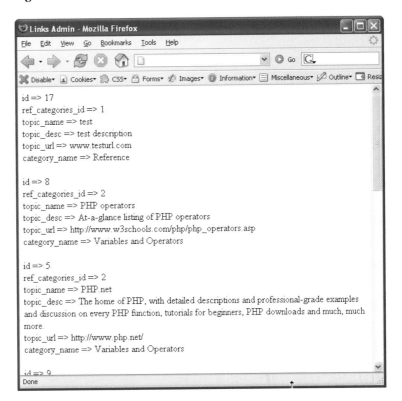

Adding the Category Headings to the Table

Now that we are sure that we are retrieving the data we want, let's proceed with the next steps of our plan:

1. Store the category ID of each listing *after* we write it to its table row.

2. As we start to write the next listing, check whether it has the same category ID as the previous one; if so, just write it, but if not, then we know we have found the first record of the next category.

3. If we have found the first record of the next category, write the new category name in a table heading that spans all the columns of the table *before* writing the listings that are in that category.

To perform step 1, simply put the category ID in a variable right at the end of the `while` loop. We'll call this variable `$last_cat`, because when we test it next time around the loop, it will contain the category ID of the last record we wrote. So, in the code, after the table row closes, but before the `while` loop closes, we add this line:

CODE 4.11: Part of links_admin4. php4

```
print "</tr>\n"; //Close the table row

   $lastCat = $row['category_name'];
```

End of while loop

```
}
```

Now at the start of the loop, we will put the category ID of the next record into a variable called $this_Cat, and, before the code that writes this record, we will add a test to compare $this_Cat and $last_Cat. If they don't match, we know that we have encountered the first listing in a new category, so we'll write a table heading with the category name of this new record.

Right after the `while` loop opens, add this code:

CODE 4.12: Part of links_admin4. php4

$thisCat is used to test whether a new heading needs to be written out

TRUE first time ($lastCat not set) and each time a new category is found; then write out a table heading with the category name

Heading spans all four columns of table

Print the next category heading

```
while ($row = mysql_fetch_array($myResult, MYSQL_ASSOC)) {

   $thisCat= $row['category_name'];

   if ($lastCat<>$thisCat) {

   print '<th colspan="4">';

   print "<h3>".$row['category_name']."</h3>";

   print "</th>\n";

   }
```

Write out listing table rows

```
   print '<tr>';

   print '<td width="150">'.$row['topic_name'].'</td>';
```

The first time the loop runs, $lastCat is not even initialized, so the test returns TRUE (because $last_cat does not equal $this_cat), and the first heading is written. After the loop has run once, $last_cat contain a value, and this value is compared with the value of $this_cat the next time the loop runs. The result is that before the first record is written, and before each record with a new ID is written, a new heading is added to the table (**Figure 4.16**).

The expression if ($lastCat<>$thisCat) *means "if last_cat is not equal to this_cat."*

FIGURE 4.16 The listing now has category headings.

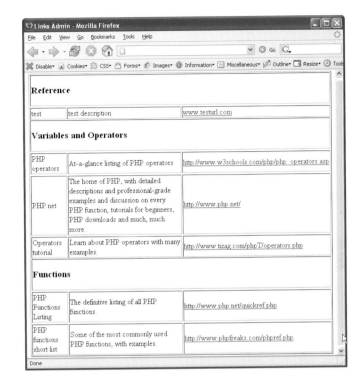

Adding Modify and Delete Links to Each Record

So that we can manage the links, we will next add a Modify and a Delete link to each record.

The Modify link will pass the ID of the listing to the Edit Links form by using a query string on the end of the URL, like this:

```
href="links_form.php4?modify_id=7"
```

This particular URL query will tell the Edit Links form page to populate the form with listing record 7, so that the record's data can be changed by the user. (In a later step, we will revisit the form script and add some code that will allow the form to load a record based on the `modify_id` value and then determine whether the submitted form data is a new record or an update and write to the database accordingly.)

Don't confuse URL query strings with queries on the database—same word, but a query string extends a URL with data that can be used by the page, whereas a database query is a means of moving data between a script and the database.

The Delete link will be similar, except it will reload the Links Admin page on which it lives:

```
href="<?php $_SERVER['PHP_SELF'] ?>?delete_id=23"
```

We will add some code at the top of this page's script to delete the record of the listing identified by the ID, right before the query we just wrote that loads all the listing records. Thus, clicking the Delete link will appear to simply refresh the page, with the deleted record instantly removed from the listing (and the database).

Coding the Modify and Delete Links

To add these two links to the page, we need to add two new cells to the right end of each record: one for each link.

After the last cell (`<td>`) of the listing table, right before we close the table row, we add two more cells that look like this:

CODE 4.13: Part of links_admin_
step5

```
print '<td><a href="'.$row['topic_url'].'" target="_
blank">'.$row['topic_url'];

print'</a></td>';

$id=$row['id'];
```

The modify link

```
print '<td><a href="links_form_step3.php4?modify_
id='.$id.'">Edit</td>';
```

The delete link

```
print '<td><a href="';

print ($_SERVER['PHP_SELF']);

print '?delete_id='.$id.'">Delete</a></td>';
```

```
print '</tr>'."\n";
```

First, we set a variable called `$id` to the ID of the record in the `$_GET` array, to avoid having to escape the new set of single quotation marks in `$row['id']`) if we include it in the URL query. Then we write the two new cells of our table.

If we now load the page and roll over one of our new links, the status bar shows the query with that listing's ID appended to it (**Figure 4.17**).

I decided to label the Modify link with the word Edit, to make the link's use clearer to the user, so in the rest of this discussion, the words modify and edit are synonymous.

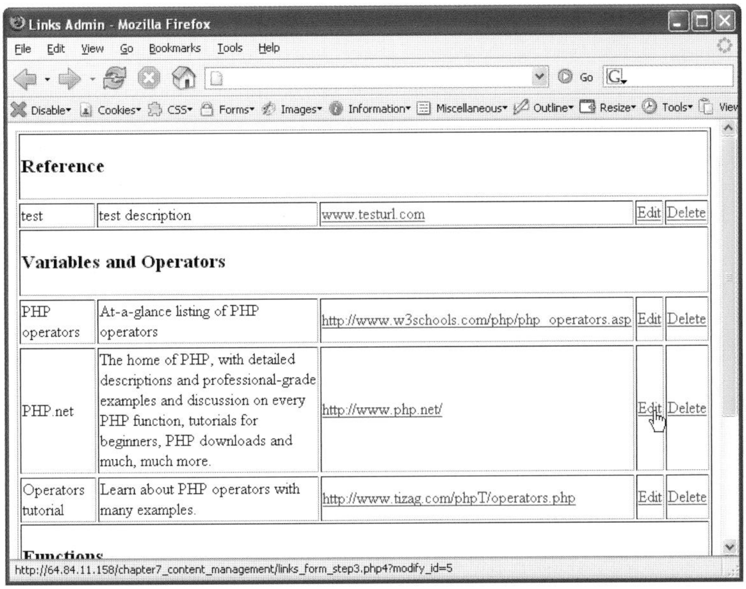

FIGURE 4.17 Pointing at one of the new links displays the URL with a query containing the record's ID in the status bar at the bottom of the window.

Coding the Delete Functionality

Now the links are working, so let's add the code to make the Delete link functional.

Deleting a record by ID is easy, as we saw in Chapter 3. When the page loads, we test whether the delete_id variable in the $_GET array is set; if it is, we use its value to delete the corresponding record. (Any data passed in the query part of a URL string is accessible from the $_GET array.) Here's the delete query in the code block:

```
if ($_GET['delete_id']) {

id = ($_GET['delete_id']);

$success = mysql_query ("DELETE FROM ref_links WHERE id =
$id", $connectID)

  or die ("Unable to delete record from database");

if ($success) { print "Record successfully deleted"; }

}
```

Be sure to include a WHERE clause with a SQL DELETE statement; without it, SQL will delete all the records in the table.

CODE 4.14: Part of list_admin6.
php4

This code goes into the script right after the SQL connection code and right before the XHTML DOCTYPE element:

```
mysql_select_db("databaseName", $connectID)
  or die ("Unable to select database");
if ($_GET['delete_id']) {
$id = $_GET['delete_id']);
$success = mysql_query ("DELETE FROM ref_links WHERE id =
$id", $connectID)
  or die ("Unable to delete record from database");
  if ($success) {
    print "Record successfully deleted";
  }
}
?>

<!DOCTYPE html PUBLIC "-//W3C//DTD XHTML 1.0 Transitional//
EN" "http://www.w3.org/TR/xhtml1/DTD/xhtml1-transitional.
dtd">
```

Let's test this code by deleting the test record that we added to the listings earlier in this chapter (**Figures 4.18** and **4.19**).

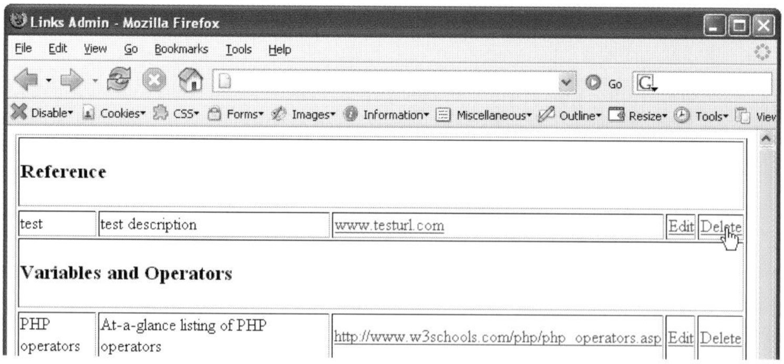

FIGURE 4.18 Clicking a delete link.

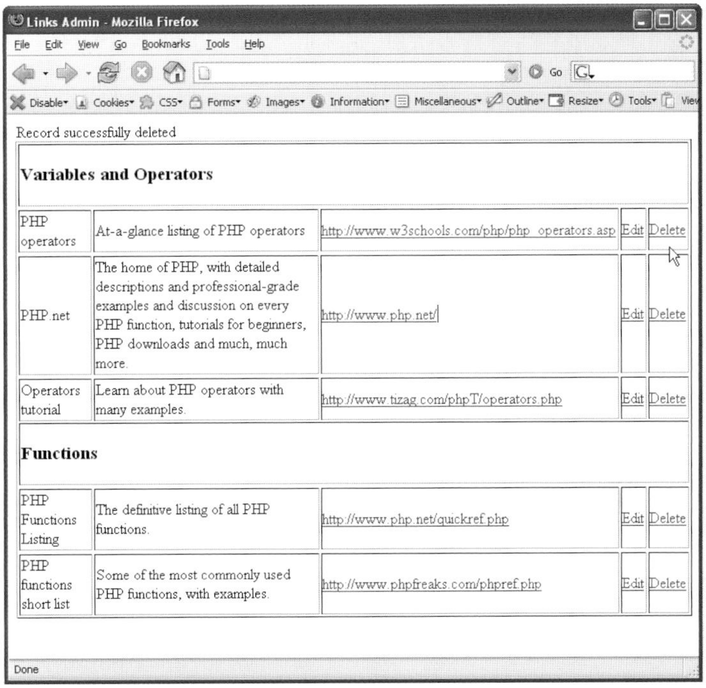

FIGURE 4.19 After the Delete link is clicked, the record is deleted and the listings are reloaded.

In Figure 4.19, note that because the deleted record was the only one in the Reference category, the Reference heading is no longer displayed either.

Modifying a Record: Going Back to the Edit Links Form Page

When the user clicks the Edit link to modify a record, the Edit Links form page loads. If we load the form in this way now, the form is blank. What we must do is load the form with the data for the record whose ID was passed to the form page in the URL's query string, so that that record's data can be viewed and modified. Our first task is to determine whether a modify request (or some other kind of request) was issued to the page.

Four Possible Edit Links Form Activities

To use the Edit Links form to modify records as well as create them, our code must be able to detect which of four possible states exists when the page loads:

- State 1: The user has loaded the page to enter a new listing:

  Test for: no form submit, no modify ID.

- State 2: The user has submitted a new listing:

  Test for: form submitted, no modify ID.

- State 3: The Links Admin page has passed the ID of a record that needs to be updated:

  Test for: no form submit, modify ID present.

- State 4: The user has submitted the form to update a listing:

  Test for: form submitted, modify ID present.

Here are the tests for states 2, 3, and 4:

- State 2: `if (($_POST['submitted']) && (!$_GET['modify_id']))`
- State 3: `if ((!$_POST['submitted']) && ($_GET['modify_id']))`
- State 4: `if ((@$_POST['submitted']) && ($_GET['modify_id']))`

Note that the only difference among these three is the "not" exclamation point operator (highlighted).

If none of these three conditions resolve to TRUE, then state 1 must be true by default.

By creating an elseif structure that includes these three tests (see Chapter 1 for details on if-else structures), we can ensure that only one of the four code sections that we will add will run each time the page loads. Here's the code to do that:

| Then the user has submitted a new listing |
| Then the administration page has passed the ID of the record to be updated |
| Then the user has submitted the form to update a listing |
| Then the user has loaded the page to enter a new listing |

```
if (($_POST['submitted']) && (!$_GET['modify_id'])) {
} elseif ((!$_POST['submitted']) && ($_GET['modify_id'])) {
} elseif (($_POST['submitted']) && ($_GET['modify_id'])) {
} else {
}
```

Let's move this code block into our form. We already have the code for adding a new listing, so we can add that into this code block at the same time. Now the code for our form page, from after the database connection code to the start of the XHTML, looks like this:

CODE 4.15: Part of links_form4.php4

| The user has submitted a new listing |

```
if (($_POST['submitted']) && (!$_GET['modify_id'])) {
    $category=($_POST['category']);
    $topic_name=($_POST['topic_name']);
    $topic_description=($_POST['topic_description']);
    $topic_url=($_POST['topic_url']);
```

| Write to database |

```
    mysql_query ("INSERT into ref_links (ref_categories_id,
topic_name, topic_desc, topic_url) VALUES ('$category',
'$topic_name', '$topic_description', '$topic_url')",
$connectID)
    or die ("Unable to insert record into database");
    print "Record successfully added";
} elseif ((!$_POST['submitted']) && ($_GET['modify_id'])) {
} elseif (($_POST['submitted']) && ($_GET['modify_id'])) {
} else {
}
?>
```

Now we can add the code that will load the Edit Links form with a listing record when the Links Admin page requests a listing update. That code will go right after the highlighted comment in the code just shown.

After making these changes to the code, run a quick test to ensure that the Edit Links form can still create new records.

Coding the Edit Links Form to Modify Records

To get the Edit Links form to display the requested record, we will need another JOIN query, only this time, instead of retrieving all the records as we did in the Links Admin form code, we are just going to retrieve the data for the one record identified by the ID that is passed in the requesting URL.

Retrieving One Record Using a SQL JOIN Query

We will start by retrieving the record we want to modify.

```
$thisRecord = mysql_query("SELECT ref_links.*,ref_categories.
category_name, ref_categories.id AS cat_id FROM ref_links,
ref_categories WHERE ref_categories.id = ref_links.ref_
categories_id AND ref_links.id = '$id'", $connectID)
```

This JOIN query is identical to one that we wrote earlier for the Links Admin page that retrieved all the records and all the categories, except for two small details.

First, there is the addition of an AND clause (highlighted). Because of this requirement for a match on a specific ID (a unique primary key), only one record is returned.

Because you will inevitably be deleting records during the testing process, remember when testing the code in this section to ensure that the URL query is referencing the ID of a record that still exists in the listing table of your database, such as http://www.yourDomain.com/chapter4_content_management/links_form7.php4?modify_id=5 The best way to ensure that the URL references an existing database record is to simply click an Edit link on the Links Admin page, which was, of course, created from records in the database. The Edit Links form page will then load, and the URL passed to the page will have the query with a valid modify ID appended to it.

Second, without the addition of the AS cat_id clause (also highlighted), the query will cause both tables to return a field called ID, and the code we are about to write may get confused as to which ID we are referring. Having fields with the same name in two different tables is a common occurrence in databases, and SQL has means for us to resolve this problem, using the AS clause. Simply put, the SQL code:

```
ref_categories.id AS cat_id
```

changes the name of the category id to cat_id, but only in the result array—a SELECT query cannot modify the actual name of the field in the database. Now we will have only one element in our results array with the name id, as we will see in a moment.

Before we run the query, we need to copy the ID of the record from the $_GET array to a variable, to make the query easier to read—it's complicated enough already.

Using our `foreach` loop trick, we can verify that we do indeed have one, and only one, record in the results array, and that each element of the record has a unique name; when running a complex query like this, it is well worth the time it takes to ensure you have the data you want before you try using it in your code.

CODE 4.16: links_form_step5. php4

Then the administration page has passed the ID of the record to be updated

Put the record ID into a variable

```
} elseif  ((!$_POST['submitted']) && ($_GET['modify_id'])) {

  $id = $_GET['modify_id']);

        $this_Record = mysql_query("SELECT ref_links.*,ref_
categories.category_name, ref_categories.id AS cat_id
FROM ref_links, ref_categories WHERE ref_categories.id =
ref_links.ref_categories_id AND ref_links.id = '$id'",
$connectID)

        or die ("Can't read the this record.");
while ($record_data = mysql_fetch_array($myResult, MYSQL_
ASSOC)) {

foreach ($record_data as $key => $value) {

  print "$key => $value<br />";

  }

}
```

The highlighted part of this code associated with the while *and* for *loops is just for testing purposes and will soon be removed.*

End of temporary code

End of while loop

Clicking the Edit link of one of the displayed listings on the Links Admin page, which happens to have this URL in the link `href`.

```
links_form_step5.php4?modify_id=18
```

—loads the Edit Links form page and causes the `foreach` loop to print the following on the page above the form (the actual data you see will, of course, be different, but should appear in this format):

```
id => 18
ref_categories_id => 2
topic_name => var test
topic_desc => something about variables
topic_url => www.variables.com/lotsavars.htm
category_name => Variables and Operators
cat_id => 2
```

Note that the last data item, which came from the ID field of the categories table, now has the name `cat_id` instead of `id`, because of the `AS` clause in the query.

Displaying the Retrieved Data in the Edit Links Form Fields

Now that we know for sure that we have the data we need, we can make the Edit Links form "sticky" and display that data in the form fields. First, we no longer need the `while` loop and the `foreach` loop; we can strip out the highlighted parts of the code in the preceding section.

Next, we will add the following code in the values of the form XHTML elements so the form displays the record data.

CODE 4.17: Part of links_form6.php4

```
<!--topic_name-->

<label for="topic_name"   >Topic Name</label>

<input name="topic_name" type="text" size="30" id="topic_name" value="<?php print $record_data['topic_name']; ?>" />

<!--topic_description-->

<label for="topic_description">Topic Description</label>

<textarea name="topic_description"><?php print $record_data['topic_desc']; ?></textarea>

<!--topic_url-->

<label for="topic_url">Topic URL</label>

<input name="topic_url" type="text" size="30" id="topic_url" value="<?php print $record_data['topic_url']; ?>" />

<input type="submit" value="Submit" name="submitted" />

</form>
```

Figure 4.20 shows the results.

FIGURE 4.20 The Edit Links form inputs (text fields) now display the data retrieved by the SQL query.

Add or modify a listing

Test Link

Topic Category
Select a Catagory ▾

Topic Name
var test

Topic Description
something about variables

Topic URL
www.variables.com/lotsavars.htm

Submit

Because we will redirect the user to the Links Admin page after a record has been successfully added or deleted, the only time we need the form to be sticky is in this particular case, when we display a record so it can be modified.

Making the Menu Sticky

For those of you who skipped *HTML 101: The Basics* in high school, each choice in a SELECT element (a drop-down menu in a form) is created with an OPTION element—for example:

```
<option value="1">Reference</option>
```

If we wanted this choice to be displayed in the menu as the default choice that's visible when the page loads, as shown in **Figure 4.21**, then all we would need to do is modify the code to look like this:

```
<option value="1" selected="selected">Reference</option>
```

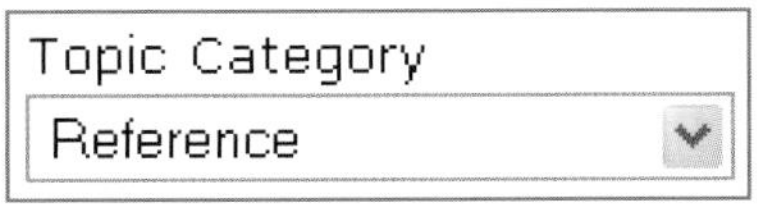

FIGURE 4.21 Default menu choice visible when the page loads.

Topic Category
Reference ▾

So to have the drop-down menu of our form display the category of the retrieved record, we need to add this bit of code to the correct OPTION element.

CODE 4.18: Part of list_form_
step6.php4

The existing code for the drop-down menu looks like this, with the part that writes the OPTION elements highlighted:

```php
<?php

print '<select name="category">'."\n";

print '<option value="none">Select a Catagory</option>'."\n";

$Categories = mysql_query('SELECT * FROM ref_categories', $connectID);while ($Category = mysql_fetch_array($Categories, MYSQL_ASSOC)){

print '<option value="'.$Category['id'].'">'.$Category['category_name']."</option>\n";

}

print '</select>'."<br />\n";

?>
```

The drop-down menu already has its own SQL query that retrieves the category IDs and names, which are then added to the OPTION elements as they are written. All we need to do is determine which of the IDs from this query match the category ID from our modify record query and then add the selected="selected" code to the corresponding OPTION element as it is written out.

The modified code that replaces the highlighted code looks like this:

CODE 4.19: Part of list_form_
step7.php4

The print *statement for the* "selected" *phrase has two sets of double quotation marks, with the inner ones escaped with backslashes so that PHP knows to treat them as part of the string defined by the outer ones.*

```php
print '<option value="'.$Category['id'].'"';

  if($record_data['cat_id']==$Category['id']) print " selected=\"selected\" ";

print '>'.$Category['category_name']."</option>\n";
```

If you compare the before and after code here, you can see that we broke the original line of code into two lines so that we could add another line in between them that checks for a modify ID match before each category ID is written and inserts the required "selected" phrase if there is indeed a match.

Now when we load the page, the menu displays the correct category name for the record (**Figure 4.22**).

FIGURE 4.22 The drop-down menu
now displays the category of the
record.

Add or modify a listing
Test Link
Topic Category
Variables and Operators ▾
Topic Name
var test
Topic Description
something about
variables
Topic URL
www.variables.com/lotsavars.htm
Submit

*This technique for making the
drop-down menu sticky can also be
applied to check boxes and radio
buttons.*

The user can now view the category and information for the listing
to be modified, make changes both to the category and the text, and
then click Submit to update the record.

As a more complete test of the menu's stickiness, go the Links
Admin page and click the Edit link of a listing in another category;
the Edit Links form page should immediately display that listing's
data, including the correct category in the menu.

There is only one more step to complete the functionality of this
form, and that is to write the code to update this modified record
when the Edit Links form is submitted.

Updating a Record

We have already seen where the code to update the listing will go:
in the section of the `elseif` statement that begins

```
elseif  (($_POST['submitted']) && ($_GET['modify_id']))
```

If you are wondering how the `$_GET` array can still contain the
`modify_id` data after the form is submitted, here's the answer: The
form is submitted to the URL of the current page, of which the
query string is a part, because of this form action:

```
<form method="post" action="<?php $_SERVER['PHP_SELF'] ?>">
```

Thus, the `$_GET` array is reset with the same `modify_id` data when
the Submit button is clicked and the page reloads, and we can again
test for its presence.

The UPDATE query we are about to write needs to modify only the
listings table. If the user assigns the listing to a new category using

the drop-down menu, we simply record the new category ID in the `ref_categories_id` field of the listings table; the categories table itself needs to be modified only if a category name is added, modified, or deleted.

This query is going to need access to some variables that are in other sections of the code, so we need to make a couple of minor changes before we can write and test our query.

Sharing Variables between Queries

When we wrote the code to add a record, we copied the `$_POST` array data (that contains the submitted data from the Edit Links form) to variables that were shorter and easier to use. Here's the start of the `ifelse` code structure, which contains the code for a new record, where these variables are currently set:

Start of elseif structure	`if (($_POST['submitted']) && (!$_GET['modify_id'])) {`
The user has submitted a new listing	`$category=($_POST['category']);`
	`$topic_name=($_POST['topic_name']);`
	`$topic_description=($_POST['topic_description']);`
	`$topic_url=($_POST['topic_url']);`

We want use those same four variables in our update, but they are within the "new record" section of our `elseif` structure and therefore will not be set when the Edit Links form is submitted for an update. We thus will move these four lines that set the variable up in the code flow, so that they are no longer within the `elseif` structure and therefore will be set regardless of whether the form is submitted for a new record or an update.

CODE 4.20: Part of list_form_step8	`$category=($_POST['category']);`
	`$topic_name=($_POST['topic_name']);`
	`$topic_description=($_POST['topic_description']);`
Start of elseif structure	`$topic_url=($_POST['topic_url']);`
The user has submitted a new listing	`if (($_POST['submitted']) && (!$_GET['modify_id'])) {`

Our UPDATE query will also use the `modify_id` value, and at the moment that variable is set within the section of the `ifelse` statement that deals with a modify request from the Links Admin form—the code we just wrote:

Then the administration page has passed the ID of the record to be updated

```
} elseif  ((!$_POST['submitted']) && ($_GET['modify_id'])) {

$id = ($_GET['modify_id']);
```

We will take that line (highlighted) and remove it from the `ifelse` structure too, so it is set both when a modify request is made and when a modified record is submitted for updating. We'll move it up with the other four newly located variables from the previous step:

```
$category=($_POST['category']);

$topic_name=($_POST['topic_name']);

$topic_description=($_POST['topic_description']);
```

Start of ifelse structure

```
$topic_url=($_POST['topic_url']);
```

The user has submitted a new listing

```
if (($_POST['submitted']) && (!$_GET['modify_id'])) {
```

These kinds of minor reorganizations of your code are common as you add functionality to a script. These two simple steps have saved us from having to write code to set these five variables in two different places. Now we can get back to the job at hand: writing a query to update a record.

Writing the UPDATE Query

Here is the UPDATE query:

Then the user has submitted the form to update a listing

```
} elseif  (($_POST['submitted']) && ($_GET['modify_id'])) {
    $success = mysql_query("UPDATE ref_links SET ref_
categories_id = '$category', topic_name = '$topic_name',
topic_desc = '$topic_description', topic_url = '$topic_url'
WHERE id='$id'", $connectID);
```

If the the update was successful, return to the administration page

```
    if ($success) {

    header ('Location: links_admin_step6.php4?updated=1');

    }
} else { …etc
```

This query is similar to the INSERT query we used to add a new record; the only differences are that it's an UPDATE query, not an INSERT query, so it modifies a record instead of creating one, and that it includes the `WHERE id='$id'` clause, which tells SQL which record to update. Note that if the record is successfully updated, the user is redirected to the Links Admin page, where the updated record will be displayed along with the others.

```
if ($success) {

header ('Location: links_admin_step6.php4?updated=1');

}
```

Because we are leaving this page at this point in the script, we do not need to display a "success" message here, but the query at the end of the URL enables us to tell the Links Admin page that the record was updated so that the Links Admin page knows to display the success message for the user. We will code the display of this message in the Links Admin form script during the final cleanup steps, which we will tackle next.

For now, note that you are at the very satisfying point where you can click the Edit link of a listing on the Links Admin page and instantly see that listing's information on the Edit Links form page, where you can modify it and submit the changes. You are then redirected to the Links Admin page, where you can see the updated record. You can then pick the next record to update and repeat the process. In this way, you can make changes to a number of listings in rapid succession.

Adding Finishing Touches to the Edit Links Form Page

There are a couple of minor additions we need to make to finish the Edit Links form page.

Redirecting When a Record Is Successfully Added

When we wrote the code for the form to add a listing, we hadn't yet created the Links Admin page. Now that the Links Admin page exists, we can send the user there when a new record is added, where that record can be viewed along with the others, just as we did when a record is updated.

Here is the current code for the INSERT (add a record) query and its success message, located in the first section of the `ifelse` structure:

```
mysql_query ("INSERT into ref_links (ref_categories_id,
topic_name, topic_desc, topic_url) VALUES ('$category',
'$topic_name', '$topic_description', '$topic_url')",
$connectID)

  or die ("Unable to insert record into database");

  print "Record successfully added";
```

Again, there is no need to display a success message on a page that we are going to leave, so we will use virtually the same code we just wrote to test for the success of the update to both redirect the user and pass notification of the record's successful creation to the Links Admin page so we can display the success message there instead. Replace the preceding highlighted code with the following:

CODE 4.21: Part of links_form_step9

```
if ($success) {

  header ('Location: links_admin_step6.php4?added=1');

}
```

Adding a Link to the Links Admin Page

If the user loads the Edit Links form page intending to add a link and then decides not to add the link, we need some way to send the user to the Links Admin page. There is a dummy link at the top of the form that currently reads Test Link; let's make it operational. Here's the current code:

CODE 4.22: Part of links_form_
step8

```
<body>

<h3>Add or modify a listing</h3>

<a href="#">Test Link</a>

<form method="post" action="<?php $_SERVER['PHP_SELF'] ?>">
```

It's a quick step to rewrite the link so that it returns the user to the Links Admin page:

CODE 4.23: Part of links_form_
step9

```
<a href="links_admin_step6.php4">Links Admin page</a>
```

With these two changes, our form is complete.

Adding Finishing Touches to the Links Admin Form

The first thing the Links Admin form needs is an onscreen title.

Also, because the Links Admin form is the primary page of this CMS, we need to offer navigation links from it to two other pages: the form page that we have already created and the listings page that visitors will see when they visit the site, which we will create (quite easily, you'll be pleased to hear) as the final part of this chapter.

Right after the body tag of the Links Admin page, add the following:

CODE 4.24: Part of links_admin_
step7.php4

```
<h2>Links Admin</h2>

<p><a href="links_form7.php4">Add new link</a><br />

<a href="link_listings4.php4">View listings page</a></p>
```

This page of listings could get very long, so we'll also add the two links at the bottom of the page right before the closing body tag, to save the user from having to scroll all the way back to the top.

```
print '</table>'."\n";

?>

<p><a href="links_form7.php4">Add new link</a><br />

<a href="link_listings4.php4">View listings page</a></p>

</body>
```

Note that the links are wrapped in a paragraph tag so we can style some space around them with CSS.

Adding CSS Styles to the Links Admin Page

The default table presentation is rather dull and puts every data element in its own box, which doesn't aid understanding of the relationships between them. To improve this situation, add the following CSS styles to the page, right after the `<title>` tag:

```
<style type="text/css">

body {font-family:verdana, arial, sans-serif; font-size:80%}

h2 {font-size:1.4em; }

h3 {padding:10px 0 0 0;margin:0; border-top:2px solid #666;}

table {border-bottom:2px solid #666}

td {padding:0 2px; vertical-align:top; border-top: 1px solid #CCC;}

a {color:#066;}

a:hover {color:#000;text-decoration:none;}

</style>
```

Then find the `<table>` tag a few lines farther down the page and remove the border attribute:

```
print '<table border="1">'."\n";
```

Load the page (**Figure 4.23**).

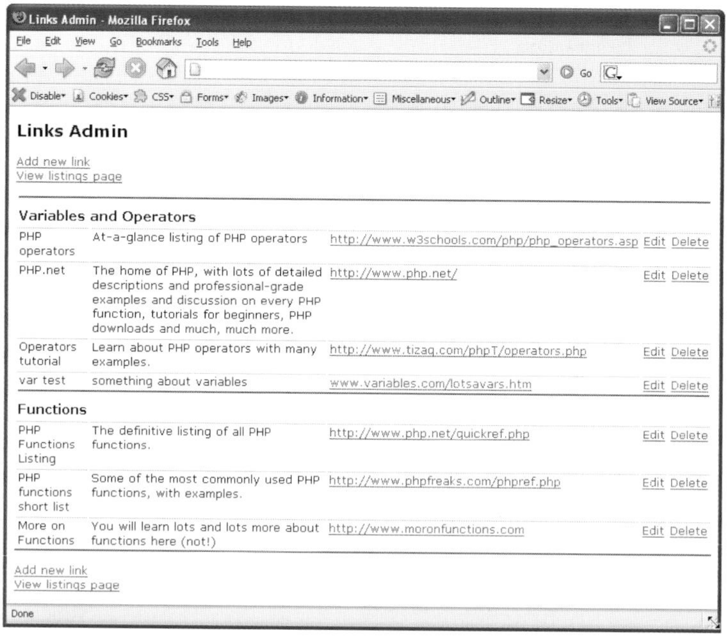

FIGURE 4.23 Now the page has navigation links at the top and bottom, and some CSS styles have changed the appearance of the listings table.

The design of the page is much improved with the addition of the CSS styles, and the removal of the vertical lines from the table certainly helps the viewer better understand what data relates to what.

Truncating the Displayed URL Strings

The problem with displaying URLs onscreen, especially in tables, is that they are one continuous, unbroken string of text, so they are always displayed on one line. Adding a link to the PHP installation information on the PHP.net site shows the problems that long URLs can cause (**Figure 4.24**).

As you can see, not only does this problem cause the column with the URL to be very wide, but also the other columns get crushed down to make room for it. No amount of adding width attributes to table cells can help you here.

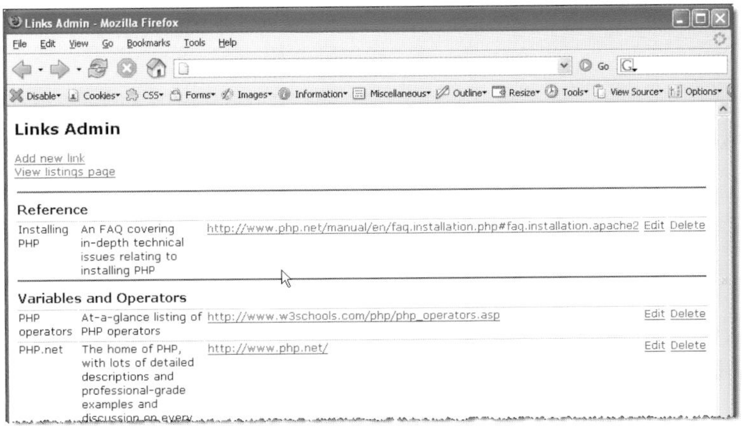

FIGURE 4.24 Long URLs force the table cell to be very wide.

The way around this problem is to truncate (cut the end off) the displayed URL using PHP's `substr` substring function.

The existing code for this cell looks like this:

CODE 4.25: Part of links_admin_step7

```php
print '<td class="description">'.$row['topic_desc'].'</td>'."\n";

print '<td><a href="'.$row['topic_url'].'" target="_blank">'.$row['topic_url'];

print'</a></td>';

$id=$row['id'];

print '<td><a href="links_form_step8.php4?modify_id='.$id.'">Edit</td>';
```

This code writes the URL into two places in the `a` link element: into `href`, which sets the target page of the link, and also between the opening and closing tags, which displays the URL onscreen. We don't want to touch the `href` URL or the link won't work; anyway, it's the second URL—the one displayed onscreen—that's our problem. Because it's used only for display purposes, we can modify this one as much as we want, as long as it remains meaningful to the viewer.

The `substr` function is a great example of the many useful string functions that PHP offers. You pass the `substr` function a string, and it returns a substring, a part of that string, according to the other arguments you define. The structure of the `substr` function is

```php
substr(string, start_position, length)
```

To see a full list of the entities used with documents written in English—that is , using the Latin-1 (ISO-8859-1) character set—see http://www.htmlhelp.com/reference/html40/entities/latin1.html.

The counting starts from zero, so this code will return the first 30 characters of the string:

```
(substr($row['topic_url'],0,29));
```

This code will return only the first 30 characters of any URL longer than 30 characters, but it looks weird if the URL is simply cut short; we need to add an ellipsis (…) at the end of any URL we truncate, to indicate that we shortened the URL on purpose, and that there is more that we are not displaying. To achieve this user-friendly detail, we turn to another handy-dandy string function, strlen(*string*), which simply returns the number of characters in the string. If it tells us that the original string length is greater than 30, it will print the ellipsis after the truncated version, using the HTML ellipsis entity (…).

CODE 4.26: Part of link_admin9.php4

```
print '<td><a href="'.$row['topic_url'].'">'.(substr($row['topic_url'],0,29));

if ((strlen($row['topic_url']) > 30)) {print "&#8230;";}

print'</a></td>';
```

Now the problem is solved (**Figure 4.25**).

FIGURE 4.25 All displayed URLs longer than 30 characters are truncated to this length, and an ellipsis is added to indicate that not all the URL is displayed.

Note that the full URL is displayed in the status bar at the bottom of the screen when the user points at the truncated URL onscreen—the status bar displays the href value, which we did not change.

Adding the Success Messages

You have seen that when the user either adds or modifies a record using the Edit Links form, the user is redirected to the Links Admin page, where the new or modified record is displayed along with all the others. In the case of both redirects, we append a URL query indicating the success of that action. We now need to check for those query strings as the Links Admin page loads and display an appropriate onscreen message.

The query on the new record URL is:

```
links_admin_step6.php4?added=1
```

The query on the modified record URL is:

```
links_admin_step6.php4?updated=1
```

Here, the purpose of 1 is to represent TRUE, so this is the code we need to add to the Links Admin page:

```
<h2>Links Admin</h2>

<p><a href="links_form7.php4">Add new link</a><br />

<a href="link_listings4.php4">View listings page</a></p>

<?php

if ($_GET['added']) print '<p style="color:red; font-weight:
bold;">Record successfully created!</p>';

if ($_GET['updated']) print '<p style="color:red; font-
weight: bold;">Record successfully updated!</p>';
```

Query the database ⟶

```
$myResult = mysql_query('SELECT ref_links.*, ref_categories.
category_name FROM ref_links, ref_categories WHERE ref_links.
ref_categories_id=ref_categories.id', $connectID)

  or die ("Unable to select from database");
```

We can test this code by simply tacking the appropriate variables onto the end of the page's URL (**Figures 4.26** and **4.27**).

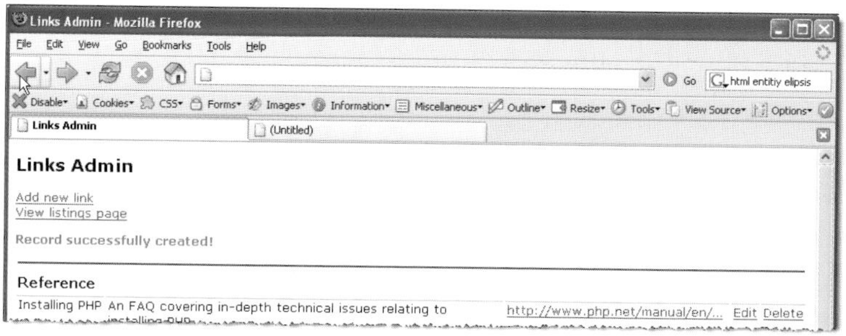

FIGURE 4.26 The add record query in the URL causes the "created" message to appear.

FIGURE 4.27 The update record query in the URL causes the "updated" message to appear.

Note the queries on the ends of the URLs in **Figures 4.26** and **4.27**. Also, I added some simple inline CSS styles to the paragraph tags to make the messages stand out in red and bold; in a multipage site, it would be better to a define a special CSS class in the style sheet for such messages and add that class to every message XHTML element.

This completes that Links Admin page. All that is left to do is to create a listing page where visitors can see and select the links that the CMS publishes to the site.

Plugging Security Holes

Notice that I passed a simple TRUE variable (for example, added=1) across to the Links Admin page from the Edit Links form page, rather than passing the actual string of text I wanted to print. This variable is then tested, and if the test resolves to TRUE, a message is displayed. You may wonder why go to all this trouble when, for example, you could easily achieve the same result by writing the URL as:

```
links_admin_step6.php4?added="Record successfully updated"
```

and simply adding:

```
print ($_GET[updated]);
```

to the Links Admin page. The reason you do *not* want to use this approach to display the message is that it creates a large and easily exploited security hole. It would be simple to request the page from anywhere on the Web, with a nasty piece of code in place of the text message in the URL's query string. This code would then be written directly into the page and executed, perhaps providing a means of digging around in your database and passing information back to the requesting page.

Hackers spend their time probing sites for exactly these kinds of vulnerabilities. Be aware that anything that the page will accept from a URL can potentially be exploited, so consider how the code you write could be vulnerable to attack, as I did here.

If you never use any data directly from the $_GET, $_POST, or $_COOKIE arrays to print to the screen or use in your database queries, you will have taken a huge step in protecting your site from attack. If you do use such data, validate it carefully, as we did in Chapter 2, to ensure that it's in the format you are expecting; see the sidebar "Validate for Public Use" later in this chapter for an example of a very simple way to check incoming data.

Creating the Public Listings Page

To create a page of the listings that will go on the Web site the public will view, we can, with very minor modifications, use the code for the Links Admin page. We simply need to remove the Edit and Modify columns, and also the navigation links above and below the table, as these all these relate to maintaining the records, which we are not going to allow our visitors to do. Go to the Links Admin page code, remove these sections of the code, and save the page under a new name, such as **links_listing.php4**.

If the page template to which you are adding the listings has side columns, the layout we used for the Links Admin page may be too wide. In this case, you can lay out the listings page in a slightly different format, as shown in **Figure 4.1**.

Technically, the listings page is virtually identical to the Links Admin page; only the visual appearance is different. Because of this, the code here is presented with minimal comment.

CODE 4.27: links_listing.php4

```php
<?php

$hostUrl = 'localhost';

$userName = 'yourUserName';

$password = 'yourPassword';

$connectID = mysql_connect($hostUrl, $userName, $password)

   or die ("Sorry, can't connect to database");

mysql_select_db("databaseName", $connectID)

   or die ("Unable to select database");

?>
<!DOCTYPE html PUBLIC "-//W3C//DTD XHTML 1.0 Transitional//
EN" "http://www.w3.org/TR/xhtml1/DTD/xhtml1-transitional.
dtd">

<html xmlns="http://www.w3.org/1999/xhtml">

<head>

<meta http-equiv="Content-Type" content="text/html;
charset=iso-8859-1" />

<title>Reference links</title>

<style type="text/css">

* {margin:0}

div#content {font-family:Arial, Helvetica, sans-serif;
margin:.75em 40px; border-bottom:2px solid #777; padding:
10px 0;}

div#content h1 {font-size:1em;}

div#content p {font-size:.8em; margin:0;}

div#content h2 {font-size:.9em; font-weight:bold;
margin:.75em 0 0 0;}

div#ref_links {margin:0 0 0 20px;}

div#ref_links h3 {font-size:.8em; font-weight:bold;
margin:.5em 0 0 0;}

div#ref_links p {font-size:.75em; margin:0;}
```

Connect to database

Select the database to read from

```
div#ref_links a {font-size:.75em; font-weight:bold; margin-
bottom:.75em;}

div#ref_links:hover a {text-decoration:none;}

</style>

</head>

<body>

<div id="content">

  <h1>Links to Codin' related sites</h1>

  <p>Many of the URLs referenced in Codin' are listed
here.</p>

<?php

$myResult = mysql_query('SELECT ref_links.*, ref_categories.
category_name FROM ref_links, ref_categories WHERE ref_links.
ref_categories_id=ref_categories.id', $connectID)

  or die ("Unable to select from database");

while ($row=mysql_fetch_array($myResult, MYSQL_ASSOC)) {

  $thisCat= $row['category_name'];

  if ($lastCat<>$thisCat) {

  print "<h2>".$row['category_name']."</h2>";

  }

  print '<div id="ref_links">';

  print "<h3>".$row['topic_name']."</h3>\n";

  print "<p>".$row['topic_desc']."</p>\n";

  print "<a href=".$row['topic_url']." target=\"_blank\
">".$row['topic_url']."</a>\n";

  $lastCat = $row['category_name'];

  print "</div>\n"; }

?>

</div>

</body>
```

TRUE first time ($lastCat not set) and each time a new category is found

Print the next category heading

Record which category this listing was in so we can test whether the category changes

End of ref_links div

End of content div

```
                              </html>

                              <?php
```

| Close the connection |—⟨ `mysql_close($connectID);`

```
                              ?>
```

Your page should look like **Figure 4.1** at the beginning of the chapter.

Validate for Public Use

Because the simple CMS shown in this chapter is intended for use by the site's administrator only, we didn't add validation to the form fields. If you plan to use this code on a site where visitors can add links, you must validate the form data as shown in Chapter 2.

Also, when you move $_GET[modify_id] into a variable, do it like this:

```
$id = ereg_replace("[^0-9]", "", $_GET['modify_id']);
```

Then you can be sure you are getting only digits; otherwise, it's easy for someone to modify the URL to include malicious code and resubmit the page. This validation is especially important because the value is used in a SQL query, and if unvalidated, it could be a vehicle for a SQL injection attack.

Summary

And with that, we come to the end of this long chapter. We have seen how to use SQL queries known as JOIN queries to combine data from multiple database tables and extract the data using the field names of the database tables.

We've seen that we can run complex conditional tests, such as `ifelse` statements, on the $_POST and $_GET arrays to determine the status of data passed to the pages from forms and URL strings respectively and run different blocks of code based on those tests.

The techniques that you have learned in this chapter allow both you and nontechnical members of your team to easily manage and publish categorized information and links for whatever topics you choose or perhaps provide access to a library of downloadable documents or music and video files.

In the next chapter, we will look at authentication and how you can sign up visitors to your site as members and then give them access to a password-protected members-only area of your site.

Cookies and Authentication

CREATE A MEMBERS-ONLY AREA FOR YOUR SITE

Sign up new members

> **Sign up**
>
> Members can download code samples access the Codin' links.
>
> **First Name required**
> Jimi
> **Last Name required**
> Hendrix
> **Email required**
> jimi@purplehaze.com
> **Password required - 4 to 8 letters/numbers**
> ******
> **Type password again required**
> ******
> [Go]

> Authenticated by member cookie.
>
> # You are a member!
>
> Test cookie - exit to non-member area, then click Go to Member Area to return.
> Go to non-member area.
>
> Log Out

Use cookies to authenticate member access to members' pages

Redirect nonmembers who try to redirect members' pages

> **You are not signed in. You must sign in to view member content.**
>
> - Member sign-in
> - Sign up to become a member
> - Email me my password

> **Sign in**
>
> Non-member page. Any visitor can access this page. Emter your user name and password to sign in.
>
> Email
> [   ]
> Password
> [   ]
> [Go]
> Email me my password!
> Sign me up.
> Go to member area.
> Closing the browser ends your session - you will then have to log in again.

Provide returning members with an easy sign-on process

Enable members to retrieve a forgotten password

> **Send me my Password!**
>
> Enter you email address and we will email y
>
> Enter Email
> [   ]
> [Go]

Have you ever clicked a link at a site only to be told "You must be a member to view this page"? When this happens, you usually are then presented with a Log In form where you can authenticate yourself as a member by entering your member credentials, such as a user name and password. There's also usually a Sign Up Now link to a longer form where nonmembers can sign up to become members.

From a security viewpoint, without some kind of viewing restrictions in place, you cannot protect documents that are meant only for certain people, such as the staff of your company, from being viewed or downloaded by others who should not see them. Here the credentials serve as the key to the lock on the vault.

From a value viewpoint, requiring authentication for users to access certain areas of your site can also have profound business implications. Once you restrict access, you can set up what brand-strategy guru Michael Moon of Gistics, Inc. (www.gistics.com), calls an info-barter: Give us your e-mail address, and we'll send you our newsletter. Fill out our survey, and then you can print a discount coupon. Give us your credit card information, and we will let you download our software product. The site visitor obtains the product or service, often at no cost, and the site organization obtains the visitor's contact information and can start to establish an online relationship.

Of course, such barters must be balanced. It's unreasonable to expect visitors to provide their physical mailing addresses and income details in exchange for an e-mail newsletter, but they might if we provide them with access to a low-rate mortgage program.

Because of the importance of info-barter to almost every online business, the mechanism for setting up restricted access to certain areas of our site and for identifying entitled visitors once they have successfully met our requirements is an essential programming skill.

A key tool for tracking visitors is cookies. In this chapter, we will discuss the role that cookies play in setting up controlled and secure areas of a Web site that require user credentials, usually in the form of a user name and password, to access. We will also discuss how to use a cookie to tag and later identify users who are members, so they can freely access areas of our site that nonmembers cannot.

Cookies and the Session State

A *cookie* is a small text file that a Web site can write on a user's machine. For security reasons, a cookie goes into a specific folder selected by the user's browser. A cookie is the only kind of file that a site can write on a user's machine without causing a dialog box to appear where the user must click OK to accept the file.

Every time a user requests a page from our site (or more specifically, our domain), any cookie data that we passed to that user on a previous visit is automatically passed back to the server along with the request. It's easy to test for the cookie's presence and provide different responses to users who do and don't have it.

Cookies are also a useful tool for keeping track of the activities of individual users on our site. They can be used to associate that visitor with data that the visitor previously supplied to us and to keep track of the user's session as the user moves from page to page.

Some people think cookies can read the data on their computer, steal their identity, and do other harm, and therefore they turn cookies off, but cookies are a legitimate and simple mechanism for implementing features such as shopping carts and member areas.

Depending on the specific browser, a site can write up to about 20 cookies on a user's machine, and most computers accept a maximum of 300 cookies from all sites combined. Browsers delete old cookies to make room for new ones.

You can think of a cookie as a label that is stuck on the user's computer by a site that the user visits. The data in the cookie usually contains either an arbitrary ID that simply differentiates each user from other users, or a specific ID, such as a database reference, that links to information that the user has previously supplied or generated by making purchases and engaging in other activity.

A cookie with a unique ID, such as an e-mail address, is typically put on the user's machine when the user first registers. The cookie then acts as a pointer to the user's information; as soon as that visitor return to our site, we can check for and read the cookie and then immediately match the visitor to his or her record in the database and to all the associated records of that person's previous transactions with us.

For security reasons, a cookie has limited scope. It can be read only by the domain that wrote it, so one site can't grab the information written in a cookie by a different site.

However, within the scope of your site, once a cookie has been written to a visitor's computer, it's easy to use it to associate every page that visitor views, every file the visitor downloads, and every link the visitor clicks, should you be so inclined. Even if the site does not have enough information to recognize a visitor personally, any number of actions can be associated with a particular cookie ID. Later, a visitor might register at the site and supply personal information. We could then associate that personal information with data the person provided when he or she was anonymous.

Because a cookie persists over months and years (and can be renewed with every visit), over time and numerous visits, we can start to identify the products that a specific visitor is interested in, or we can send e-mails customized just for that person. So although a cookie is just a tiny data file, it enables our site to see each visitor as an individual, and if we choose to do so, we can record and analyze every move each visitor makes. This is what makes some people uneasy about cookies.

Maintaining the Session State

The primary reason that cookies are useful is that they help us maintain the *session state* with the user. A session is simply the period of time from when the user arrives on our site to when the user leaves.

HTTP is a *stateless* protocol, so the Web is essentially a stateless place—that is, from the HTTP perspective, there is no concept of a user being at a Web site for a period of time, or even of the existence of an individual user. Each request for an HTML page that is made to a Web server is a discrete event: the page is requested, and the page is served. If, after viewing that page for a few seconds or minutes, the user then requests another page, that request is an entirely separate event—the server has no way of knowing that the previous request came from this same computer, no concept of you, the individual, traversing the site.

For online transactions to be successful, we need a means of keeping track of the page requests that each user makes. When, for example, the user adds items to a shopping cart, we need to keep track, from page to page, of which items are in that user's cart. Similarly, when an authorized user moves through a number of pages that are unavailable to unauthorized users, we have to be able to check, before serving each page, that the user has access rights.

In short, we need to maintain session state for users so that we can mange each individual user's page requests as a related group of events—a session—instead of as an unrelated stream of requests for pages. We do this with cookies.

Using Cookies

Two types of cookies are associated with PHP: session cookies, which are created when we start a session by calling the `session_start()` function and which are managed by PHP and regular cookies, which we create and can add data to and delete as needed.

In this book, we will focus on regular cookies, but you can learn about PHP sessions and URL rewriting (using sessions to maintain the session state for users who have cookies turned off) at the Zend Web site: http://www.zend.com/zend/tut/session.php.

Cookies or Sessions?

I think regular cookies are easier for novice programmers to understand and use, so I am going to demonstrate them in this chapter, but be aware that if you are authenticating users into areas of your site where they can perform financial transactions or access sensitive information, then sessions are a safer way to go, as the session cookie information is stored on the server, and the related cookie data is much harder to access; with sessions, only the session ID number travels between the server and the browser, not the actual data.

Additionally, sessions can work even if cookies are turned off. If configured correctly, PHP will pass the session ID between pages as a URL query (a process known as URL rewriting) if it cannot pass it as a cookie.

Amazon.com and many other e-commerce sites append the session ID that normally resides in the cookie to the end of every URL string as an alternative method of identifying users as they move from page to page. This is their fallback mechanism in case a visitor has cookies turned off. It's more work to implement such a system, but this approach ensures that every visitor can shop—more specifically, that their activities during the session can be tracked—whether they have cookies on or not.

PHP can append session data to URLs automatically. To learn more, see "Session ID Propagation" at http://www.zend. com/zend/tut/session.php, which is an excellent page for getting a good grounding in the use of sessions.

For those of you who want to use sessions instead of cookies, I have provided a second set of files in the Chapter 5 downloads folder at the *Codin'* Web site, in a folder called code_session. Here, I use sessions instead of cookies, so you can compare the difference. Also see the sidebar "Differences between Coding Cookies and Sessions" later in this chapter for information on the basics of coding session cookies.

A cookie can hold about 3KB of data, which is equal to few hundred words of text. Usually, however, all you need to store is enough information to identify a user's record in the database.

Creating a Cookie

Cookies are created using the `setcookie` function. This function can accept six arguments, in this format:

`setcookie (name, value, expire, path, domain, secure)`

- `name`: The cookie's name, the only required argument.

- `value`: Up to 3 or 4KB of data, the cookie's payload.

- `expire`: The time when the cookie expires. If this value isn't set, the cookie expires when the browser closes..

- `path`: The scope of the cookie within the site. For instance, `/cart` limits the reading of the cookie to pages below the level of the cart folder. The default argument is the root folder.

- `domain`: The domain in which the cookie returns data. The default argument is the host name. If you want the cookie to be visible across subdomains such as shop.mydomain.com and members.mydomain.com, this argument must be set to `.mydomain.com` (note the starting dot). Note that this setting will not work on a URL such as http://mysite.com, where no subdomain, such as www., is stated.

- `secure`: If TRUE, returns the cookie only over an HTTPS connection. The default setting is FALSE.

  Because only the cookie name is required, you can set a cookie as simply as this:

  `setcookie ("visited");`

  The default values will then be used for all the other settings.

Updating and Deleting Cookies

To update a cookie, simply set a new one with the same name.

There is no PHP command to actually delete a cookie. You delete a cookie by setting its expiration time to some time past, such as two years ago, like this:

The current time minus two years' worth of seconds —— `time()-(2*365*24*60*60)`

Note the minus sign to get a time in the past. Not everyone's computer clock is accurate, so don't use a small time period such as –1 second.

Using Single-Session Cookies

In the example in this chapter, the session starts when the user receives the cookie and ends when the user closes the browser and the cookie is deleted.

The simplest way to create a cookie is to use a single argument, the cookie's name, like this:

```
setcookie ("member");
```

The setcookie function creates the cookie called member. Its undeclared value (its data) is effectively TRUE. Because no expiration time is set for this particular cookie, it lasts until the user closes the browser. This expires-on-close feature is useful if you are trying to track a logged-in user; you write the cookie on the user's machine after the user logs in, and you can check for its presence every time the user attempts to view content that is available only to logged-in users, using code like this:

```
if(isset($_cookie("member")) {

        echo "Welcome to the member's area!"

} else {

    echo "You must be logged in to view this page";

    exit;

}
```

The page stops loading

The rest of the code to display info for members goes here

As soon as the user closes the browser, the user is effectively logged out, because the cookie automatically expires. If the user wants to view the same content even a few seconds later, the user must log in again. This approach is a very simple way to ensure that only authorized people are viewing these areas of your site. We will see this code in action when we set up a sign-up and sign-in system for members later in this chapter.

Setting a Cookie

Here's an example of how to set and test a cookie. Because a cookie is returned to the server only when a visitor requests a page, after the cookie is set, we cannot test for its presence until the page is reloaded.

CODE 5.1: `cookies_create_basic_cookie.php4`

Set the cookie

Then the cookie was created on a previous page load

```
setcookie ('userID');
if (isset($_COOKIE['userID'])) {
    echo "Cookie is set! Welcome back!";
} else {
    echo "Reload the page to test if a cookie is present.";
}
```

Refresh the page to see that the cookie is recognized. The session is still in progress. If we quit the browser, the cookie is deleted, as no time was defined for its existence, so if we then reopen the page, we will be given a new cookie and be told that we must reload the page a second time to test for the cookie.

Another use of cookies is to determine whether a visitor is a new visitor or has been to the site before, so we can get a true count of unique visitors. If we put a cookie on the computer of every visitor, with an expiration date so the cookie persists after the user closes the browser, then we can know for certain, when a visitor returns another day, that the person is a repeat visitor. We may want to set such cookies to expire after a year; it would be a reasonable business decision to say that anyone who hasn't visited our site for a year should be considered a new visitor. If we renew the one-year cookie each time a visitor returns, then we can tell, over any period in the next year, when that visitor last visited.

Here we set the cookie with an expiration date:

One-year expiration date

```
setcookie ("visit", date( ), date( ) +(60*60*24*365))
```

This cookie contains three pieces of information: its name, the date it was created (the cookie's data), and the expiration date. The `date()` function is what makes this cookie work. This function is useful for managing all kinds of time-related activities on your site, so let's look at this function in more detail.

Using the time Function

The function `time()` returns the current time in seconds (from the Unix epoch of January 1, 1970—it's a very large number, which, fortunately, we don't actually need to see or deal with because PHP just gets it and sticks it in the cookie). We use the `time()` function in the second argument, the cookie's data, to record the moment (to the second) that the cookie was created. We could use this data to calculate, when the visitor returns to the site, how much time has elapsed since the first visit. For the third argument, the cookie's expiration date, we again use the `time( )`function (which effectively means Now!), and add to it the number of seconds in a year—so the cookie in this example will expire in one year.

He's Baaaack!

When a visitor comes to our site, we can immediately check whether that person has visited before by testing whether the cookie is set.

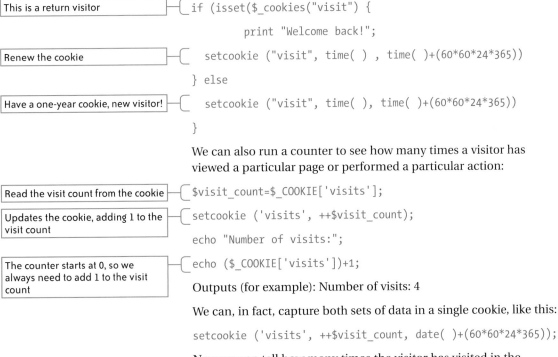

```
This is a return visitor    —⎡ if (isset($_cookies("visit") {

                                      print "Welcome back!";

Renew the cookie            —⎡   setcookie ("visit", time( ) , time( )+(60*60*24*365))

                               } else

Have a one-year cookie, new visitor! ⎡   setcookie ("visit", time( ), time( )+(60*60*24*365))

                               }
```

We can also run a counter to see how many times a visitor has viewed a particular page or performed a particular action:

```
Read the visit count from the cookie —⎡ $visit_count=$_COOKIE['visits'];

Updates the cookie, adding 1 to the —⎡ setcookie ('visits', ++$visit_count);
visit count
                               echo "Number of visits:";

The counter starts at 0, so we —⎡ echo ($_COOKIE['visits'])+1;
always need to add 1 to the visit
count
```

Outputs (for example): Number of visits: 4

We can, in fact, capture both sets of data in a single cookie, like this:

```
setcookie ('visits', ++$visit_count, date( )+(60*60*24*365));
```

Now we can tell how many times the visitor has visited in the past year.

Creating Data-Rich Cookies

Cookies can hold between 3 and 4KB of data (the amount varies between browsers), so it's perfectly feasible to load not just one but several data elements into the payload of a cookie. If you want to save a list of shopping cart items using the product IDs you assigned to them when you added them to the database, for instance, you can store the items in a cookie as a comma-delimited string:

| Product IDs of items in cart | `ScookieData = "456, 567, 313, 482";` |
| Three weeks until cookie expires | `setcookie ("cart_items", ScookieData, date ( ) +(60*60*24*21)` |

With this cookie and some nifty coding on our part, a user could return to the site up to three weeks after shopping and still find the items in his or her cart.

Using explode and implode to Convert between Arrays and Strings

Our shopping cart code would typically manage the cart items in an array, adding a new item ID to the array and updating the cookie with the array's data each time the user adds an item to the cart, so we need to be able to convert the array data into a string of delimited elements for storage in the cookie, a process known as serializing the data. Later, when the user comes back to the site, we want to unserialize it and convert the string of data elements in the cookie back into an array for use in our code. We perform these conversions using the implode and explode functions: we *implode* an array to pack it down into a single string, and we *explode* a string into pieces to create the array elements again.

When the user puts an item in the cart, we need to write to the cookie:

```
function updateCartCookie (itemNumber){
```

| Create the array if it doesn't exist | `if (!isset($cookieData)) {` |

```
        $cookieData [];

    }
```

Add the new item to the array	`$cookieData [] = $itemNumber`
Convert the array into a comma-delimited string	`ScookieData = implode (',' , $cartArray);`
Write the cookie—expires in 3 weeks	`setcookie ("cart_items", ScookieData, date ( ) +(60*60*24*21)`
End of function	`}`

If the user comes back to the site and the cart cookie exists, we reverse the process:

```
if ($_COOKIE [cart_items]) {

$cartArray = explode ( ',' , $_COOKIE [cart_items]);

}
```

Now we can access the array as usual.

```
foreach ($cart_array as $item) {

    print $item."<br />";

}
```

Display each item number on the shopping cart page

In reality, as we iterate through the array, we would look up each item in the database and display the relevant text and images relating to that product.

Cookies and Security

Cookies can be a security risk if used carelessly, but such risks can be mitigated considerably if you follow a few simple steps. As always, this is just advice. Consult a Web security expert for your specific case.

Don't put critical data in cookies.

Don't write passwords and other personal user data, such as credit card numbers, in a cookie, because the cookie files on the user's machine can easily be located and opened. If you write a user ID in a cookie, don't use the actual database primary key ID; instead, use a long, hard-to-guess number that references the ID in the database, or reference a different piece of data. Generally, it's okay to use e-mail addresses; each is a unique identifier without being the primary key for the user's record.

Let authentication cookies expire after every session, so the visitor must log in at each new visit.

A cookie is related to the browser, not to a specific person, so it is inaccurate, as well as dangerous, to assume that the presence of an identifying cookie means that a specific person is at your site. The cookie means only that your site is again being accessed by the browser to which you gave the cookie, so don't use the presence of a cookie as authorization for a user to perform tasks such as conduct financial transactions.

Shoppers who return to Amazon having shopped there previously are recognized using session cookie data and welcomed back by name; there is no great risk associated with saying "Welcome back, Joe" when in fact Joe's spendthrift roomie Tom is on the machine. But as soon as Tom tries to buy something using Joe's One-Click account, essentially attempting to using Joe's credit card without having to enter the information again, Amazon will ask for a password, which Joe has hopefully kept to himself, before finalizing the transaction. Amazon does this to prevent Tom from making fraudulent charges when Joe goes out to get a six-pack and pizza and forgets to close his browser.

You would be wise to consider whether your own site has danger points where you should ask users to reauthenticate, even when they have already been identified by the system. eBay asks for your password to the point of annoyance before you can undertake a variety of tasks, but because your session ID is changed each time you enter your password (check the ID string at the end of the URL), the eBay site is a much safer place to do business. People don't always do the smart thing, such as logging out at the end of a shopping session, and cookies' data can be spoofed (impersonated via code, URLs, or other means), so don't rely on cookies alone for authentication of returning visitors.

Authentication Basics

Just to see how authentication works, let's look at an example of a cookie that expires after a period of time. In this example, the cookie will expire very quickly, in just 15 seconds, so that we can repeatedly create it and then see what happens when it expires. In reality, of course, a cookie might be set to last for months or years.

Here we have two pages. The first is a log-in page, which, if we log in successfully, gives us a cookie and then sends us to the member's page with information that can be viewed only if we have the cookie (**Figure 5.1**). Here's the key part of the code:

CODE 5.2: Part of cookies4.php4

If the entered and stored passwords match, set the cookie

Then send the user to the member's page

```php
if ($password == $validPassword) {

    setcookie ("member", time(), time()+15);

    header ('Location: cookies4a.php4');

} else {

    $errMsg = "<p style='color:red;'>The password is wrong. Try again!</p>";

}

}
```

FIGURE 5.1 If the user logs in successfully, the user is forwarded to the member's page.

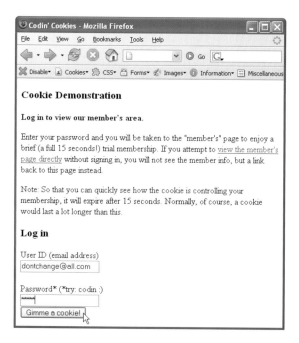

The member's page, to which we are redirected if our log-in is successful, is coded so that clicking the "How much time do I have left?" link reloads the page and displays the time left on the cookie (**Figure 5.2**).

CODE 5.3: Part of cookies4a.php4

If the cookie exists

```php
if (isset($_COOKIE['member'])) {

    $timeElapsed = (time() - ($_COOKIE['member']));
```

Calculate the time left

```php
    $timeLeft = 15 - $timeElapsed;
```

Display member info

```php
    print "<h3>Welcome, member!</h3>";

    print "<h4>We hope you enjoy your 15 second membership!</h4>";

    print ("<p>You are a member for $timeLeft more seconds!</p>");
```

Reloads the page and shows time left on cookie

```php
    print ("<p><a href='cookies4a.php4'>How much time do I have left?</a></p>");

    print ("<p>Only members can read this!</p>");
```

Cookie has expired—display nonmember info

```php
} else {

    print "<h3>Sign up for a 15 second membership!</h3>";

    print ("<p>It appears you are not a member.</p>");

    print ("<a href='cookies4.php4'>Sign me up!</a>");

}

?>
```

FIGURE 5.2 In this example, the cookie expires very quickly.

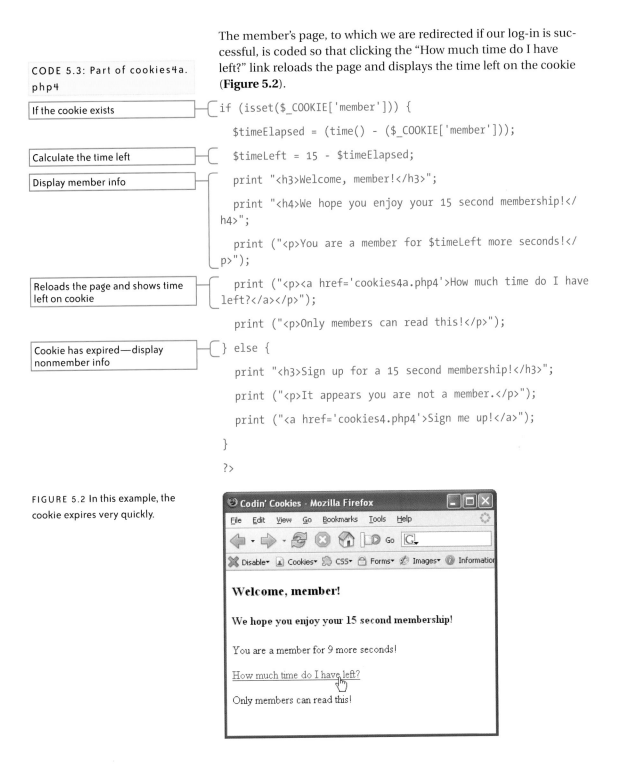

When the time reaches 0, the cookie expires. The reloaded page then no longer displays the member information but instead tells us that we are not authorized to view the content and offers a link back to the log-in page (**Figure 5.3**).

FIGURE 5.3 After the cookie expires, the member information is no longer available.

Cookies can be deleted by the user or replaced by a different cookie if the browser's cookies limit (usually around 200) is reached, so always provide authentication (member sign-in), and not just new member sign-up, options for visitors who don't have your cookie; they may be members who simply lost their cookies since their last visit.

Always Authenticate with Two Credentials

Note in Figure 5.1 that the form has fields for both the e-mail address and password, even though using the e-mail address made no sense in this demonstration, as we don't check any records. I put it there as a reminder to always authorize with two credentials. When you enable a user to log in with a password, always require a second credential, such as an e-mail address and or user name, to prevent password guessing.

Once the user has entered the user name (e-mail address) and password, look up the record using the e-mail address or user name and then check that that record has the matching password. This forces the user to know both pieces of information. If you leave this security hole open by authenticating members only with a password, you're inviting people to type passwords until they find one that works—and there are some very common pet names out there, if you know what I mean.

However, a cookie with a user ID can act as that other credential, because it too can identify the specific record that the password should match. So if you are registered with eBay or Amazon, the site's ID cookie is already on your machine. If the site wants to reauthenticate you at some point, it need only ask for a password; it already knows who you are and which record to check for the password. The PayPal site, where lots of money changes hands, makes use of this kind of reauthentication at the start of transactions and when you are about to update a record; PayPal can then be reasonably confident that you are actually who you say you are at that point: the same person who set up the account in the first place.

Creating an Authentication System

Now it's time to take these concepts and use them in a practical example that you can use on your own site.

Sign Up, Sign In: Registration and Credentials

Let's first get clear on the nomenclature here: A user will *sign up*, or *register*, only once as *member*, or *authorized visitor*, but the user will *sign in*, or *log in*, upon every subsequent visit to the site (at least if the user wants to view the member's area).

We have discussed why *verification* (confirmation) of membership is usually achieved by having a member sign in with a user name and password, known collectively as the member's *credentials*. If the credentials match the database record for that member, then that person is *authenticated* within the system, and because the user gets the member cookie upon authentication, the user can then visit members-only pages.

Creating the Authentication System Architecture

Let's now put the concepts discussed in this chapter to work to create a system whereby we use a database and cookies to register and authenticate members. **Figure 5.4** shows the flowchart for our system.

FIGURE 5.4 Flow chart for
the user authentication system

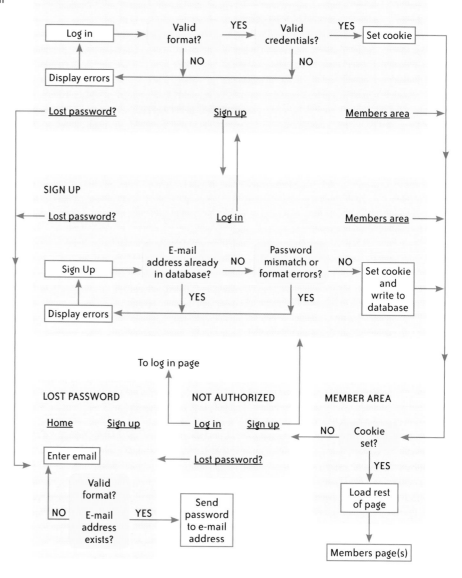

Every person who wants to view the member's pages of our site must first sign up as a member (**Figure 5.5**).

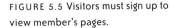

FIGURE 5.5 Visitors must sign up to view member's pages.

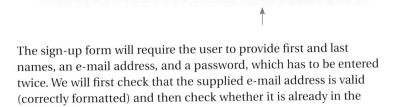

The sign-up form will require the user to provide first and last names, an e-mail address, and a password, which has to be entered twice. We will first check that the supplied e-mail address is valid (correctly formatted) and then check whether it is already in the database.

An e-mail makes a good credential only if we don't allow duplicate e-mail addresses to appear in our database, so we must ensure that it's impossible to register with an e-mail address that's already in the database.

If the e-mail address passes these tests, we validate the other fields (check whether they contain only acceptable characters) and ensure that the password is the right length and that both versions entered match (**Figure 5.6**). It's important to have the user enter the password twice and then check that the entries match because the user cannot see the password as it is entered and so this process helps ensure that the user accurately typed the desired password.

Interestingly, it doesn't matter whether the stored password is the same as someone else's, as we will not use it as a means to look up a specific record but simply to compare with the password supplied at sign-up or sign-in.

If the sign-up data passes these tests, the data is stored in the member table in the database, a member cookie is written to the visitor's computer, and our new member's browser is redirected to the member's area (a single page in this example).

On subsequent visits, we will require members to sign in.

FIGURE 5.6 We validate the sign-up field entries and password.

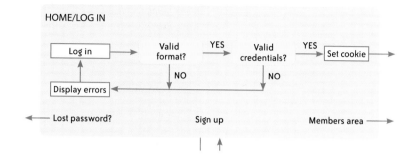

Sign-in requires just two credentials: an e-mail address and password. First, again, we validate the format of the data. Then we validate the supplied credentials: we use the e-mail address to look up the record in the database and then check whether that record's password matches the supplied password. If it does, the visitor is a member and so receives a member cookie and is redirected to the member's area (**Figure 5.7**).

FIGURE 5.7 We check whether the cookie is present.

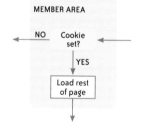

The first piece of code in each member area page checks whether the cookie is present.

If it the cookie is present, the rest of the page loads; if it is absent, the user is immediately redirected to a "not authorized" page (**Figure 5.8**).

FIGURE 5.8 If the cookie is missing, the user is redirected to a "not authorized" page.

The "not authorized" page informs rejected visitors that they are not authorized to view the member's pages and offers links to the sign-up, sign-in, and lost password pages.

The lost password page offers a way for members who can't remember their passwords to retrieve them (**Figure 5.9**).

FIGURE 5.9 The lost password page allows users to retrieve forgotten passwords.

On this page, members who have forgotten their passwords can submit their e-mail addresses; if an e-mail address exists in a member record, the corresponding password is e-mailed to the e-mail address. The password is e-mailed rather than displayed onscreen to help ensure that this mechanism is used only to retrieve a person's own password.

Creating the Database Table

CODE 5.4: create_members_db_script.txt

You can copy this code from the create_members_db_script.txt file in the Codin' Web site downloads and then click the SQL tab in phpMyAdmin. Paste the SQL code in the query field and click Go. The table will immediately be created. Of course, you can also perform this process in phpMyAdmin by setting the parameters for each field as we did in Chapter 3.

FIGURE 5.10 The key details shown in phpMyAdmin after the table is created using the SQL query. (The table is very wide, so the irrelevant middle part is not shown.)

We are going to start by creating a database table to hold the records of our members. We already have a table called members from Chapter 3, so let's call this table members2.

For sign-up, we are going to require the visitor to provide first and last names, an e-mail address, and a password. We want to record this information and also add a record ID and the date and time that the user signed up. We will use the following SQL query to create the database table (**Figure 5.10**).

```
CREATE TABLE `members2` (

`id` INT NOT NULL AUTO_INCREMENT PRIMARY KEY ,
`first_name` VARCHAR( 40 ) NOT NULL ,
`last_name` VARCHAR( 40 ) NOT NULL ,
`email` VARCHAR( 64 ) NOT NULL ,
`date_joined` TIMESTAMP NOT NULL DEFAULT CURRENT_TIMESTAMP ,
`cred` VARCHAR( 10 ) NOT NULL

) ENGINE = MYISAM COMMENT = 'authentication chapter
database';
```

	Field	Type		Default	Extra	
☐	**id**	int(11)			auto_increment	
☐	**first_name**	varchar(40)				
☐	**last_name**	varchar(40)				
☐	**email**	varchar(64)				
☐	**date_joined**	timestamp		CURRENT_TIMESTAMP		
☐	**cred**	varchar(10)				

Adding Database Functions

We need to be able to perform several database operations to create our members-only area, so we will write some functions that will enable us to perform the associated queries on the database. The functions we will write will be used more than once in our pages, so we will store them in separate include files, to avoid duplicating this code in several places.

For the functions presented here, I will give the name of the function, the key lines of code, and a description of what the function does, so you can easily understand the functions as you read the code for the individual pages. You can download the full versions of these functions from the *Codin'* Web site.

The code shown here consists of code fragments and does not include code for establishing and closing the connection with the database.

The @ suppresses the error that results if no record is found

Return first item of the first (and only) result

SIGN-UP FUNCTIONS

● Check whether an e-mail address exists before recording a new member's information.

```
function checkEmail ($email) {

$myDataID = mysql_query("SELECT id FROM members WHERE
email = '$email'", $connectID)

  or die ("Unable to select from database");

$matching_id = @mysql_result($myDataID,0,0);

return $matching_id;

}
```

The checkEmail function accepts one argument: the member's e-mail address. It uses this address to find the member's record and returns that record's ID.

● Record a new member's information.

```
function writeMemberSignup ($first_name, $last_name,
$email, $credential){

mysql_query ("INSERT into members (first_name, last_name,
email, cred, active) VALUES ('$first_name', '$last_name',
'$email', '$credential', $active)", $connectID)

  or die ("Unable to insert record into database");

}
```

The writeMemberSignup function's arguments accept the four pieces of sign-up information entered by the visitor and write them in a new record in the database. The ID and date joined are automatically added to the record by mySQL.

LOG-IN FUNCTIONS

● Return a record for a supplied ID.

```
function readMemberRecord ($id) {

$myDataID = mysql_query("SELECT * FROM members WHERE id =
'$id'", $connectID)

  or die ("Unable to select from database");

return $myDataID;
```

The `readMemberRecord` function accepts one argument—the member's ID (the ID is obtained by calling `checkEmail` first)—and returns the data from all fields of the record.

VALIDATION FUNCTIONS

• Check that the first name, last name, and e-mail address are correctly formed (only allowed characters are used). These two functions were used in the forms examples earlier.

```
function verifyAlphaNum ($testString) {

    return (eregi ("^([[:alnum:]]|-|\.| |')+$",
$testString));
```

Ensure the use of only letters, numbers, dashes, periods, spaces, and single quotation marks

Check for a valid e-mail address

```
function verifyEmail ($testString) {

    return (eregi("^([[:alnum:]]|_|\.|-)+@([[:
alnum:]]|\.|-)+(\.)([a-z]{2,4})$", $testString));

}
```

• Check that the password uses only allowed characters.

```
function verifyPassword ($testString) {
```

Check for only letters, numbers, dashes, periods, spaces, and single quotation marks

```
    return (eregi("^([[:alnum:]]|-|\.| |\?|\!|\"|')+$",
$testString));

}
```

The `verifyAlphaNum`, `verifyEmail`, and `verifyPassword` functions each accept a text string as an argument and check that it contains alphanumeric characters and certain symbols. There are slight difference betweens them with regard to which symbols are accepted.

• Check that the password is between 4 and 10 characters.

```
if (((strlen($password1)) < 4) or ((strlen($password1)))
> 10){

$error_msg[]="Password must be between 4 and 10
characters in length.";

}

if ($password1 !== $password2) {

$error_msg[]="Both password fields must match. Please try
again.";

}
```

These last two password tests are written right in the sign-up page, rather than being stored in functions in include pages, as this is the only time we will need them. The first uses the `strlen` (string length) function to check the number of characters in the password, and the second checks whether the two passwords match.

Creating the Authentication System Pages

Now that we have some functions that we can use to test the data the user enters, let's look at each of the pages in our member authentication system.

Creating the Sign-Up Page

Let's start by creating the sign-up page (**Figure 5.11**). It will be similar to the forms we have seen earlier, so the code will be familiar.

FIGURE 5.11 The sign-up page.

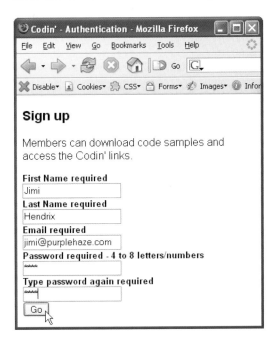

```php
<?php
```

Include the includes

```php
require_once ("includes/validation/validation_functions.
php4");

require_once ("includes/files/write_to_a_flat_file4.php4");

require_once ("includes/sql/write_signup_db.php4");

require_once ("includes/sql/email_exists_check_db.php4");

if (@$_POST['submitted']) {
```

Move post array data into variables

```php
    $first_name = @$_POST['first_name'];

    $last_name = @$_POST['last_name'];

    $email = @$_POST['email'];

    $password1 = @$_POST['password1'];

    $password2 = @$_POST['password2'];
```

Check whether e-mail address is already in database—if so, function returns 1; see error output in following form

```php
    $returnedID = checkEmail($email);
```

Intialize error array for form errors

```php
    $error_msg=array();

$valid = verifyAlphaNum ($first_name);
```

The validation functions are in a separate include file—see above

Test for invalid data

```php
if (!$valid){

$error_msg[]="First Name must be letters and numbers, spaces,
dashes and ' only.";

}

$valid = verifyAlphaNum ($last_name);
```

Test for invalid data

```php
if (!$valid){

$error_msg[]="Last Name must be letters and numbers, spaces,
dashes and ' only.";

}

$valid = verifyEmail ($email);
```

Test for invalid data

```php
if (!$valid){

$error_msg[]="Email must be a valid format (e.g. john@yahoo.
com).";

}

if (((strlen($password1)) < 4) or ((strlen($password1))) >
10){
```

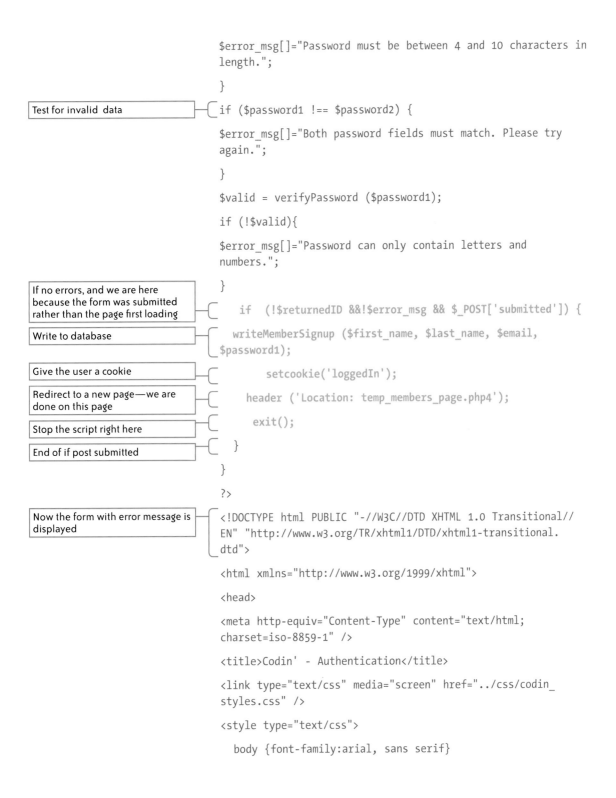

```
                                     $error_msg[]="Password must be between 4 and 10 characters in
                                     length.";

                                     }
Test for invalid data                if ($password1 !== $password2) {

                                     $error_msg[]="Both password fields must match. Please try
                                     again.";

                                     }

                                     $valid = verifyPassword ($password1);

                                     if (!$valid){

                                     $error_msg[]="Password can only contain letters and
                                     numbers.";

If no errors, and we are here        }
because the form was submitted
rather than the page first loading       if  (!$returnedID &&!$error_msg && $_POST['submitted']) {

Write to database                       writeMemberSignup ($first_name, $last_name, $email,
                                     $password1);

Give the user a cookie                      setcookie('loggedIn');

Redirect to a new page—we are           header ('Location: temp_members_page.php4');
done on this page

Stop the script right here               exit();

End of if post submitted              }

                                     }

                                     ?>

Now the form with error message is   <!DOCTYPE html PUBLIC "-//W3C//DTD XHTML 1.0 Transitional//
displayed                            EN" "http://www.w3.org/TR/xhtml1/DTD/xhtml1-transitional.
                                     dtd">

                                     <html xmlns="http://www.w3.org/1999/xhtml">

                                     <head>

                                     <meta http-equiv="Content-Type" content="text/html;
                                     charset=iso-8859-1" />

                                     <title>Codin' - Authentication</title>

                                     <link type="text/css" media="screen" href="../css/codin_
                                     styles.css" />

                                     <style type="text/css">

                                       body {font-family:arial, sans serif}
```

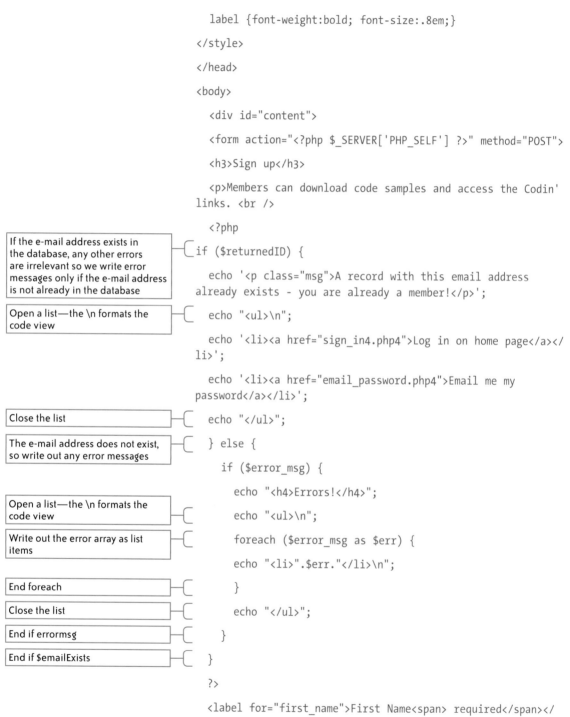

```
    label {font-weight:bold; font-size:.8em;}
    </style>
    </head>
    <body>
      <div id="content">
      <form action="<?php $_SERVER['PHP_SELF'] ?>" method="POST">
      <h3>Sign up</h3>
      <p>Members can download code samples and access the Codin'
      links. <br />
      <?php
      if ($returnedID) {

        echo '<p class="msg">A record with this email address
        already exists - you are already a member!</p>';

        echo "<ul>\n";

        echo '<li><a href="sign_in4.php4">Log in on home page</a></
        li>';

        echo '<li><a href="email_password.php4">Email me my
        password</a></li>';

        echo "</ul>";

      } else {

        if ($error_msg) {

          echo "<h4>Errors!</h4>";

          echo "<ul>\n";

          foreach ($error_msg as $err) {

          echo "<li>".$err."</li>\n";

          }

          echo "</ul>";

        }

      }

      ?>

      <label for="first_name">First Name<span> required</span></
      label><br />
```

Annotations (left margin):

- If the e-mail address exists in the database, any other errors are irrelevant so we write error messages only if the e-mail address is not already in the database
- Open a list—the \n formats the code view
- Close the list
- The e-mail address does not exist, so write out any error messages
- Open a list—the \n formats the code view
- Write out the error array as list items
- End foreach
- Close the list
- End if errormsg
- End if $emailExists

```
            <input name="first_name" type="text" size="20"
id="first_name" value="<?php echo ($first_name) ?>" /><br />

            <label for="last_name">Last Name<span> required</
span></label><br />

            <input name="last_name" type="text" size="20" id="last_
name" value="<?php echo ($last_name) ?>" /><br />

            <label for="email">Email<span> required</span></
label><br />

            <input name= "email" type="text" size="20" id="email"
value="<?php echo ($email) ?>" /><br />

            <label for="password1">Password<span> required - 4 to
8 letters/numbers</span></label><br />

            <input name= "password1" type="password" size="10"
id="password1" /><br />

            <label for="password2">Type password again<span>
required</span></label><br />

            <input name= "password2" type="password" size="10"
id="password2" /><br />

            <input type="submit" value="Go" name="submitted"/>

        </form>

    </div>

</body>

</html>
```

Although this might look like a lot of code, it's actually only four steps:

1. Include the external functions.

2. Put the POST array form data into variables.

3. Validate the supplied data.

4. After the data passes validation, write the data in the database, give the user the cookie needed to view the member's page, and redirect the user to the member's page (highlighted in the code).

Figure 5.12 shows the new record in the database.

FIGURE 5.12 A new record in the database.

←T→	id	first_name	last_name	email	date_joined	cred
☐ ✎ ✗	1	Jimi	Hendrix	jimi@purplehaze.com	2006-07-30 15:51:08	fire

---

Passwords and Encryption

You can see that the password in the `cred` (credential) column is not encrypted in any way. Sometimes you will want to encrypt information you store in the database, and sometimes you won't.

Encryption is a process that turns text and numbers into an incomprehensible string by applying an encryption algorithm to the string. Using the md5 encryption function in PHP, a given string is consistently turned into the same string of apparently random characters. It is virtually impossible for anyone to decrypt an md5 string.

For example, let's use PHP's md5 encryption function on the string "codin' for the web".

```
print md5("codin' for the web");
```

Outputs: b0682aa07076f0f5d1ff05eac2c7266e

The primary advantage of using encryption for a password is that if someone should manage to hack your database, the person won't be able to steal the encrypted data. However, there is no way to convert an md5-encrypted string back to text. If you want to compare a submitted password with an md5-encrypted password, you'll need to encrypt the submitted password as well and see if it then matches the one in the database; there is no need to know the actual password.

Here we will not encrypt the passwords. In the unlikely event that someone should decide to hack this database, all the person will obtain is access to some links to Web pages about PHP and maybe some e-mail addresses—not exactly information of great value. By leaving the passwords unencrypted, we can set up a mechanism to e-mail users their passwords if they forget them.

Sites that encrypt passwords (such as your online banking service) almost always ask you at registration time to provide a password hint (such as the name of your furry friend) that is not encrypted when stored. If you forget the password, you are sent the hint, and hopefully that is enough to jog your memory; otherwise, you are you-know-what out of luck and cannot log in again. Even the service provider cannot decrypt the password for you.

Creating the Members-Only Page

Once the sign-up code has done its job, the newly signed-up member, with a shiny new member cookie on the computer, is redirected to the home page of the member area of the site (**Figure 5.13**). Every member area page has a piece of code that checks for the member cookie. If the cookie is present, the page is displayed; otherwise, visitors are redirected to a page telling them that they can't view member's pages and offering links to sign up, to sign in if they simply forgot to do that, or to return to the main home page.

FIGURE 5.13 Only visitors with the member cookie get to view this page.

We saw a simple example of this process earlier; now let's revisit it in the context of our real-world example. Here is the code for the member page to which our newly-signed up member is redirected.

CODE 5.5: members_page.php4

This if statement code runs only if the page is reloaded after the Log Out link is clicked	
Delete cookie by setting its expiration date to the past	
Force a page reload so the cookie is checked and found absent	
End of if ($_GET…)	
Check whether the cookie exists	
Visitor is a member	
Not-a-member page does not load, and visitor is redirected	
Sends unauthenticated visitor to a different page	

```php
<?php
if ($_GET['log_out']) {
setcookie ('loggedIn', 0, time() - (365*24*60*60));
$loc=($_SERVER['PHP_SELF']);
header ("Location: $loc");
}
if (isset($_COOKIE['loggedIn'])) {
print "Authenticated by member cookie.";
} else {
header ('Location: no_credentials.php4');
}
?>
<!DOCTYPE html PUBLIC "-//W3C//DTD XHTML 1.0 Transitional//
EN" "http://www.w3.org/TR/xhtml1/DTD/xhtml1-transitional.
dtd">

<html xmlns="http://www.w3.org/1999/xhtml">
```

```
<head>

<meta http-equiv="Content-Type" content="text/html;
charset=iso-8859-1" />

<title>Codin' - Authentication</title>

</head>

<body>

<h1>You are a member!</h1>

<p>Test cookie - exit to non-member area, then click Go to
Member Area to return.<br /><a href="sign_in4">Go to non-
member area.</a></p>

<p><a href="<?php $_SERVER['PHP_SELF'] ?>?log_out=1">Log
Out</a></p>

</body>

</html>
```

This page (when further developed) would be the member's home page, with links to all the member-only content. For now, it just offers users a chance to return to a nonmembers page. If you then link back here again, you'll be able to view this page without logging in; once you have the member cookie, you can move freely between the nonmember and member areas of the site.

This page also provides a Log Out link that destroys the cookie. However, because the cookie data is passed to the server from the user's browser only when page loads, after deleting the cookie we then force a page reload, so the page once again tests for the cookie. Because the cookie is now deleted, the user is unceremoniously booted out to the not-signed-in page.

Creating the Not-Signed-In Page

When a user who is not signed in attempts to use the site, the not-signed-in page appears (**Figure 5.14**).

FIGURE 5.14 If you attempt to view a member's page without the required cookie, you are redirected to this page.

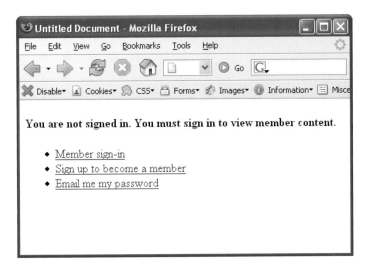

The code for this page looks like this:

CODE 5.6: no credentials.php4

```
<!DOCTYPE html PUBLIC "-//W3C//DTD XHTML 1.0 Transitional//
EN" "http://www.w3.org/TR/xhtml1/DTD/xhtml1-transitional.
dtd">

<html xmlns="http://www.w3.org/1999/xhtml">

<head>

<meta http-equiv="Content-Type" content="text/html;
charset=iso-8859-1" />

<title>Untitled Document</title>

</head>

<body>

<h4>You are not logged in. You must log in to view member
content.</h4>";

    <ul>

    <li><a href="sign_in4.php4">Log in</a></li>

    <li><a href="sign_up.php4">Sign up as a member</a></li>

    <li><a href="email_password.php4">Email me my password</
a></li>

    </ul>

</body>

</html>
```

Unlike virtually every other example in this book, there is no PHP code logic associated with this page; it simply uses XHTML to write a number of links. Of these three links, we have already seen the sign-up page, so let's examine the other two.

Creating the Lost Password Page

Most of us have numerous passwords that we use for different purposes, and many sites add to the confusion by insisting that a password contain letters and numbers and uppercase and lowercase letters and be of a certain minimum length, forcing us to invent weird passwords we have little chance of remembering for long.

Unless you want your site's support team (you?) to receive an endless stream of requests for forgotten passwords, it makes sense to automate a process by which members can easily retrieve forgotten passwords.

As discussed earlier, the process involves asking the user for his or her e-mail address, using the address to look up the password, and then sending the password to the supplied e-mail address (**Figure 5.15**).

FIGURE 5.15 If the submitted e-mail address exists in the database, the corresponding password is e-mailed to the e-mail address.

Here's the code to do this:

```php
<?php
require_once ("includes/sql/read_member.php4");

require_once ("includes/sql/email_exists_check_db.php4");

require_once ("includes/validation/validation_functions.
php4");

$msg = "Enter your email address and we will email your
password.";

if ($_POST['submitted']) {

    $email = $_POST['email'];

$valid = verifyEmail ($email);

if (!$valid){

$error_msg="Email must be a valid format (e.g. john@yahoo.
com).";

}

    $id = checkEmail($email);

    $returnedRecord = readMemberRecord($id);

    $password = @mysql_result($returnedRecord,0,'cred');

    ////Print "the password is ".$password;

    if ($password) {

    $email_subject="From the Codin' site";

    $email_body = "Here is the information you requested:
".$password;

    mail ($email, $email_subject, $email_body);

    $msg = "Your password has been emailed to ".$email.".";

    } else {

    $msg = "Sorry, the email ".$email." was not found.";

    }

}

?>
```

Check for a well-formed e-mail address

Look up the id with the e-mail address

This function converts the e-mail address to its corresponding id

Use the id to retrieve the member's record

Extract the password from the record

Read field credentials from row 0—there is only one row

If a password is found, e-mail it to the member

Set up variables for use in the mail function

Send the e-mail

Set message variable

End if submitted

```
<!DOCTYPE html PUBLIC "-//W3C//DTD XHTML 1.0 Transitional//
EN" "http://www.w3.org/TR/xhtml1/DTD/xhtml1-transitional.
dtd">

<html xmlns="http://www.w3.org/1999/xhtml">

<head>

<meta http-equiv="Content-Type" content="text/html;
charset=iso-8859-1" />

<title>Untitled Document</title>

</head>

<body>

<h3>Send me my Password!</h3>

<?php

if ($error_msg) {

  print '<p class="error">'.$error_msg.'</p>';

  } else{

  print '<p class="message">'.$msg.'</p>';

  }

  ?>

    <form action="<?php $_SERVER['PHP_SELF'] ?>" method="POST">

        <label for="email">Enter Email</label><br />

        <input name= "email" type="text" size="20" id="email"
value="<?php echo ($email) ?>" /><br />

        <input type="submit" value="Go" name="submitted"/>

    </form>

</body>

</html>
```

If the e-mail address format is invalid, display error; else display message

Once the member receives the e-mailed forgotten password, the user can sign in again on the sign-in page.

Creating the Sign-In Page

Because the member cookie is destroyed when the visitor clicks Log Out or closes the browser, a member will need to reauthenticate when returning to the site. Obviously, we don't want (and don't allow) members to sign up a second time, so this is where we will ask them to log in instead (**Figure 5.16**).

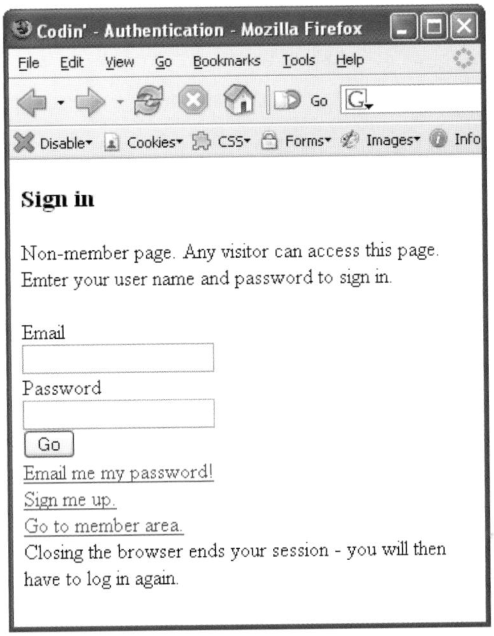

FIGURE 5.16 Returning members can sign in using their e-mail address and password.

We already have the member's information; we just want proof that the visitor is a member, so we present a simple form that requires the member's e-mail address and password. Typically, you will see this form on a sidebar of the home page. Once the visitor provides this information, we check that the supplied password matches the one in the record that we found using the supplied e-mail address. If this criterion is met, this person is a member, and we set the member cookie and redirect the user to the member area.

Here's the code for the log-in page.

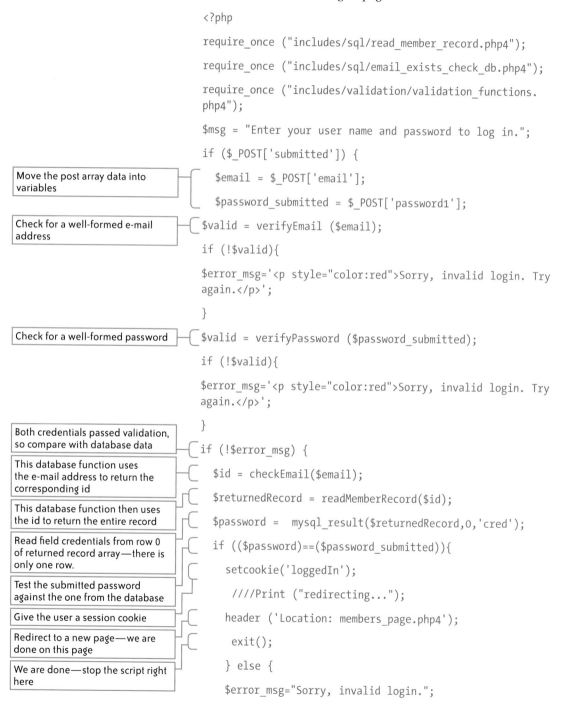

```php
<?php

require_once ("includes/sql/read_member_record.php4");

require_once ("includes/sql/email_exists_check_db.php4");

require_once ("includes/validation/validation_functions.
php4");

$msg = "Enter your user name and password to log in.";

if ($_POST['submitted']) {

    $email = $_POST['email'];

    $password_submitted = $_POST['password1'];

$valid = verifyEmail ($email);

if (!$valid){

$error_msg='<p style="color:red">Sorry, invalid login. Try
again.</p>';

}

$valid = verifyPassword ($password_submitted);

if (!$valid){

$error_msg='<p style="color:red">Sorry, invalid login. Try
again.</p>';

}

if (!$error_msg) {

    $id = checkEmail($email);

    $returnedRecord = readMemberRecord($id);

    $password =  mysql_result($returnedRecord,0,'cred');

    if (($password)==($password_submitted)){

        setcookie('loggedIn');

        ////Print ("redirecting...");

        header ('Location: members_page.php4');

        exit();

    } else {

        $error_msg="Sorry, invalid login.";
```

Move the post array data into variables

Check for a well-formed e-mail address

Check for a well-formed password

Both credentials passed validation, so compare with database data

This database function uses the e-mail address to return the corresponding id

This database function then uses the id to return the entire record

Read field credentials from row 0 of returned record array—there is only one row.

Test the submitted password against the one from the database

Give the user a session cookie

Redirect to a new page—we are done on this page

We are done—stop the script right here

```
End if error-msg ─┤        }

End if submitted ─┤     }

                     }

                     ?>

<!DOCTYPE html PUBLIC "-//W3C//DTD XHTML 1.0 Transitional//
EN" "http://www.w3.org/TR/xhtml1/DTD/xhtml1-transitional.
dtd">

<html xmlns="http://www.w3.org/1999/xhtml">

<head>

<meta http-equiv="Content-Type" content="text/html;
charset=iso-8859-1" />

<title>Codin' - Authentication</title>

</head>

<body>

<style type="text/css">

p {margin:0}; //Reduces vertical height of page for this demo

</style>

<h3>Log in</h3>

<p>Non-member page. Any visitor can access this page.</p>

<?php
```

If there is an error message, display the error; else display message ─┤
```
if ($error_msg) {

  print '<p class="error">'.$error_msg.'</p>';

  } else{

  print '<p class="message">'.$msg.'</p>';

  }

  ?>

  <form action="<?php $_SERVER['PHP_SELF'] ?>" method="POST">

      <label for="email">Email</label><br />

      <input name= "email" type="text" size="20" id="email"
value="<?php echo ($email) ?>" /><br />

      <label for="password1">Password<span></span></label><br />
```

```
        <input name= "password1" type="password" size="20"
id="password1" /><br />

        <input type="submit" value="Go" name="submitted"/>

    </form>

    <p><a href="email_password.php4">Email me my password!</
a></p>

    <p><a href="sign_up.php4">Sign me up.</a></p>

    <p><a href="members_page.php4">Go to member area.</a></p>

    <p>Closing the browser ends your session - you will then
have to log in again.</p>

</body>

</html>
```

The code where we use the e-mail address to obtain the password is virtually identical to the code used for a similar purpose in the lost password script, except that instead of e-mailing the password in the database after we retrieve it, we compare it with the submitted password.

Summary

As mentioned at the start of the chapter, being able to selectively admit visitors into certain areas of your site opens a wide range of possibilities for publishing information on the Web in a secure and controlled way. Be aware, though, that regular cookies can be spoofed, and that you should use session cookies in situations where security is important. You should consult an Internet security expert if you want to work with financial data or social security or credit card numbers. However, for most situations, simple cookie authentication as described in this chapter can be an easy way to set up premium offerings for which users will exchange information useful to your business; it is also a useful way to ensure that only certain groups of visitors can access the more valuable pages and capabilities of your site.

Differences between Coding Cookies and Sessions

Although cookies and sessions perform both maintain the state during a user session so we can track specific users as they move from page to page and even between visits, cookies and sessions work in slightly different ways.

As discussed at the start of this chapter, a cookie has six specific pieces of data associated with it, the most significant of which are the name, data, and expiration time.

Session cookies are simply an associative array, and each element of the array can be given a name and associated values of your choosing.

To start a session, write

```
session_start();
```

A 32-character ID (called PHPSESSID) is generated automatically, and this value is passed back and forth between the server and browser. You can view this string using

```
print ($_COOKIE['PHPSESSID']);
```

The data we assign to the session cookie remains on the server and is not passed with each page request as in the case of regular cookies, which is why session cookies are inherently safer.

Because a session cookie is an array, we can give our session cookie a descriptive name, like this:

```
$_SESSION['name']="loggedIn";
```

We can add more values the same way:

```
$_SESSION['id']=20;
```

We can then access those values as in any array:

```
print ($_SESSION['id']);    //Outputs 20
```

We can test whether the session cookie exists:

```
if (isset($_SESSION['loggedIn'])) { echo "Welcome, member!"};
```

We can also change the PHPSESSID string without affecting the associated data:

```
session_regenerate_id();
```

This is what Amazon and others do when they ask you to log in a second time before performing a transaction such as a purchase, to prevent someone who obtains this ID by examining the page headers from impersonating you and buying with your 1-Click account.

You destroy a session cookie with the following:

```
session_destroy();
```

Note that you must call `session_start();` on every page where you want to use the session cookie before attempting to set or read the session cookie data.

Larry Ulman has a great introduction to sessions and cookies in his book *PHP and MySQL for Dynamic Web Sites* published by Peachpit Press.

Regular cookies are easier to use than session cookies, but session cookies, though more complex, are more secure. It's up to you to decide which you want to use.

Building a Web Site
with PHP

All pages share underlying XHTML markup, stylesheets, headers, footers, and navigation elements; only the page title and content area are unique to each page

CREATE A DYNAMIC WEB SITE

Included header is common to every page

Dynamic navigation area adds links a folders are added to the site structure

Member log-in and content management systems are integrated from the previous chapters

Included footer is common to every page

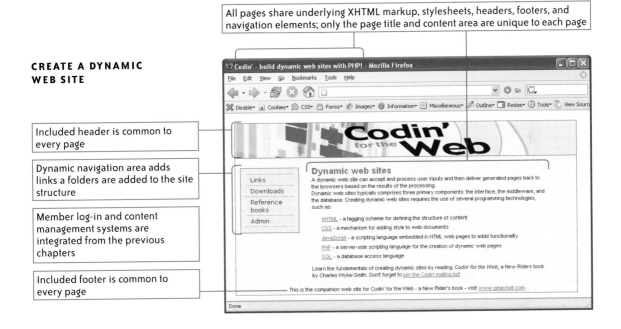

Now it's time to assemble many of the ideas and code from previous chapters into a framework for a complete Web site. In this chapter, we will make more extensive use of include files, integrate the content management and authorization code developed in Chapters 4 and 5, build a dynamic navigation system that displays links according to the site's folder structure, and explore many new PHP functions and the techniques for using them.

Using include Files to Build Pages

We have seen how to use include files to share code, such as database queries, among multiple pages. Now we will use include files to add much of the markup of our page, such as the page's head and footer—the boilerplate XHTML that appears on every page. Then if we ever want to change the design of one of these parts of our pages, we have to do it in just one place.

Figure 6.1 shows the XHTML template. (This same template is used in Chapter B at the *Codin'* Web site.)

FIGURE 6.1 Our XHTML template.

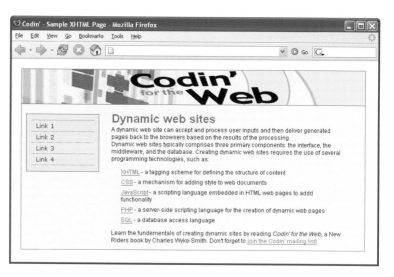

The chapter6_web_site folder in the downloadable examples at the *Codin'* Web site contains a folder called code, and in this is a folder called step1. We will create additional folders, called step2, step3, and so, on as we work through this chapter, so you can review the stages of the site's development. The downloadable examples are set up exactly as shown in this chapter.

We start by copying the code for the Chapter B template page to the step1 folder, creating the file structure shown in **Figure 6.2**.

FIGURE 6.2 The folder setup for Chapter 6.

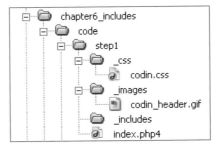

The names of the folders currently in the step1 folder all start with an underscore, to differentiate them from other folders that we will add later, which will be named without underscores at the start of their names. In a later step of this chapter, when we dynamically display these top-level folder names as links in our navigation bar, the ones that start with underscores will be excluded; we don't want to provide navigation to the _css folder, for example.

CODE 6.1: basic_xhtml_
markup12.html

The step*x* folder will act as the root folder of the site for the demonstrations in this chapter, although the root folder of a site would normally be wwwroot, which is several folder levels above this location. The index.php4 file at this pseudo-root is our home page, and at the same level are the folders _css, _images, and _includes. The _includes folder is currently empty.

Here is the code of the code/step1/index.php4 file:

```
<!DOCTYPE html PUBLIC "-//W3C//DTD XHTML 1.0 Transitional//
EN" "http://www.w3.org/TR/xhtml1/DTD/xhtml1-transitional.
dtd">

<html xmlns="http://www.w3.org/1999/xhtml">

<head>

<meta http-equiv="Content-Type" content="text/html;
charset=iso-8859-1" />

<title>Codin' - Sample XHTML Page</title>

<link href="css/codin.css" media="screen" rel="stylesheet" />

</head>

<body>

<div id = "wrapper">

  <div id="header">

    <!-- -->

  </div>

  <div id="navigation">

    <ul>
```

```
        <li><a href="#">Link 1</a></li>

        <!--other links removed here-->

    </ul>

  </div>

  <div id="content">

    <h1>Dynamic web sites</h1>

    <p>A dynamic web site... (text removed here) ... requires the
use of several programming technologies, such as:</p>

    <ul>

    <li><a href="#">XHTML</a> - a tagging scheme for defining
the structure of content</li>
```

> Other links removed here to save space

```
    </ul>

    <p>Learn the fundementals of creating dynamic sites by
reading <em>Codin' for the Web</em>, a New Riders book by
Charles Wyke-Smith. Don't forget to <a href="#">join the
Codin' mailing list!</a></p>

  </div>

  <div id="footer"><p>This is the companion web site for Codin'
for the Web - a New Rider's book - visit <a href="http://
www.peachpit.com">www.peachpit.com</a></p></div>

  <!--end of wrapper div-->

  </body>

  </html>
```

The highlighted code indicates content specific to this page. The rest of the code will appear on every other page of our site. Rather than adding this common code in the markup of every page—meaning that we would have to edit every page if we wanted to change the code in these areas—we will move the code above and below the highlighted content into two include files that can be shared by all the pages. Then if we later want to change something at the top or bottom of the pages, we need only change one file and not every file in the entire site.

Creating the XHTML include Files

We will move all the code above the highlighted content into a file called page_top.inc.php4, and we will move all the code below the highlighted content into a file called page_bottom.inc.php4. Now the code for our page can be reduced to the following:

CODE 6.2: step1/index.php4

```
<?php

include "_includes/page_top.inc.php4";

?>

<h1>Dynamic web sites</h1>

    <p>A dynamic web site... (text removed here) ...
requires the use of several programming technologies, such
as:</p>

    <ul>

    <li><a href="#">XHTML</a> - a tagging scheme for defining
the structure of content</li>
```

Other links removed here

```
    </ul>

    <p>Learn the fundamentals of creating dynamic sites by
reading <em>Codin' for the Web</em>, a New Riders book by
Charles Wyke-Smith. Don't forget to <a href="#">join the
Codin' mailing list!</a></p>

<?php

include "_includes/page_bottom.inc.php4";

?>
```

The page will look the same in the browser, but now our folder structure looks like **Figure 6.3**.

FIGURE 6.3 The index page's top and bottom chunks of code, which bookend the page's content, are now in two include files.

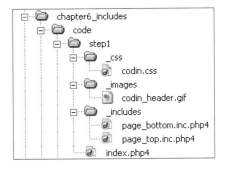

Creating the Navigation include Files

Because we are only using one page template in this example, the navigation bar element could remain in the page top include file, but we are going to move into its own include file. This element is going to become more complex, as later it will dynamically display links according to the names of top-level folders of the site (and thereby be updated automatically as new folders are added), and for this reason it's worth managing it in its own include file. Also, if you decide to create an additional page template, which would mean creating additional page top and page bottom include files, you could then share this navigation element between both templates if it is in its own include file.

Our page top include file currently looks like this:

CODE 6.3: step1/page_top.inc.php4

```
<!DOCTYPE html PUBLIC "-//W3C//DTD XHTML 1.0 Transitional//
EN" "http://www.w3.org/TR/xhtml1/DTD/xhtml1-transitional.
dtd">

<html xmlns="http://www.w3.org/1999/xhtml">

<head>

<meta http-equiv="Content-Type" content="text/html;
charset=iso-8859-1" />

<title>Codin' - Sample XHTML Page</title>

<link href="_css/codin.css" media="screen" rel="stylesheet"
/>

</head>

<body>

<div id = "wrapper">

  <div id="header">

    <!-- -->

  </div>

  <div id="navigation">

    <ul>

      <li><a href="#">Link 1</a></li>

      <li><a href="#">Link 2</a></li>
```

```
      <li><a href="#">Link 3</a></li>

      <li><a href="#">Link 4</a></li>

    </ul>

  </div>

  <div id="content">
```

We will cut the highlighted code and paste it into its own include file, which we will save in the _includes folder as navigation.inc. php4. Then we will replace the code we removed with the following line:

CODE 6.4: Part of step2/page_top. inc.php4

```
<div id="navigation">

  include "_includes/navigation.inc.php4";

</div>
```

Now we have an include within an include, a capability that is a powerful feature of PHP. Our navigation element could now be shared among numerous page templates.

Again, after this step, our page looks again identical in the browser, but the underlying PHP is now structured in way that is very economical and easy to manage. **Figure 6.4** shows our new folder structure.

FIGURE 6.4 The navigation element is now in its own include file.

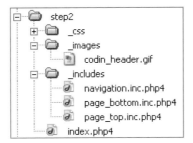

Let's now start integrating the code that allows us to display and manage the reference links of the site that we created in Chapter 4.

Creating the Reference Links Folder

The first step is to create a folder called links at the top level of our site and copy (not move) our existing index.php4 file into it (**Figure 6.5**). Then we will have the framework of our new page with the include functions at the top and bottom of it, and we can modify it by replacing its existing content code with the code that displays the links.

FIGURE 6.5 The new links folder and its index file.

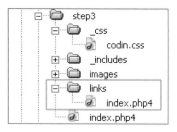

Now we can go to the Chapter 4 file and grab the code for this page. We'll first simply replace the existing content of our links/index.php4 file with the content of the file links_listing1.php4 in the Chapter 7 folder—at least, everything within the content div tag. Our script looks like this:

CODE 6.5: step3/links/index1.php4

The advantage of leaving this file's name as index.php4 is that it will automatically load when a URL references the folder. This behavior will be handy when we dynamically generate navigation URLs later: we need only have these URLs reference the folder for the folder's index file to load and don't have to worry about appending a file name to the folder name. However, we need to keep in mind that several files will have the same name. The server will have no problem with this as the files are in different folders, but we'll need to keep track of which file we are modifying at any given moment.

```php
<?php

include "_includes/page_top.inc.php4";

?>

<h1>Links to Codin' related sites</h1>

    <p>Many of the URLs referenced in Codin' are listed
here.</p>


<?php

$myResult = mysql_query('SELECT ref_links.*, ref_categories.
category_name FROM ref_links, ref_categories WHERE ref_links.
ref_categories_id=ref_categories.id', $connectID)

    or die ("Unable to select from database");

    while ($row=mysql_fetch_array($myResult, MYSQL_ASSOC)) {
```

TRUE first time $lastCat not set and each time a new category is found

Print the next category heading

Record which category this listing was in so we can test whether the category changes

End of ref_links div

```php
$thisCat= $row['category_name'];

   if ($lastCat<>$thisCat) {

      print "<h2>".$row['category_name']."</h2>";

   }

   print '<div id="ref_links">';

   print "<h3>".$row['topic_name']."</h3>\n";

   print "<p>".$row['topic_desc']."</p>\n";

   print "<a href=".$row['topic_url']." target=\"_blank\
">".$row['topic_url']."</a>\n";

   $lastCat = $row['category_name'];

   print "</div>\n";

}

?>

<?php

include "_includes/page_bottom.inc.php4";

?>
```

Figure 6.6 shows the results in the browser.

FIGURE 6.6 When we load the page, the _includes folder path is wrong, and the database query throws an error instead of writing the list of links.

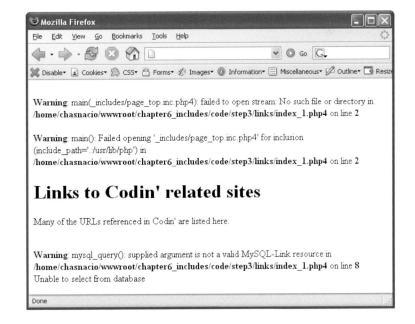

As Figure 6.6 shows, we need to fix a few things here. Because our index.php4 file is down one level (in the links folder), the relative path to the _includes folder

```
include "_includes/page_bottom.inc.php4";
```

which worked for this page in its original location at the top level of our site, doesn't work here. From this new location, the correct URL is

```
include "../_includes/page_bottom.inc.php4";
```

—in other words, up one level and then into the _includes folder. These are both relative paths—they work because they specify the relationship between the page containing the code and the referenced resource (in this case, the include file). We could make the simple modification shown in the second of the two links, but if we adopt this approach, every single URL on a page will require custom modification like this, and if we move a page for any reason, all such links will break because they are relative, not absolute.

So now we will create a configuration file that enables us to provide paths to the _includes folder and the top level folder of our site that works from any page. This configuration file will also be an include file, and it will contain code that sets a variable that contains a top-down absolute path reference that we can append to the front of each URL. Every page will reference this config file, so the path variables are available to every page; this will enable us to write a standardized URL that contains this variable for every link in every page, so that every page can find the associated include files and other resources no matter where they in relation to that page.

Creating a Config File

Here is what is needed in the configuration file, which will go in our _includes folder:

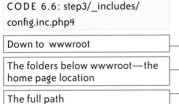

CODE 6.6: step3/_includes/ config.inc.php4

Down to wwwroot

The folders below wwwroot—the home page location

The full path

```php
<?php

$serverPath =$_SERVER['DOCUMENT_ROOT'];

$folderPath = "/chapter9_includes/code/step3/";

$fullPath = $serverPath.$folderPath;

$includePath = $fullPath."_includes/"

?>
```

If you have come this far through this book, this code shouldn't require much explanation, but in brief, if we were to simply run the code

```php
print $_SERVER['DOCUMENT_ROOT'];
```

the output would be /home/codin/wwwroot.

You can see from this that $_SERVER['DOCUMENT_ROOT'] gives us the path above our site's root folder. Next, because the demonstration site's home page is actually several folders below the root folder (which is unusual, but necessary for me to show you these step-by-step versions of the site's development), we also have to create a variable called $folderPath that shows the path down from the root folder to the step$x$ folder that we are currently looking at—you wouldn't need this $folderPath variable if you were creating a site where the home page is in the root folder, as is typical.

We combine $_SERVER['DOCUMENT_ROOT'] and $folderPath to create $fullPath, which contains the full URL of the pseudo-home folder.

```php
print $fullPath;
```

Outputs: /home/codin/wwwroot/chapter6_includes/code/step3/

If you are using this demonstration code to modify a site you are creating and working with a home page at the root level, you can either delete the $folderPath *reference here (and remove or modify it on every page where it occurs), or leave the variable in the code and convert its value to an empty string, like this:*
$folderPath = "";

Because I am not working from the root folder but several folder levels down, the include path for the config file must be relative and so does need to be customized for each page, like this:

```
include "../_includes/
config.inc.php4;
```

This would not be the case if I were building a site in the normal manner, where the _includes folder could be at the root level. Then I would be able to write

```
include $_SERVER['DOCUMENT_
ROOT']."_includes/config.
inc.php4";
```

and this code would work in every page. As it is, I have to set one relative path to the config file in each script, and after that, I have use of the absolute path variables. This approach is still far better than having to write a unique relative path for every resource reference in the file.

From that, we create $includesPath, which provides a path to the _includes folder.

```
print $includesPath
```

Outputs: /home/codin/wwwroot/chapter6_includes/code/step3/_includes/

Now we can use these variables to prefix the names of the files we want to reference. For example, the absolute (top-down) path to the include file can be written as

```
include $includesPath."page_bottom.inc.php4";
```

We can now use the same references to the include files on every page. It doesn't matter how many folders down in our site a page might be; this include path will always point at the _includes folder, because it is a full absolute path, from the top level of the server down to the _includes folder.

Note that a URL in a link does not take the full path from the very top of the server like the include files do; a URL is relative to the root folder, so when we want to write a URL, in this case to the links folder, we can write href=$folderPath."links".

The bottom line is that a config file with absolute path references is key to creating links that don't break as you reorganize your site, and config files can also hold database credentials and other unchanging data that your pages need to reference. It's much better to store such information in a config file than to repeat it in many different places in your code.

Once you have adopted the labor-saving methodology of include files, you also take on the task of tying all the scripts together to build your pages. It can be challenging to make everything link together at first, but setting up absolute-path variables in a config file can greatly simplify this process, by standardizing the format of include URLs for every page. Hopefully this discussion gives you some pointers for taking control of this important task.

Anyway, with the includes path now using our config file, things are looking much better (**Figure 6.7**).

FIGURE 6.7 The config file now provides the paths to link the include files to the page.

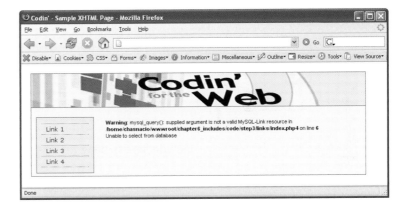

With the page `include` functions now working, we can turn our attention to the database query error.

Setting Up the Database include Files

As you may have noticed, when we moved the content of the links page to our script, we didn't bring the code that establishes and closes the connection with the database, which is why we are seeing the database error, so let's now add this code. Because we will be establishing and closing the database connection from many pages in this site, let's put these two pieces of code in include files also.

Here's the code that establishes the database connection:

```php
<?php

$hostUrl = 'localhost';

$userName = 'userName';

$password = 'userPassword';

$connectID = mysql_connect($hostUrl, $userName, $password)
    or die ("Sorry, can't connect to database");

mysql_select_db("databaseName", $connectID)
    or die ("Unable to select database");

?>
```

Connect to database ⎯⎯⎯ `$connectID = mysql_connect($hostUrl, $userName, $password)`

Select the database to read from ⎯⎯⎯ `mysql_select_db("databaseName", $connectID)`

We'll save this code in a file called db_connect.inc.php4.

Here's the code that closes the database:

```php
<?php

mysql_close($connectID);

?>
```

Close the connection → `mysql_close($connectID);`

We'll save this code in a file called db_close.inc.php4. Both files are saved in the _includes folder.

Now we add the code for these two include files our links page.

```php
<?php

include "../_includes/config.inc.php4";

include $includesPath."page_top.inc.php4";

include $fullPath."_includes/db_connect.inc.php4";

?>
```

```php
<?php

$myResult = mysql_query('SELECT ref_links.*, ref_categories.
category_name FROM ref_links, ref_categories WHERE ref_links.
ref_categories_id=ref_categories.id', $connectID)

  or die ("Unable to select from database");

  while ($row=mysql_fetch_array($myResult, MYSQL_ASSOC)) {

  $thisCat= $row['category_name'];

  if ($lastCat<>$thisCat) {

        print "<h2>".$row['category_name']."</h2>";

    }

    print '<div id="ref_links">';

    print "<h3>".$row['topic_name']."</h3>\n";

    print "<p>".$row['topic_desc']."</p>\n";

    print "<a href=".$row['topic_url']." target=\"_blank\
">".$row['topic_url']."</a>\n";

  $lastCat = $row['category_name'];

    print "</div>\n";

  }

?>
```

- TRUE first time $lastCat not set and each time a new category is found → `if ($lastCat<>$thisCat) {`
- Print the next category heading → `print "<h2>".$row['category_name']."</h2>";`
- Record which category this listing was in so we can test whether the category changes → `$lastCat = $row['category_name'];`
- End of ref_links div → `}`

```php
<?php

include $includesPath."page_bottom.inc.php4";

include $fullPath."_includes/db_close.inc.php4";

?>
```

Now our page is functioning as it did when we first developed this code back in Chapter 4, except now it is presented in the page template (**Figure 6.8**).

FIGURE 6.8 The links display code (chapter4/links_listing_step1) is now functional within the page template.

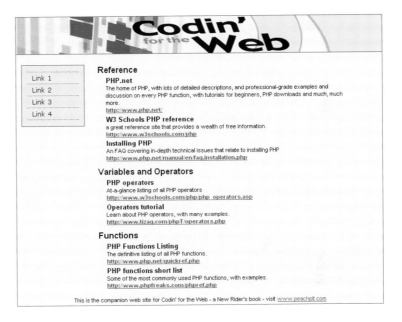

By using include files to open the database connection at the start of the page and close it at the end, we can have as many database queries within a page as we like and not have to establish a connection for each query; for as long as the script is running, the connection is open. Of course, we add these two database include files only in scripts that need access to the database.

For now, we are hard-wiring the navigation. Later in this chapter, we will make the navigation elements dynamically update based on the names of the top-level folders.

CODE 6.7: step3/_includes/ navigation.inc.php4

Activating the Navigation Links

To finish this section of our site development work, let's make the navigation work, so that we can move between the home page and the links page.

We open the navigation include file and modify it to look like this:

```
<ul>

    <li><a href="<?php print $folderPath ?>/links">Links</a></li>

    <li><a href="#">Link 2</a></li>

    <li><a href="#">Link 3</a></li>

    <li><a href="<?php print $folderPath ?>">Home</a></li>

</ul>
```

Figure 6.9 shows the results.

FIGURE 6.9 The navigation links.

Now we can use the navigation links to move between our links page and the home page. We'll add more links as we proceed.

Adding the Administration Pages

Now it's time to add the administration pages for the links. By the time we finish doing this, the links page, which displays the links, will be viewable only to signed-up members, and the pages in the admin folder, which allow links to be added and edited, will be accessible only to a superuser, who must log in with a special administrator password.

We will start by adding a folder called admin (**Figure 6.10**). This folder will contain the pages that allow the site administrator to add and edit links on the links page.

FIGURE 6.10 The admin folder added to the site structure.

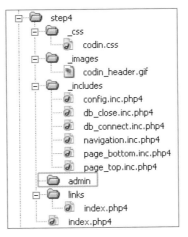

Transferring the Admin Page Code to the Page Template

Next, we'll copy the index.php4 page from the links folder to the new admin folder, to use it as a page template with the include functions already in place. Then we'll replace its links-related code with the code of the links admin page from Chapter 4. The only bit we won't copy from the Chapter 4 code is the database connect and database close code from the top and bottom of the file, as we have that in our page top and page bottom include files already. Before we look at the code, though, we'll look at the related CSS.

Moving the CSS to the Style Sheet

The Chapter 4 code also contains a big chunk of CSS, so we'll next move that CSS into a style sheet, taking care to remove the XHTML <style> tags that enclosed the CSS in its former location because those tags are not needed in a style sheet.

In this new context of a style sheet for the whole site, the generic CSS selectors in this piece of CSS that simply read table, h3, and so on could have unwanted effects on other pages of the site where such tags are also present. So we need to modify the selectors in this piece of CSS by adding div#admin in front of each one—for example,

div#admin table {CSS definitions here}

Then we add a div tag with the ID admin for the code for the admin page. Now these CSS style affect only the code within the admin div tag on this one page. And that is all that's needed to make this page functional within our page template.

Here's the finished code with the changes highlighted and the CSS moved into the style sheet:

CODE 6.8: Part of step 4/_css/ codin.css

```php
<?php

include "../_includes/config.inc.php4";

include $fullPath."_includes/db_connect.inc.php4";

include $fullPath."_includes/page_top.inc.php4";


if ($_GET['delete_id']) {

  $id = ($_GET['delete_id']);

    $success = mysql_query ("DELETE FROM ref_links WHERE id
= $id", $connectID)

    or die ("Unable to delete record from database");

  if ($success) {

    print "Record successfully deleted";

  }

}

?>

<h2>Links Admin</h2>
```

```
<p><a href="links_form.php4">Add new link</a><br />

<a href="<?php print $folderPath ?>links">View listings
page</a></p>

<?php

if ($_GET['added']) print '<p style="color:red; font-weight:
bold;">Record successfully created!</p>';

if ($_GET['updated']) print '<p style="color:red; font-
weight: bold;">Record successfully updated!</p>';

$myResult = mysql_query('SELECT ref_links.*, ref_categories.
category_name FROM ref_links, ref_categories WHERE ref_links.
ref_categories_id=ref_categories.id', $connectID)

    or die ("Unable to select from database");

print '<div id="admin">';

print '<table>'."\n";

while ($row = mysql_fetch_array($myResult, MYSQL_ASSOC)) {

    $thisCat= $row['category_name'];

    if ($lastCat<>$thisCat) {

        print '<th colspan="6" align="left">';

        print "<h3>".$row['category_name']."</h3>";

        print "</th>\n";

    }

    print '<tr>';

    print '<tr>'."\n";

    print '<td>'.$row['topic_name'].'</td>'."\n";

    print '<td class="description">'.$row['topic_desc'].'</
td>'."\n";

    $id=$row['id'];

    print '<td><a href="links_form.php4?modify_
id='.$id.'">Edit</td>';

    print '<td><a href="';

    print ($_SERVER['PHP_SELF']);

    print '?delete_id='.$id.'">Delete</a></td>';
```

Query the database

Start of admin div

Loop through the returned records

$thisCat is used to test whether a new heading needs to be written out; TRUE first time $lastCat not set and each time a new category is found

Then write out a table heading with the category name

Heading spans all columns of the table

Print the next category heading

Trim the displayed URL down to 60 characters (0 thru 59)

Otherwise, long URLs force the table to be very wide

Add ellipsis if URL is trimmed (> 60 chars)

Finally, store the current category so next time the loop repeats, we can tell whether the next item is in a new category

If so, write out a new heading— see if ($lastCat<>$thisCat) above

End of admin div

The ref links on the admin page

CODE 6.9: Part of step4/_css/ codin.css

```php
    print '</tr>'."\n";
    print '<tr><td class="url" colspan=6><a
href="'.$row['topic_url'].'">'.(substr($row['topic_
url'],0,59));
    if ((strlen($row['topic_url']) > 60)) {print "&#8230;";}
    print'</a></td></tr>';
    $lastCat = $row['category_name'];
  }
  print '</table>'."\n";

  print '</div>';
?>

<p><a href="links_form.php4">Add new link</a><br />
<a href="<?php print $folderPath ?>links">View listings
page</a></p>

<?php

include $fullPath."_includes/page_bottom.inc.php4";

include $fullPath."_includes/db_close.inc.php4";

?>
```

The new CSS added to the style sheet looks like this:

```css
div#admin table h3 {padding:10px 0 0 0;margin:0; border-
top:2px solid #666;}

div#admin table {border-bottom:2px solid #666; width:530px;}

div#admin table td {padding:0 2px; vertical-align:top;
border-top: 1px solid #CCC;}

div#admin table td:first-child {font-weight:bold; width:25%;}

div#admin table td.url {border-top:0; font-weight:normal;}
```

You can see in the main code block above that we have already modified the URLs for the links form, where we enter new links, in anticipation of adding this page to our site in the next step. We've also put in the correct URL for the link to the existing links listing page, so that as we edit the links from this page, we can click to see how they will appear on what will be the public page of the site. Note that we only need to reference the folder in this URL; the index.php4 file within it will load automatically.

Figure 6.11 shows the displayed page.

FIGURE 6.11 The Links Admin page
displayed within the page template.

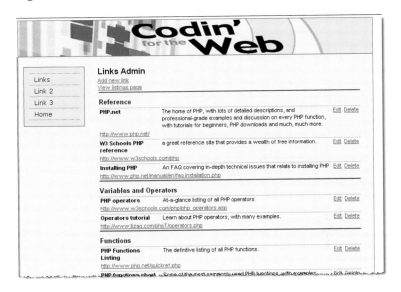

Normally at this point, we would test the Edit and Delete links, but we are going to wait to do this. The Delete link does, in fact, already work, because its functionality is implemented at the top of this same page, but we are not going to test it until we can add a test link that we don't mind deleting, and we can't do that until the links form is working.

We also can't test the Edit link until we have the links form working as that form is where a link is displayed for editing, so let's now add this page and then test the Edit and Delete links.

Building the Links Form Page

We originally created the links form in Chapter 4; the final version is called links_form_step9.php4.

You can copy this file directly from the Chapter 4 folder into the admin folder. Be sure then to rename it links_form.php4. If you don't rename it and then you copy another index.php4 file into that folder as a template to modify, you will overwrite the page we just created that is also named index.php4.

After you move the Chapter 4 file links_form_step9.php4 into the admin folder and rename it links_form.php4, you can copy the include code to the top and bottom of the page and strip out the XHTML head code, which is already in the page top include file.

Note that the XHTML <head> part of the code from the Chapter 4 links_form_step9.php4 file also contains the CSS that styles the form, so once again, we move that CSS into the style sheet and add a div ID to each selector, like this:

```
div#links_admin_form  h3 {some CSS definitions}
```

We then add a div tag with the same ID, links_admin_form, to the markup for the form. This tag ensures that these styles are applied only to this piece of code and that there are no other XHTML tags with the same name in other pages.

What you want to end up with is this:

CODE 6.10: step4/admin/links_ form.php4

> The page top include has been moved down below the elseif code so that we don't send XHTML headers before the redirects and get an error

> The user has submitted a new listing

> The admin page has passed the ID of the record to be updated

```php
<?php

include "../_includes/config.inc.php4";

include $fullPath."_includes/db_connect.inc.php4";

    $category=($_POST['category']);

    $topic_name=($_POST['topic_name']);

    $topic_description=($_POST['topic_description']);

    $topic_url=($_POST['topic_url']);

    $id = ($_GET['modify_id']);

if (($_POST['submitted']) && (!$_GET['modify_id'])) {

    $success = mysql_query ("INSERT into ref_links (ref_
categories_id, topic_name, topic_desc, topic_url) VALUES
('$category', '$topic_name', '$topic_description', '$topic_
url')", $connectID)

    or die ("Unable to insert record into database");

    if ($success) {

    header ('Location: index.php?added=1');

            }

} elseif  ((!$_POST['submitted']) && ($_GET['modify_id'])) {

            $this_Record = mysql_query("SELECT ref_links.*,ref_
categories.category_name, ref_categories.id AS cat_id
FROM ref_links, ref_categories WHERE ref_categories.id =
ref_links.ref_categories_id AND ref_links.id = '$id'",
$connectID)

            or die ("Can't read the this record.");
```

```php
            $record_data = mysql_fetch_array($this_Record, MYSQL_ASSOC);
```

The user has submitted the form to update a listing

```php
    } elseif  (($_POST['submitted']) && ($_GET['modify_id'])) {

            $success = mysql_query("UPDATE ref_links SET ref_
    categories_id = '$category', topic_name = '$topic_name',
    topic_desc = '$topic_description', topic_url = '$topic_url'
    WHERE id='$id'", $connectID);

            if ($success) {

            header ('Location: index.php?updated=1');

            }
```

The user has loaded the page to enter a new listing

```php
    } else {

    //do nothing - just let the page load

    }
```

Page top include moved down to here to prevent Headers Already Sent error

```php
    include $fullPath."_includes/page_top.inc.php4";

    ?>
```

Start of links_admin div

```html
    <div id="links_admin_form">

    <h3>Add or modify a listing</h3>

    <a href="index.php">Links Admin page</a>

    <form method="post" action="<?php $_SERVER['PHP_SELF'] ?>">

    <label for="category">Topic Category</label>

    <?php
```

Drop-down menu

```php
    print '<select name="category">'."\n";

    print '<option value="none">Select a Catagory</option>'."\n";

    $Categories = mysql_query('SELECT * FROM ref_categories',
    $connectID);while ($Category = mysql_fetch_array($Categories,
    MYSQL_ASSOC)){

    print  '<option value="'.$Category['id'].'"';

      if($record_data['cat_id']==$Category['id']) print "
    selected=\"selected\" ";

    print '>'.$Category['category_name']."</option>\n";

    }

    print '</select>'."<br />\n";
```

```
                                        ?>
```

topic_name

```
<label for="topic_name">Topic Name</label>

<input name="topic_name" type="text" size="30" id="topic_
name" value="<?php print $record_data['topic_name'] ?>" />
```

topic_description

```
<label for="topic_description">Topic Description</label>

<textarea name="topic_description"><?php print $record_
data['topic_desc'] ?></textarea>
```

topic_url

```
<label for="topic_url">Topic URL</label>

<input name="topic_url" type="text" size="30" id="topic_url"
value="<?php print $record_data['topic_url'] ?>" />

<input type="submit" value="Submit" name="submitted" />

</form>
```

End links_admin_form

```
</div>

<?php

include $fullPath."_includes/page_bottom.inc.php4";

include $fullPath."_includes/db_close.inc.php4";

?>
```

The CSS looks like this:

This CSS is the stylesheet

```
div#links_admin_form h3 {padding:10px 0 0 0; margin:0;}

div#links_admin_form label {display:block; margin:8px 0 2px
0;}

div#links_admin_form a {display:block; color:#066; margin:3px
0 10px;}

div#links_admin_form a:hover {color:#000; text-decoration:
none;}

div#links_admin_form input[type="submit"] {display:block;
margin-top:8px;}
```

Figure 6.12 shows the displayed page with some test form data
ready to be submitted.

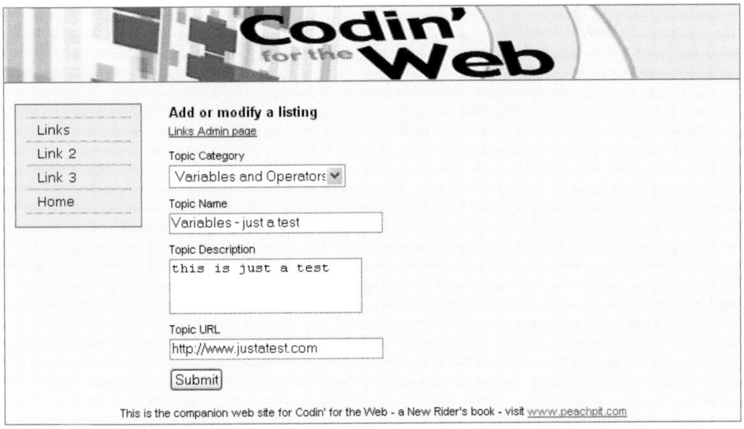

FIGURE 6.12 The displayed form with some test data ready for submission.

Note that URLs within the code have been modified to reference the administration page with simply the URL index.php4; no path information is needed because the form and the administration page are in the same folder.

Beware the Headers Already Sent Error Message

In the code we just entered, the page top `include` function

```
include $fullPath."_includes/page_top.inc.php4";
```

which contains the XHTML for the top of the page, is not in its usual position at the beginning of the script with the other include files. This `include` function does not appear in the script until after the PHP code that processes the form—you can see it highlighted about 35 lines down the script. It appears down here because otherwise a Headers Already Sent error message would appear when the form is submitted. This error would occur because we use a redirect in the large opening block of PHP code to send the user to another page after submitting the form, and this redirect must occur before any XHTML is output. See the "Headers Already Sent Error Message" sidebar for more information.

The Headers Already Sent Error

Observe that the `include` function that contains the XHTML for the top of the page is now moved down to a line below the PHP that processes the links form page. If we didn't do this, the following error message would appear when we tried to submit the form:

```
Warning: Cannot modify header information - headers already sent by (output started at /home/
chasnacio/wwwroot/chapter6_includes/code/step4/_includes/page_top.inc.php4:6) in /home/chasna-
cio/wwwroot/chapter6_includes/code/step4/admin/links_form.php4 on line 20
```

Line 20 in this case is the line with the redirect that returns the user to the main administration page after the form has been successfully submitted (and there is another redirect further down the script that acts after the user updates a listing). The message also tells us that the problem originated in line 6, indicated by `:6`. This is the line where the `include` function was originally located.

The first step toward understanding this common error is to realize that when the first scrap of XHTML of a PHP script is output, PHP precedes such output with the HTTP headers. The HTTP headers are lines of data that you never see in normal circumstances, even if you view the source code of the page; but they are the first thing sent to the browser in every HTTP transaction and so must precede any XHTML code that your PHP page outputs.

The HTTP headers contain data that helps the browser understand how to display the page, and they also contain any redirect and cookie information. So once your script outputs as little as a single white space of XHTML, the HTTP headers are immediately output (and then that white space would be output). If later in the script, even in the very next line, you then attempt to write a cookie or use `Location: "some URL"` to redirect the user to another page, you will get the Headers Already Sent error message: it's now too late for this information to be added to the headers—you've missed the bus. So you must, in the case of the list form code shown here, have the redirect precede the `include` function for the page top code. The page top code contains lots of XHTML and so triggers the output of the XHTML headers as soon as it is executed.

Headers Already Sent is a very common and frustrating error for beginners, so remember that when you see it, it is appearing because you are attempting to write a cookie, redirect the page, or perform some task that affects the HTTP headers after you have already output some XHTML from the script. Even a `print $someVariable;` line that you add temporarily to view a variable's value can trigger this message. Simply backtrack to see where XHTML is being output prior to attempting to set the cookie or redirect the page, and then delete the problem code or reorganize the script so that these events are reversed, as we did here. In this case, the fix was simple; we just moved the page top `include` function down to a line after the PHP that redirects the page, and the error went away.

Testing the Form

If we submit the form after entering the data shown in Figure 6.12, the data is written to the database and then the redirect sends us back to the Links Admin page, where we can see the new data displayed (**Figure 6.13**).

FIGURE 6.13 The test record is added to the listing.

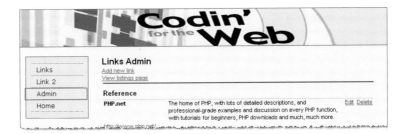

If we then click the Edit link, we see the record displayed in the form, where we can edit the data if we wish. Clicking Submit once again updates the record and returns us to the Links Admin page.

Adding the Admin Link to the Navigation

Now that our two administration pages are working, we can add the Admin link to the navigation (**Figure 6.14**).

```
<ul>
    <li><a href="<?php print $folderPath ?>links">Links</a></li>
    <li><a href="#">Link 2</a></li>
    <li><a href="<?php print $folderPath ?>Admin">Admin</a></li>
    <li><a href="<?php print $folderPath ?>">Home</a></li>
</ul>
```

FIGURE 6.14 The Admin link is added to the navigation.

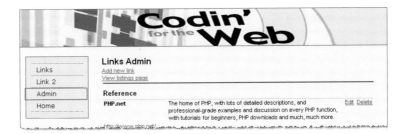

Clicking the Admin link loads the main administration page, from which we can access the form.

Now it's time to use the authentication code we created in Chapter 5 to restrict access to some of our content so that we can create a members-only area and also prevent anyone but a site administrator accessing the Admin area.

Implementing the Authentication System

We are going to use the authentication code we created in Chapter 5 for authentication here, but it's going to do a little more in our new site. Not only will we will use it to sign up and sign in members and give members access to areas restricted to regular visitors, but we will also use it to set up a special administrator superuser who has exclusive access to the Admin area.

We have created several pages for this site, so you should now understand how to assemble a new page for our site from a stand-alone page from earlier chapters:

1. Add the appropriate `include` functions.

2. Move the CSS from the stand-alone pages into the site's style sheet.

3. Remove any XHTML that is already in the page top and page bottom include files.

I will now simply show you the code as it is developed.

Setting Up the Admin include Files

We first put the include files from Chapter 5 in the _includes folder of this project as shown in **Figure 6.15**.

FIGURE 6.15 Four include files are added from the Chapter 5 includes subfolders.

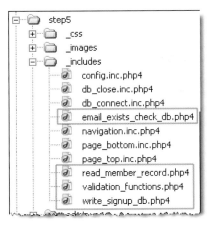

Next, we need to copy the code from each of the pages from the Chapter 8 exercise and modify the pages so that they follow the page template of our site. We will use the same page names for the site as we used in Chapter 8. Here's the sign-up page (sign_up.php4) after it has been modified for our site:

CODE 6.11: step5/sign_up.php4

```php
<?php
include "_includes/config.inc.php4";
include $includesPath."db_connect.inc.php4";
require $includesPath."email_exists_check_db.php4";
include $includesPath."validation_functions.php4";
if ($_POST['submitted']) {
    $first_name = $_POST['first_name'];
    $last_name = $_POST['last_name'];
    $email = $_POST['email'];
    $password1 = $_POST['password1'];
    $password2 = $_POST['password2'];
    $error_msg=array();
    $valid = verifyAlphaNum ($first_name);
    if (!$valid){
        $error_msg[]="First Name must be letters and numbers, spaces,
        dashes and ' only.";
    }
```

Password must be entered twice correctly—passwords don't have to be unique

intialize error array for form errors

The validation functions are in the validation_functions include file—see above

Test for invalid data

| Test for invalid data | ```
$valid = verifyAlphaNum ($last_name);

if (!$valid){

$error_msg[]="Last Name must be letters and numbers, spaces,
dashes and ' only.";

}
``` |

| Test for invalid data | ```
$valid = verifyEmail ($email);

if (!$valid){

$error_msg[]="Email must be a valid format (e.g. john@yahoo.
com).";
``` |

| The e-mail address format is good | ```
} else {
``` |

| Check whether the e-mail address already exists—returns the ID of an existing record if it does | ```
$returnedID = checkEmail($email);

print $returnedID;

}
``` |

| Check password length | ```
if (((strlen($password1)) < 4) or ((strlen($password1))) >
10){

$error_msg[]=  "Password must be between 4 and 10 characters
in length.";

}

if ($password1 !== $password2) {

$error_msg[]="Both password fields must match. Please try
again.";

}
``` |

| Test for invalid data | ```
$valid = verifyPassword ($password1);

if (!$valid){

$error_msg[]="Password can only contain letters and
numbers.";

}
``` |

| If no errors, and we are here because the form was submitted rather than the page has first loaded | ```
    if  (!$returnedID && !$error_msg && $_POST['submitted']) {
``` |

| Write to database | ```
       $success = mysql_query ("INSERT into members (first_name,
last_name, email, cred) VALUES ('$first_name', '$last_name',
'$email', '$password1')", $connectID)
``` |

```
    or die ("Unable to insert record into database");
  if ($success) {
    setcookie('loggedIn');
    header ('Location: members_page.php4');
     exit();
    }
  }
}
include $includesPath."page_top.inc.php4";
?>
  <form action="<?php $_SERVER['PHP_SELF'] ?>" method="POST">
  <h3>Sign up</h3>
  <p>Members can download code samples and access the Codin'
links.</p>
  <?php
  if ($returnedID) {
  echo '<p class="msg">A record with this email address
already exists - you are already a member!</p>';
  echo "<ul>\n";
  echo '<li><a href="sign_in.php4">Log in on home page</a></
li>';
  echo '<li><a href="email_password.php4">Email me my
password</a></li>';
  echo "</ul>";
  } else {
    if ($error_msg) {
      echo "<h4>Errors!</h4>";
      echo "<ul>\n";
      foreach ($error_msg as $err) {
      echo "<li>".$err."</li>\n";
      }
```

Give the user a cookie

Redirect to a new page—we are done on this page

Stop the script right here

End if success

End of if post submitted

Present errors to the user; if the e-mail address exists in the database, any other errors are irrelevant

Open a list—the \n formats the code view

Close the list

The e-mail address does not exist, so write out any errors

Open a list—the \n formats the code view

Write out the error array as list items

End foreach

Close the list

End if $error_msg

End if $returnedID

```
            echo "</ul>";

        }

    }

    ?>

    <label for="first_name">First Name<span> required</span></
label><br />

        <input name="first_name" type="text" size="20"
id="first_name" value="<?php echo ($first_name) ?>" /><br />

        <label for="last_name">Last Name<span> required</
span></label><br />

        <input name="last_name" type="text" size="20" id="last_
name" value="<?php echo ($last_name) ?>" /><br />

        <label for="email">Email<span> required</span></
label><br />

        <input name= "email" type="text" size="20" id="email"
value="<?php echo ($email) ?>" /><br />

        <label for="password1">Password<span> required - 4 to
8 letters/numbers</span></label><br />

        <input name= "password1" type="password" size="10"
id="password1" /><br />

        <label for="password2">Type password again<span>
required</span></label><br />

        <input name= "password2" type="password" size="10"
id="password2" /><br />

        <input type="submit" value="Go" name="submitted"/>

    </form>

<?php

include $includesPath."page_bottom.inc.php4";

include $includesPath."db_close.inc.php4";

?>
```

Figure 6.16 shows the displayed page.

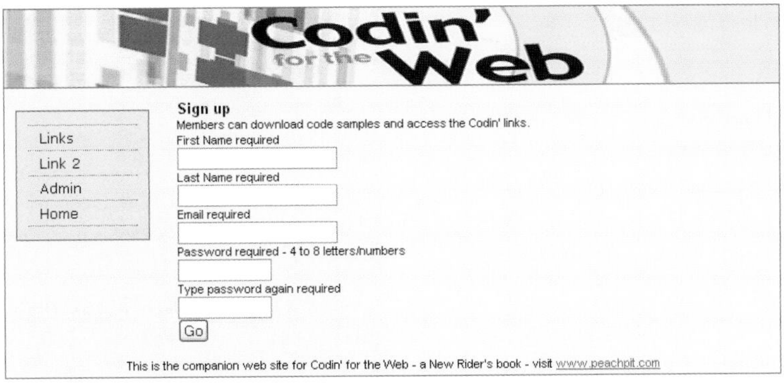

FIGURE 6.16 The displayed sign-up page.

FIGURE 6.16 The displayed sign-up page.

As you will observe if you compare this code with the version in Chapter 5, little has changed, with the exception of the page top and page bottom `include` functions at the top and bottom of the code.

Again (see the three highlighted lines), the page top `include` function does not appear until after the PHP code that processes the page, because this code both gives the user a cookie and redirects the user to the member's page (which we will add in a moment) after the user's sign-up information is validated successfully. Either of these events would trigger the Headers Already Sent error if the page top `include` function appeared before it occurred.

If you now fill out this form and submit it, it will put the data in the database, but it will then display a Page Not Found error message because, after writing to the database, the code redirects the user to the member's page, which we haven't yet added. We'll do that next.

Adding the Member's Page

As you may remember from Chapter 5, you can think of the member's page as a home page especially for members, where you offer links to all the available member content. It appears after the visitor has either signed in or signed up and so received the member cookie. Without the cookie, visitors cannot view the member's page, and if they attempt to access it, they are redirected to the not-authorized page, where they get options to sign up, sign in, or return to the nonmember areas of the site.

Here is the code for the member's page after we have added it to our site:

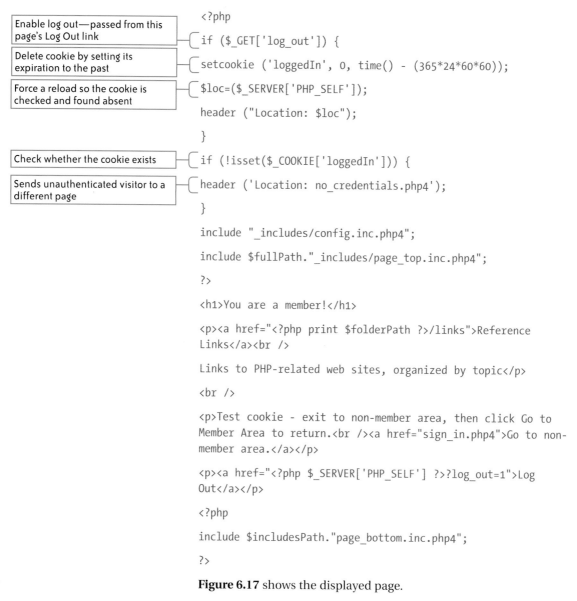

```php
<?php

if ($_GET['log_out']) {

setcookie ('loggedIn', 0, time() - (365*24*60*60));

$loc=($_SERVER['PHP_SELF']);

header ("Location: $loc");

}

if (!isset($_COOKIE['loggedIn'])) {

header ('Location: no_credentials.php4');

}

include "_includes/config.inc.php4";

include $fullPath."_includes/page_top.inc.php4";

?>

<h1>You are a member!</h1>

<p><a href="<?php print $folderPath ?>/links">Reference
Links</a><br />

Links to PHP-related web sites, organized by topic</p>

<br />

<p>Test cookie - exit to non-member area, then click Go to
Member Area to return.<br /><a href="sign_in.php4">Go to non-
member area.</a></p>

<p><a href="<?php $_SERVER['PHP_SELF'] ?>?log_out=1">Log
Out</a></p>

<?php

include $includesPath."page_bottom.inc.php4";

?>
```

Labels for code lines:
- Enable log out—passed from this page's Log Out link
- Delete cookie by setting its expiration to the past
- Force a reload so the cookie is checked and found absent
- Check whether the cookie exists
- Sends unauthenticated visitor to a different page

Figure 6.17 shows the displayed page.

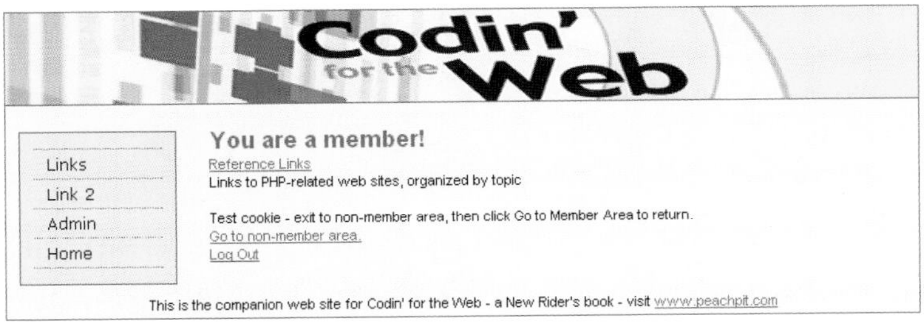

FIGURE 6.17 The displayed member's page, now with a link to a member's only page: Links.

Note the addition of a link to the Links page, a members-only link that we will add to this page.

Adding the Sign-in Page

Adding the Chapter 5 sign-in page is equally easy:

CODE 6.12: step5/sign_in.php4

```php
<?php
include "_includes/config.inc.php4";
include $includesPath."db_connect.inc.php4";
include $includesPath."email_exists_check_db.php4";
include $includesPath."read_member_record.php4";
include $includesPath."validation_functions.php4";

$msg = "Emter your user name and password to sign in.";
if ($_POST['submitted']) {
```

Convert the POST variables to regular variables

```php
    $email = $_POST['email'];
    $password_submitted = $_POST['password1'];

$valid = verifyEmail ($email);
```

Test for invalid data

```php
if (!$valid){
```

Here we provide minimal feedback if data is invalid

```php
$error_msg='<p style="color:red">Sorry, invalid login. Try again.</p>';
}
```

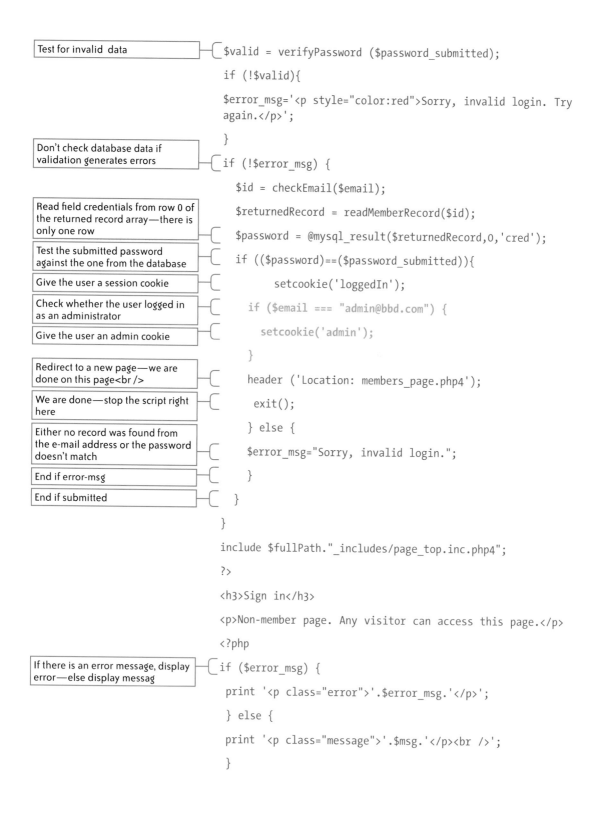

Test for invalid data

```php
$valid = verifyPassword ($password_submitted);

if (!$valid){

$error_msg='<p style="color:red">Sorry, invalid login. Try
again.</p>';

}
```

Don't check database data if validation generates errors

```php
if (!$error_msg) {

    $id = checkEmail($email);

    $returnedRecord = readMemberRecord($id);
```

Read field credentials from row 0 of the returned record array—there is only one row

```php
    $password = @mysql_result($returnedRecord,0,'cred');
```

Test the submitted password against the one from the database

```php
    if (($password)==($password_submitted)){
```

Give the user a session cookie

```php
        setcookie('loggedIn');
```

Check whether the user logged in as an administrator

```php
    if ($email === "admin@bbd.com") {
```

Give the user an admin cookie

```php
      setcookie('admin');

    }
```

Redirect to a new page—we are done on this page

```php
    header ('Location: members_page.php4');
```

We are done—stop the script right here

```php
     exit();
```

Either no record was found from the e-mail address or the password doesn't match

```php
    } else {

    $error_msg="Sorry, invalid login.";
```

End if error-msg

```php
    }
```

End if submitted

```php
  }

}

include $fullPath."_includes/page_top.inc.php4";

?>

<h3>Sign in</h3>

<p>Non-member page. Any visitor can access this page.</p>

<?php
```

If there is an error message, display error—else display messag

```php
if ($error_msg) {

  print '<p class="error">'.$error_msg.'</p>';

} else {

  print '<p class="message">'.$msg.'</p><br />';

}
```

```
?>

   <form action="<?php $_SERVER['PHP_SELF'] ?>" method="POST">

      <label for="email">Email</label><br />

      <input name= "email" type="text" size="20" id="email"
value="<?php echo ($email) ?>" /><br />

      <label for="password1">Password<span></span></label><br
/>

      <input name= "password1" type="password" size="20"
id="password1" /><br />

      <input type="submit" value="Go" name="submitted"/>

   </form>

   <p><a href="email_password.php4">Email me my password!</
a></p>

   <p><a href="sign_up.php4">Sign me up.</a></p>

   <p><a href="members_page.php4">Go to member area.</a></p>

   <p>Closing the browser ends your session - you will then
have to log in again.</p>

<?php

include $includesPath."page_bottom.inc.php4";

include $includesPath."db_close.inc.php4";

?>
```

Figure 6.18 shows the displayed page.

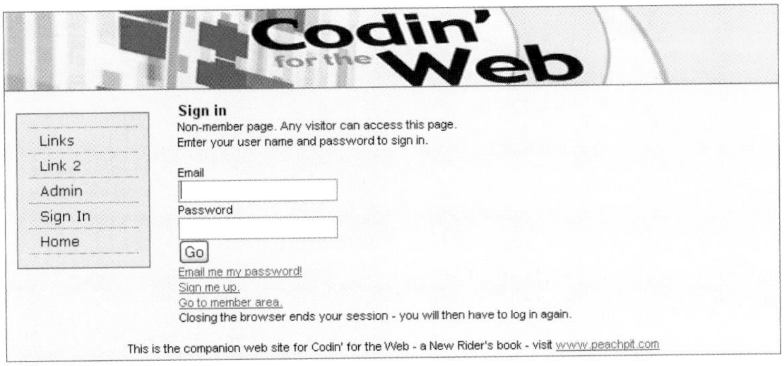

FIGURE 6.18 The displayed sign-in page.

The only part of this code that is significantly different from the version we developed in Chapter 5 is some added code that gives the user a second cookie called admin if the user logs in with the e-mail address admin@bbd.com. Of course, the user also must log in with a corresponding password—set up by signing up with the e-mail address admin@bbd.com and choosing a password. The code simply checks, after ensuring that the user is logged in with a matching user name (e-mail address) and password, that the user's e-mail address is admin@bbd.com. If it is, the user gets the admin cookie—and becomes the system administrator. Once a person has registered with that user name, no one else can, because a unique e-mail address is needed to register.

We also add a link to the sign-in page in the left navigation area.

```
<ul>

    <li><a href="<?php print $folderPath ?>links">Links</
a></li>

        <li><a href="#">Link 2</a></li>

        <li><a href="<?php print $folderPath ?>sign_
in.php4">Sign In</a></li>

        <li><a href="<?php print $folderPath ?>">Home</a></li>

    </ul>
```

Securing the Admin Area

Now that we have a mechanism for uniquely identifying an administrator, by using the admin cookie, we will lock down the Admin area so that only the administrator can access it. We add the following code to the Links Admin page:

CODE 6.13: step5/admin/index.php4

```php
<?php

include "../_includes/config.inc.php4";

include $fullPath."_includes/db_connect.inc.php4";

if (!isset($_COOKIE['admin'])) {

$redirectPath =$folderPath.'no_credentials.php4';

header ("Location: $redirectPath?notadmin=1");

}

include $fullPath."_includes/page_top.inc.php4";
```

Check whether the admin cookie exists

Sends unauthenticated visitor to a different page

```php
if ($_GET['delete_id']) {

  $id = ($_GET['delete_id']);

    $success = mysql_query ("DELETE FROM ref_links WHERE id
= $id", $connectID)

    or die ("Unable to delete record from database");

  if ($success) {

    print "Record successfully deleted";

  }

}

?>
```

If the cookie is not set (note the negating exclamation point), then
the user is sent to the not-authorized page (which we'll add next).
Note also that we append the URL query ?notadmin=1 to the end of
the redirect URL, so that the not-authorized page will know that the
user was sent there after failing to access the Admin area and a special error message can be displayed.

Now the only person who can view this page is someone who has
logged in successfully with the log-in name admin@bbd.com; only
this user will have the admin cookie. Everyone else who tries to
access this page will be redirected to the not-authorized page. Let's
add that page now.

Adding the No-Credentials Page

The not-authorized page requires little modification from its original form in Chapter 5; we just need to test whether the user was
directed there after failing to access the Admin area, in which case
the notadmin variable in the $_GET array is set to 1 (TRUE).

CODE 6.14: step5/no_credentials.
php4

```php
<?php

include "_includes/config.inc.php4";


include $fullPath."_includes/page_top.inc.php4";

  if($_GET['notadmin']) {

    print "<h4>Sorry, only an administrator can view the Admin
pages.</h4>";

  } else {
```

Visitor attempted to view admin
area

```
    print "<h4>You are not signed in. You must sign in to view
member content.</h4>";

    }

?>

    <ul>

        <li><a href="sign_in.php4">Member sign-in</a></li>

        <li><a href="sign_up.php4">Sign up to become a member</
a></li>

        <li><a href="email_password.php4">Email me my password</
a></li>

    </ul>

<?php

include $includesPath."page_bottom.inc.php4";

?>
```

If the user is sent to this page after trying to access the Admin area, the message "Sorry, only an administrator can view the Admin pages." appears (**Figure 6.19**).

FIGURE 6.19 The user attempted unsuccessfully to access the Admin page.

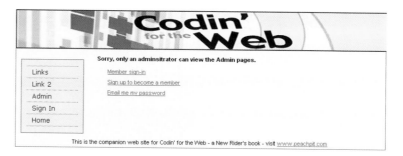

Otherwise, the user must have been sent to this page after attempting to access a member's page without having the member's cookie and so receives the default message: "You are not signed in. You must sign in to view member content." (**Figure 6.20**).

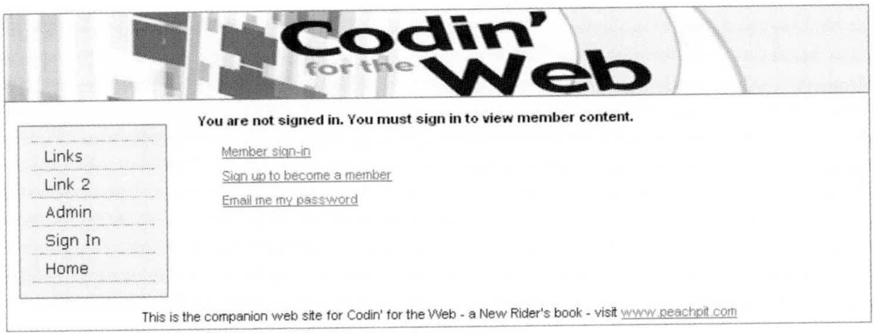

FIGURE 6.20 The user attempted unsuccessfully to access a member's page.

Now we have protected both the member's and administration pages from unauthorized viewing.

Adding the Lost Password Page

The final piece of the authentication system is the page that e-mails a forgotten password. This page can be taken from Chapter 8 almost as is and requires only the addition of the config, page top, and page bottom include functions.

```php
<?php

include "_includes/config.inc.php4";

include $includesPath."db_connect.inc.php4";

include $includesPath."email_exists_check_db.php4";

include $includesPath."read_member_record.php4";

include $includesPath."validation_functions.php4";

$msg = "Enter you email address and we will email your
password.";

if (@$_POST['submitted']) {

  $email = @$_POST['email'];

  $valid = verifyEmail ($email);

  if (!$valid){

  $error_msg="Email must be a valid format (e.g. john@yahoo.
com).";

  }

    $id = checkEmail($email);

    $returnedRecord = readMemberRecord($id);

    $password = @mysql_result($returnedRecord,0,'cred');
```

Test for invalid data

This function converts the e-mail address to its corresponding ID

Read field credentials from row 0 —there is only one row

Set up variable for use in the mail function

Assemble the e-mail body text in a variable

Send the e-mail—uncomment to send mail

End if submitted

If the e-mail address format is invalid, display error—else display message

```php
            if ($password) {
                $email_subject="From the Codin' site";

                $email_body = "Here is the information you requested:
".$password;

            $headers = 'From: Charles Wyke-Smith' . "\r\n" .
                'Reply-To: charles@bbd.com' . "\r\n";

            mail ($email, $email_subject, $email_body, $headers);

            $msg = "Your password has been emailed to ".$email.".";
            } else {
                $msg = "Sorry, the email ".$email." was not found.";
            }

        }
    include $fullPath."_includes/page_top.inc.php4";
    ?>
    <h3>Send me my Password!</h3>
    <?php
    if ($error_msg) {
        print '<p class="error">'.$error_msg.'</p>';
    } else{
        print '<p class="message">'.$msg.'</p>';
    }
    ?>
        <form action="<?php $_SERVER['PHP_SELF'] ?>" method="POST">
            <label for="email">Enter Email</label><br />
            <input name= "email" type="text" size="20" id="email"
value="<?php echo ($email) ?>" /><br />
            <input type="submit" value="Go" name="submitted"/>
        </form>
    <?php
    include $includesPath."page_bottom.inc.php4";
```

```
include $includesPath."db_close.inc.php4";

?>
```

Figure 6.21 shows the displayed page.

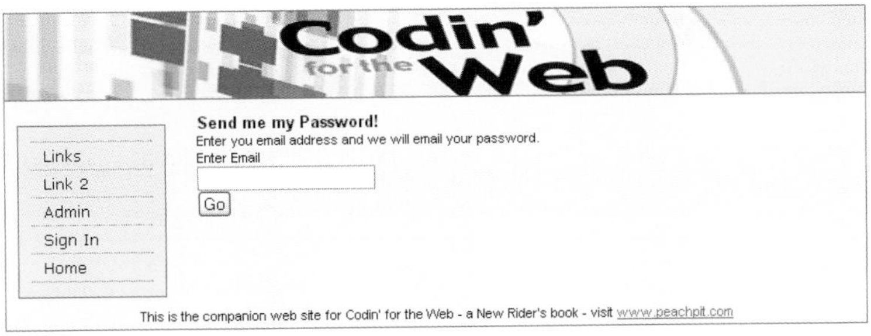

FIGURE 6.21 The displayed lost password page.

At this point, we have successfully integrated the content management functionality we created in Chapter 4 with the authentication functionality we created in Chapter 5.

By now, you should know how to add pages to the site and, if needed, add the cookie check code to pages that should be accessed only by logged-in users.

Adding a Downloads Page

As a simple demonstration of how easy it now is to add new pages, here is a page that enables users to download a .zip file of all the code examples in this book. We will create a folder called downloads and add to this folder a file called index.php4 that contains the following code:

```
<?php

include "../_includes/config.inc.php4";

include $fullPath."_includes/db_connect.inc.php4";

if (!isset($_COOKIE['loggedIn'])) {

$redirectPath =$folderPath.'no_credentials.php4';

header ("Location: $redirectPath");

}

include $fullPath."_includes/page_top.inc.php4";

?>
```

Check whether the member cookie exists

Sends unauthenticated visitor to a different page

```
<h1>Codin' downloads</h1>

<p>Download the files referenced in the book here.</p>

<p><a href="codin.zip">Complete set of files as zip file</
a>

<p>Unzip this file and you will find a folder for each
chapter with the files referenced according to the figure
references in the book.

<?php

include $fullPath."_includes/page_bottom.inc.php4";

include $fullPath."_includes/db_close.inc.php4";

?>
```

Figure 6.22 shows the displayed page.

FIGURE 6.22 The downloads page enables visitors to obtain the code samples shown in the book.

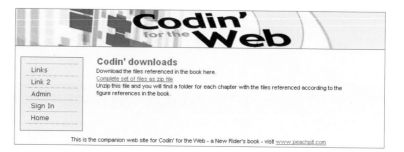

This page references large amounts of code in include files, but the code for this page is a mere 19 lines—a great demonstration of the efficiencies of the modular include function method of constructing pages shown in this chapter.

Because the URL of the link on this page references a .zip file rather than a Web page, the user's browser automatically downloads the file instead of attempting to load it in the browser (**Figure 6.23**).

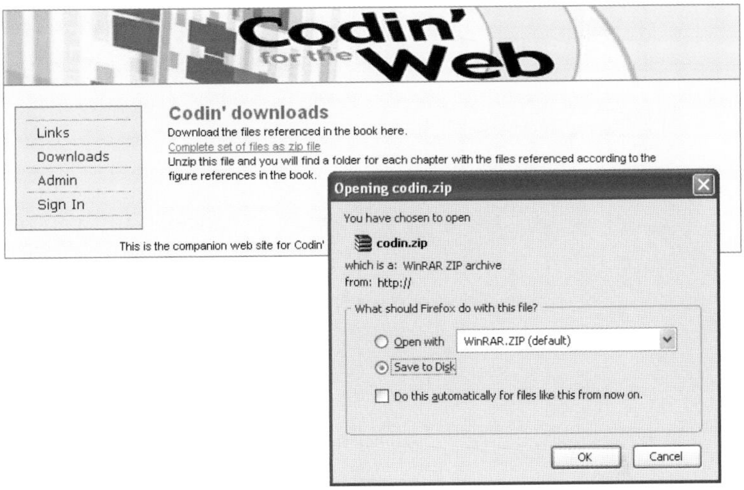

FIGURE 6.23 Because the download link's URL references a file and not a Web page, the browser asks how you want to download the file instead of attempting to display it in the browser.

The files for the book can be obtained from the Codin' *Web site. The file in the downloads folder for this chapter is just a dummy file for demonstration purposes (actually a zipped version of Figure 6.23).*

Improving the Navigation Bar

CODE 6.15: step5/_includes/ navigation.inc.php4

We'll now make some final improvements to the navigation bar so that users can find their way around our site, including adding the Downloads link and removing the Home link.

```
<ul>
    <li><a href="<?php print $folderPath ?>links">Links</a></li>
    <li><a href="<?php print $folderPath ?>links">Downloads</a></li>
    <li><a href="<?php print $folderPath ?>admin">Admin</a></li>
    <li><a href="<?php print $folderPath ?>sign_in.php4">Sign In</a></li>
</ul>
```

Here, we removed the Home link and instead made the *Codin'* graphic across the top of the page the link to the home page. This is an accepted convention; Web users know that page banners, especially any logo element within them, usually link back to the site's home page.

CODE 6.16: Part of step5/_
includes/page_top.inc.php4

To accomplish this, we modify the code in the page top include file by adding a link inside the header div tag:

```
<div id="header">

<a title="Go to the Codin' home page" href="<?php print
$folderPath ?>"></a>

</div>
```

Formerly, the header div tag had no XHTML element nested inside it; the header graphic is specified as a background image in the CSS and so does not appear in the markup. Now there is an empty link (with no displayed text) within the header div tag. However, simply adding a link within the tag is not enough to make the image in the background clickable. Because the image is not part of the markup but is a CSS-specified background, we can't just wrap a link element around the image element, which is the usual way to make an image clickable.

Making a Background Image Clickable

A link like the one in the markup here, without any associated text content (there is no text between the opening and closing tags), has no height or width. A link is an inline element and so always shrink-wraps its contents, and in this case there are no contents. However, by going into the style sheet and setting this particular link's display property to block (from its default inline value) and setting both its height and width properties to 100%, we make the link element entirely fill the header div element in which it is nested in the markup. The entire area of the header now becomes "hot"—responsive to a click.

Now that the link fills the entire area of the header's div tag, the user will seem to be clicking the background image, although this is not, in fact, the case. Actually, the click goes to our supersized but invisible link, which now overlays exactly the same area as the image.

Here's the CSS for the header div tag and the link:

```
div#header {

        width:712px;

    height:72px;

    background-image:url(../_images/codin_header.gif);

    border-bottom:#067EC5 2px;
```

```
  }
div#header a {
  display:block;
  height:100%;
  width:100%;
  }
```

Note the tool tip that appears when the user scrolls over the header area to confirm that it is indeed clickable (**Figure 6.24**). This tool tip is generated by the `title` attribute of the link.

FIGURE 6.24 Clicking the header image redirects the user to the home page.

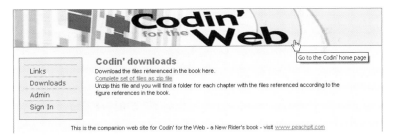

Creating Dynamic Navigation

As a final improvement to the navigation of the site and to see some powerful features of PHP, we will make the site navigation dynamic, so that the links that appear are automatically generated, based on the names of the folders that we create at the top level of our site.

Making the site navigation dynamic is optional. If you prefer to update the navigation bar manually as you add new top-level folders to the site, you have to make such changes in only one place: the navigation include file.

However, creating dynamic navigation elements makes it easier for others to make modifications to the site. It also demonstrates how you can harness the power of PHP to respond to the current state of the system at any given time and shows some more advanced PHP coding techniques.

It's entirely up to you if you want to enhance the site navigation in this way.

Setting Up the Site Navigation Structure

Figure 6.25 shows our site's current top-level file structure.

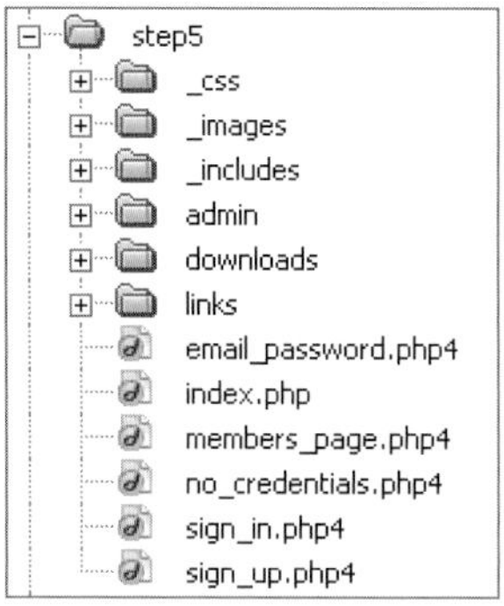

FIGURE 6.25 Our almost-completed Web site has six top-level folders.

There are six folders at the top level of our site. The dynamic navigation system we are about to create will display some of these folder names in the navigation bar automatically, and if we later add new folders to contain the pages of new sections of our site, the names of those folders will be added to the navigation bar and linked to the index page of that folder, without any additional coding. This automation will make ongoing site development much easier.

Folders with names that begin with underscores will not appear in our navigation, because we don't want users to be able to navigate to our _css, _images, and _includes folders. In fact, there are going to be several rules like this affecting both how we will select the folder names to be displayed and the way in which we will format the selected folder names before displaying them.

We will add a leading number to each of the folders we want to display in the menu (**Figure 6.26**).

FIGURE 6.26 The numbers in front of the folder names that are going to be displayed as links will be used to sort the navigation elements into the desired order.

We will use these numbers to sort the menu into the order we want. We'll then remove the numbers from the folder names before we display them in the navigation bar.

The step6 folder now contains three distinct elements:

- Folders with names that start with a number followed by a lowercase letter (a to z)

- Folders with names that start with an underscore

- Files

We'll want the process that determines which names to display in the navigation bar to filter out folder names that start with an underscore and all files.

The first step in building our dynamic navigation is to write some code that will display every file and folder in the top-level folder. Then we will write the code to filter out the elements that we don't want.

Displaying the Contents of the Top-Level Folder

To display the contents of a folder, we can use one of PHP's original object-oriented programming (OOP) functions: dir().

Because dir() is OOP based, it is a little tricky to understand, but all we need to know is that calling this function with a folder name as its argument provides access to an array containing the names of all the subfolders and files in that folder.

Here is the code to display all the files and folders in the step6 folder (which contains the site as it now stands plus all the step-by-step development versions of this navigation include file):

You can read more about the dir() function at the PHPdig Web site, at http://www.phpdig. net/ref/rn17re242.html. (PHPdig is a PHP-based Web spider and search engine. I haven't tried it, but it looks interesting.)

CODE 6.17: Code navigation1. inc.php4

Read the top-level folder's contents ──┐

The top-level folder of our site; the while loop repeats for each file and subfolder ──┐

Read each folder or file item ──┐

```php
<?php

$folder=dir($fullPath);

while($thisItem=$folder->read()){

print $thisItem."<br />";

}

$folder->close();

?>
```

Figure 6.27 shows the results.

FIGURE 6.27 All the files and folders in the site's top-level folder are displayed in the navigation area without formatting. Note the first two items, which are simply dots. Where did they come from?

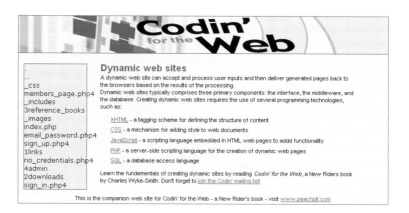

As you can see, this code just writes the names of all the files and folders in the top-level folder. The first two items—the dots—represent Unix folders, which we'll discuss in a moment.

This is the most complicated part of the code in this chapter, so let's look more closely at what is going on.

The first line

| The top-level folder of our site |

```
$folder=dir($fullPath);
```

returns an instance of the `dir` object: a pointer reference to the top-level folder that the next line of the code will use. The argument `$fullPath`, as you may remember, references the top-level folder.

The next line

```
while($thisItem=$folder->read())
```

is rather bizarre; we haven't encountered anything like this so far. It sets `$thisItem` to the next item (file or folder) each time the `while` loop executes. It does this because

```
$folder->read()
```

The use of objects is an extensive subject and beyond the scope of this book, but this technique is quite simple to apply and works well, so as long as you understand how to use it, how it works is not so important.

runs the `dir` object's read method (function) on the `$folder` instance, which returns the next item in the folder. So each time the `while` loop runs, `$thisItem` is set to the next item in the folder.

Now all we have to do is write that item within the `while` loop to get a list of all the items:

```
print $thisItem."<br />";
```

Then we close the `while` loop and clear the instance of the object from memory:

```
$folder->close();
```

Distinguishing between Folders and Files

Of course, we want our navigation to display folder names, not file names, so now our code must be modified to write out only the folders.

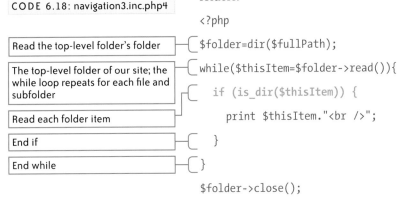

CODE 6.18: navigation3.inc.php4

Read the top-level folder's folder

The top-level folder of our site; the while loop repeats for each file and subfolder

Read each folder item

End if

End while

```php
<?php

$folder=dir($fullPath);

while($thisItem=$folder->read()){

    if (is_dir($thisItem)) {

        print $thisItem."<br />";

    }

}

$folder->close();

?>
```

Figure 6.28 shows the results now.

FIGURE 6.28 The is_dir function filters out all the file names, so now we see only the names of the folders.

The `is_dir` function returns TRUE if the item is a directory (folder), so now the output consists of only the folder names.

Creating an Absolute Path to the Top-Level Folder

If we view our navigation element from a page other than the pages at the top level of the site, such as the page links/index.php, the page doesn't display the file names. The $thisItem variable contains only the name of the folder, so from this lower-level page, the code is_dir($thisItem) fails, as the folder specified by $thisItem does not exist in the links folder; it's at one folder level higher.

We need to use a combination of the $fullPath variable and the $thisItem variable to create a new variable that provides an absolute reference to the top-level folder, like this:

```
$folderItem = $fullPath.$thisItem;

 if (is_dir($folderItem))
```

Now $folderItem contains the following: home/codin/wwwroot/chapter6_includes/code/step6/

This value provides a path to the target folder, and so $thisItem will work from any folder in which the current page is located.

As you may be realizing, one of the toughest issues in building dynamic code is ensuring that references to folders and files resolve correctly. Use temporary print commands to display the path-related variables, such as $folderItem, to ensure that such variables contain the correct information.

With this tedious issue resolved, let's next filter out the two folders that have dots for their names.

Filtering Out the Unix Folders

All Unix folders (but not Windows folders) contain two normally invisible folders named . (single period) and .. (double period). These odd names refer to, respectively, the current folder and the one above it—the current folder's parent folder.

Clearly, we don't want these folder displayed in our navigation bar, so let's write a bit of code that ensures that any folder that starts with a period will be filtered out.

Because this is one of several processes that we will run on the folder names (we will also test for underscores at the start of the names, for example), we will set a variable called $printThis to 1 (TRUE) at the start of the while loop that tests each item in the folder. If that item fails any of our tests (indicating that we don't want to display it), we will set $printThis to 0 (FALSE). At the end of the while loop, if $printThis has not been set to 0, we will store that folder name in an array of "good" folder names, which we will call $navArray. We will write the contents of this array into the navigation listing after all the folder names have been checked and rejected or formatted for display.

We first need to set up the $printThis variable and the $navArray array; then we can test for the presence of dots in the folder names and store the names of the folders that don't contain dots.

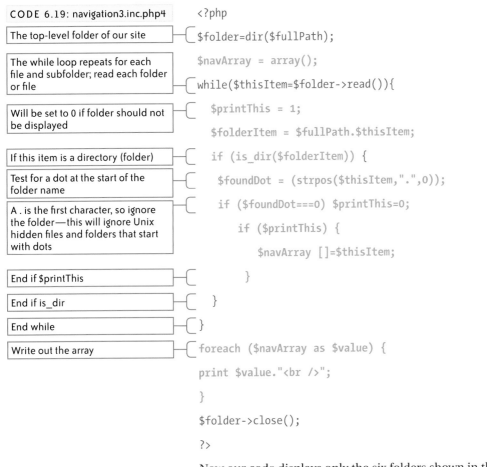

CODE 6.19: navigation3.inc.php4	```<?php```
The top-level folder of our site	```$folder=dir($fullPath);```
The while loop repeats for each file and subfolder; read each folder or file	```$navArray = array();``` ```while($thisItem=$folder->read()){```
Will be set to 0 if folder should not be displayed	```$printThis = 1;``` ```$folderItem = $fullPath.$thisItem;```
If this item is a directory (folder)	```if (is_dir($folderItem)) {```
Test for a dot at the start of the folder name	```$foundDot = (strpos($thisItem,".",0));```

A . is the first character, so ignore the folder—this will ignore Unix hidden files and folders that start with dots	```if ($foundDot===0) $printThis=0;```
	```if ($printThis) {```
	```$navArray []=$thisItem;```

End if $printThis	```}```
End if is_dir	```}```
End while	```}```
Write out the array	```foreach ($navArray as $value) {```

```
print $value."<br />";

}

$folder->close();

?>
```

Now our code displays only the six folders shown in the file structure in Figure 6.25 (**Figure 6.29**).

FIGURE 6.29 All the files and the Unix folders, which have dots for names, are now filtered out of the listing.

The test for the dots in the file names looks like this:

```
$foundDot = (strpos($thisItem,".",0));
```

Here we use the string position function, which take three arguments:

```
strpos(haystack,needle,offset)
```

The haystack argument is the data we are testing, and the needle argument, of course, is what we are searching for in haystack. The offset argument states the point in the string at which the search should start—in our case, from the first character at position 0.

This function returns the position at which the character in question (. in our case) is found, and returns 0 (FALSE) if it is not found. The problem in our case is that the function will also return 0 if the character *is* found because that's the location of the dot: at 0, the first position.

So it's not enough to test for equality here with the == operator, as that will not discern between 0 meaning FALSE and 0 meaning position 0. What we need instead is the exact-match operator: ===.

The line

```
if ($foundDot===0) $printThis=0;
```

means "If a dot is found at position 0 of the string (the first position), then set the $printThis variable to 0"—in other words, we don't want this folder.

However, if the first character is not a dot, then $printThis remains set to 1, and we want to add that item to the array. We use this code:

| If $printThis = 1 |
| Then add it to the array |

```
if ($printThis) {

    $navArray []=$thisItem;

}
```

 This array is initialized outside the while loop because we want to perform this operation only once, before we start to loop through the file names. The $thisItem variable, on the other hand, is inside the while loop because we want to reinitialize it to 1 at the start of each loop cycle.

All that is left to do is to write the array so we can see the items we've accumulated.

```php
foreach ($navArray as $value) {

print $value."<br />";

}
```

So far so good. Now let's filter for folder names that start with an underscore. This code is very similar to that for checking for names that start with a dot.

Right after the test for the dots, we add two virtually identical lines (highlighted):

CODE 6.20: Part of navigation4.
inc.php4

Don't list the two weird hidden folders that show up as dots

A . is the first character, so ignore

Returns 0 if position 0 (the first character) is an underscore

An _ is the first character, so ignore

```php
$foundDot = (strpos($thisItem,".",0));

if ($foundDot===0) $printThis=0;

$result = strpos($thisItem,"_",0);

if ($result===0) $printThis=0;

    if ($printThis) {

    $navArray []=$thisItem;
```

End if $printThis

```php
    }
```

End if is_dir

```php
}
```

Now we've also eliminated the folder names that start with an underscore (**Figure 6.30**). Except for changing the needle character to an underscore, the code is exactly the same as the code that found the leading dots.

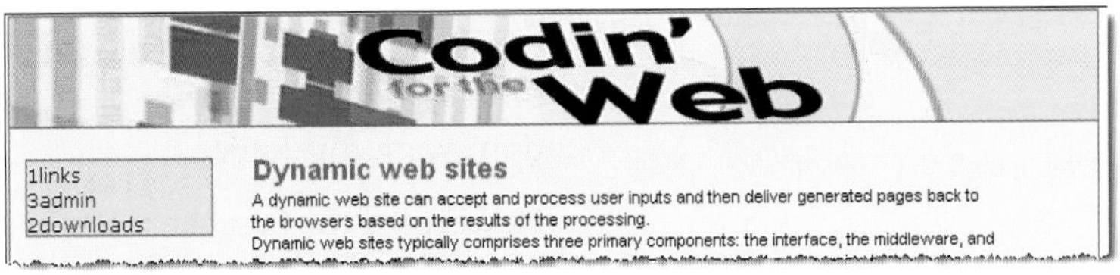

FIGURE 6.30 Now the folders that start with underscores are also removed from the listing, although they are not displayed in the correct order.

To see our dynamic navigation in action, let's add another folder to the site that we might use for a listing of reference books. The name we want on the navigation bar is "Reference books," so we'll name the folder reference_books. It's standard practice to use underscores rather than spaces in multiple-word folder names, as spaces get replaced with the entity %20 in URL strings, making them hard to read. However, we want spaces in place of such underscores in the displayed names, and we also want to capitalize the first word of each displayed name; we will later convert the folder name to the desired display formatting.

We also will want the reference_books link to appear as the third item in the navigation bar, so we'll append a 3 to its name. To accommodate this order, we'll change the number of the admin folder to 4.

Our folder structure now looks like **Figure 6.31**.

FIGURE 6.31 A new folder called 3reference_books is added to the site.

This change is automatically reflected onscreen when the browser page is refreshed (**Figure 6.32**). However, the names don't yet appear in the order that we want.

FIGURE 6.32 The new folder appears on the screen when we refresh the page.

Changing the Folder Names to Display Names

The next step is to modify the folder names so that they appear onscreen in a more user-friendly and better looking way. We will do this by running three functions on the folder names that have survived the "no leading dots" and "no leading underscore" tests. These functions will do the following:

- Remove any underscores between words.

- Remove any leading numbers.

- Capitalize the first letter of each link name.

We will store the results of this process in a new variable called $thisItemDisplay. We are using a different variable for this display version of the names because we want to keep the unmodified version of the folder names intact in the $thisItem variable for later use in the link's URL.

Here are our three functions:

```
if ($printThis) {

  $thisItemDisplay = str_replace ("_", " ", $thisItem);

  $thisItemDisplay = ereg_replace('^[0-9]+', "",
$thisItemDisplay);

  $thisItemDisplay = ucfirst($thisItemDisplay);

  $navArray []=$thisItemDisplay;

}
```

CODE 6.21: Part of navigation5.inc.php4

If folder name contains underscores, replace them with spaces

Now remove any leading numbers

Set the first letter of each link to uppercase

End if $printThis

Let's look at each of these functions in detail.

To replace any underscores between the words of the folder names, we use the string replace function, formatted like this:

str_replace (*needle*, *new needle*, *haystack*);

This function simply replaces a needle (a string of characters, consisting of only one character in this case) in our haystack (the folder name) with another needle (different characters).

Next, we use a simple regular expression (remember the validation scripts in Chapter 2?) to get rid of any numbers at the beginning of the folder name. When we used the ereg() regular expression function in Chapter 2 (to test, for example, whether an e-mail address was formatted correctly), the result that the function returned was either 1 or 0 (TRUE or FALSE)—the supplied e-mail address string either matched the structure defined in the regular expression or it didn't.

Here, we use a different regular expression function, ereg_replace(), where we pass a string to the function, and the function returns a modified version of the string. The ereg_replace() function takes the use of regular expressions to a whole new level, as we can now write regular expressions that perform complex modifications of strings according to rules defined in our regular expression.

For example, although there is a string function that can find all instances of particular characters in a string and replace them with other characters (as we saw in the use of the str_replace() function in the previous step), if we want to be more specific and state *where* the characters to be replaced must appear in the string, string functions can't help us. In such a case, we turn to the power of regular expressions and `ereg_replace()`.

The format of `ereg_replace()` is very similar to that of `str_replace()`:

```
ereg_replace(expression defining characters to be replaced,
replacement characters, string to test);
```

The regular expression `^[0-9]+` means "at the start of the string, any numerical character, in any quantity." The `^` symbol represents "at the beginning," and `+` represents "any quantity." Thus, the expression

```
ereg_replace('^[0-9]+', "", $thisItemDisplay);
```

will remove all numbers at the beginning of the supplied string because the replacement characters string `""` is empty.

The expression matching on the string will stop only when a nonnumerical character within the string is encountered. Thus, we could have folders numbered into the thousands in our navigation bar, and this expression would still strip out those numbers at the beginning of the names. (If you have more than nine folders, though, be sure to number the folders 01, 02, … 09, 10, and so on; otherwise, folder 11 will appear before folder 2.)

Finally, we use the string function `ucfirst()` simply to return the supplied argument string, but with the first letter capitalized (in uppercase):

```
$thisItemDisplay = ucfirst($thisItemDisplay);
```

So, for example, the folder name links is converted to Links.

Now the folder names appear in the format in which we want them displayed in the navigation bar (**Figure 6.33**). However, they are not yet correctly sorted, nor are they structured as clickable links.

FIGURE 6.33 Now the names are formatted correctly, but they are not yet correctly sorted or set up as links.

Generating the Links

So now we get to the conclusion of this example: creating the click-able links. A link requires two pieces of data, as illustrated here:

```
<a href="URL">Displayed name</a>
```

In our case, we want

```
<a href="folder path + unmodified folder name">Modified
folder name</a>
```

Or, for example, more specifically, we want

```
<a href="/chapter6_includes/code/step6/1links">Links</a>
```

So we'll now convert the $navArray array (which is currently an indexed array, where each element is simply the modified folder name) into an associative array—that is, an array where each array element has both a name and a value. The name will be the modified version of the folder name, which we will use in the displayed name part of the link, and the value will be the unmodified version of the folder name that starts with the number, which we will use both to sort the array and as the URL of the link. In terms of the array, here is what we are aiming for:

```
<a href="folder path + array element value">array element
name</a>
```

CODE 6.22: navigation6.inc.php4

This is the code we need to accomplish our goal:

```php
<?php
$folder=dir($fullPath);
$navArray = array();
while($thisItem=$folder->read()){
    ////Print $thisItem."<br />";
    $printThis = 1;
    if (is_dir($thisItem)) {
        $foundDot = (strpos($thisItem,".",0));
        if ($foundDot===0) $printThis=0;
        $result = strpos($thisItem,"_",0);
        if ($result===0) $printThis=0;
            if ($printThis) {
```

The top-level folder of our site

Array for "good" folders

Read each folder or file

Will be set to 0 if folder should not be displayed

Don't list the two weird hidden folders that show up as dots

A . is the first character, so ignore folder

Don't list folders with underscores as the first character

An _ is the first character, so ignore folder

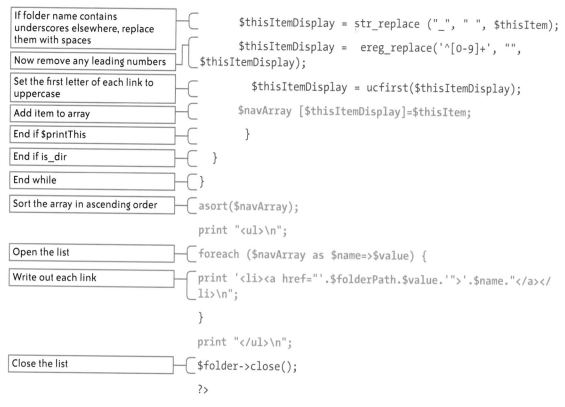

If folder name contains underscores elsewhere, replace them with spaces	`$thisItemDisplay = str_replace ("_", " ", $thisItem);`
Now remove any leading numbers	`$thisItemDisplay = ereg_replace('^[0-9]+', "", $thisItemDisplay);`
Set the first letter of each link to uppercase	`$thisItemDisplay = ucfirst($thisItemDisplay);`
Add item to array	`$navArray [$thisItemDisplay]=$thisItem;`
End if $printThis	`}`
End if is_dir	`}`
End while	`}`
Sort the array in ascending order	`asort($navArray);`
	`print "<ul>\n";`
Open the list	`foreach ($navArray as $name=>$value) {`
Write out each link	`print '<li><a href="'.$folderPath.$value.'">'.$name."</a></li>\n";`
	`}`
	`print "</ul>\n";`
Close the list	`$folder->close();`
	`?>`

Now the navigation links are correctly formatted and sorted according to the number at the beginning of each folder name (**Figure 6.34**).

FIGURE 6.34 The completed dynamic navigation element, formatted for display and sorted according to the numbering of the folder names from which the displayed names are derived.

Here is the XHTML output from our script:

```
<div id="navigation">

<ul>

<li><a href="/chapter6_includes/code/step6/1links">Links</a></li>
```

```
<li><a href="/chapter6_includes/code/step6/
2downloads">Downloads</a></li>

<li><a href="/chapter6_includes/code/step6/3reference_
books">Reference books</a></li>

<li><a href="/chapter6_includes/code/step6/4admin">Admin</
a></li>

</ul>

</div>
```

Observe that the URLs end with the name of the folder, so each folder must contain an index.php or index.html file (and your server can be configured to read other page names by default) that will automatically load when the link is clicked.

Adding the Reference Books Page

You can add the Reference books page on your own. Use the code from the Links page because the Reference books page will have the same functionality. Go to phpMyAdmin and copy the Links database tables structure and rename the tables and book_categories, for example. Then copy the pages that relate to the links into the new folder and make the necessary modifications to those new pages—mainly to the URLs, database queries, and other file references in the code.

Making the Page Titles Dynamic

One problem that results from using a common include file for the head of every page, as we are doing here, is that every page can end up with the same page title displayed in the top bar of the browser window. This occurs because the `<title>` element is in the `<head>` element of the markup, and in our site and many others, that part of the code is in a page top include file that is shared by every page, so the page title ends up being the same on every page. There are good reasons to have a unique title for every page: it helps your site's visitors see the subject of the page at a glance, and it improves your site's visibility to search engines (see the sidebar "Page Titles and Search Engines"). So let's now see how to overcome this problem and enable the inclusion of a unique title on each page.

The page title is the text that appears in the `<title>` element in the `<head>` element of each Web page. This text is displayed at the top edge of the browser window (**Figure 6.35**).

FIGURE 6.35 The text in the `<title>` tag is displayed at the top the browser window.

Because our page titles all currently derive from the same piece of code, the `<title>` tag in the page top include file that is shared by all pages, we need to get creative to enable a unique title to appear every page.

Page Titles and Search Engines

Search engines weight the titles of your pages very heavily; that is, a search engine will consider the words you use here to relate closely to the content of the page, and therefore if someone searches on a word or phrase that appears in the title of your page, that page is more likely to appear, and to appear higher, in the search results.

Also, if such is page *is* returned in the search results, it's the title of the page that is displayed, along with (usually) a snippet of text for the page text that also includes the search phrase, so you also want that page title to appeal to the person who is searching. So what this all means is that *page titles are an important factor in bringing visitors to your site from search engines*. Don't waste this opportunity with the all-too-common useless page title "Welcome to Our Web Site!" No one is searching for that phrase.

Ideally, each page of your site will have a unique title that summarizes the contents of that page. Also, it's good practice to spread all the search phrases that you think search engine visitors might type when looking for a site like yours across the title text of all the pages of your site, one or two phrases to a page, so that you maximize the chance of a search phrase matching at least one of your pages.

I always try to make each page title both summarize the page content and include some search phrase relating to the site as whole. For example, for the Links page, I might use the title "PHP Reference Sites and Links—Programming and Coding Tutorials." A search on *PHP reference sites* would be the most likely to match, as the title starts with these words in this order, but this title might also appear as a match to the search phrases *PHP programming tutorials*, *PHP coding links*, and so on.

Using the same phrases in page headings (`<h1>`, `<h2>`, and so on) further confirms to the search engine that the page is truly about the subject stated in the title tags, and using the same phases early in the body text can add further weight to your title page keywords. Just don't overdo it and repeat the same phrases over and over consecutively in titles, heads, and page copy, because search engines will blacklist sites that appear to overuse keywords in an effort to affect page rankings.

Adding Dynamic Page Title Code to the Page Top include File

Here's the `<head>` element of the page top include file (page_top.inc.php4):

```
<head>

<meta http-equiv="Content-Type" content="text/html;
charset=iso-8859-1" />

<title>Codin' - Sample XHTML Page</title>

<link href="<?php print $folderPath ?>_css/codin.css"
media="screen" rel="stylesheet" />

</head>
```

Right now the placeholder title Codin'—Sample XHTML Page appears on every page of our site—not very useful, so we'll modify the title tag (highlighted in the preceding code) to look like this:

```
<title>

<?php

if ($pageTitle) {

 print $pageTitle;

} else {

 print "Codin' for the Web - a designer's guide | learn PHP
and build dynamic web sites";

}

?>

</title>
```

This code says "If the `$pageTitle` variable is set, print that variable's text; otherwise, print a default title." Now, because this code is in the page top include file, it appears in every script, so if we add the following code at the top of the Links page, before the page top include file appears in the script, then the Links page will have a unique title (**Figure 6.36**).

CODE 6.25: Part of step6/
_includes/1links/index.php4

```php
<?php

$pageTitle = "PHP reference sites and links - PHP programming
and coding tutorials";

include "../_includes/config.inc.php4";

include $fullPath."_includes/db_connect.inc.php4";

if (!isset($_COOKIE['loggedIn'])) {

$redirectPath =$folderPath.'no_credentials.php4';

header ("Location: $redirectPath");

}

include $fullPath."_includes/page_top.inc.php4";
```

FIGURE 6.36 We set the $pageTitle variable at the top of the script, before the page top include file, so the variable's text appears in the page title.

If we don't set the $pageTitle variable at the top of a page, that page will display the default title text defined in the page top include file.

Now it's easy to selectively add page titles to any page of the site we want, by setting the $pageTitle variable at the top of that page's script. We can add unique metatags and other <head>-related data to the pages in the same manner.

And that completes the final example of this book.

Reviewing Our Dynamic Site

Our site, while it needs more pages of content to be truly useful, now has quite extensive functionality.

We can easily create more pages because each page's structural code is contained in include files, which can easily be linked to any script.

We can sign up new members and allow existing members to sign in. We can make any pages we want accessible to members only and reject anyone else who tries to access them.

We can add and edit content through an administrator area that is accessible only with a specific administrator's user name and password. Our visitors can view our links, and link to the listed pages on third-party sites, and they can download files from a special downloads page.

Most of all, we have created a site that is easy to maintain, modify, and expand over time.

By designing using Web standards, separating the presentational aspects of the site into a CSS style sheet and having only structural XHTML in the pages themselves, we have created a site where we can easily modify either the content or presentation without disrupting the other.

It would be easy to present the site's content within an entirely different page design by simply modifying the CSS style sheet and recoding the page top and page bottom include files; the actual pages of the site, which contain the page's marked-up content and the code to process that content, would not need to be touched.

We could rapidly create a version of this site that could be displayed on a cell phone or PDA, again by modifying only the CSS style sheet and the page top and page bottom include files, to create page layouts that would fit the form factor of these devices' smaller screens.

By sharing common functionality of the pages through include files, we can easily change the database to which the pages are connected or update the navigation mechanism of every page by modifying a single script.

Adopting the kinds of development techniques shown in *Codin' for the Web* greatly simplifies a Web site's development process and lays the groundwork for its ongoing evolution.

Once you master the concepts of gathering and processing data, then you can create a Web site that is a two-way connection between you and your site's visitors, and if you wish, you can build an entire business around your Web site.

By applying the techniques you have learned in this book and by recycling the book's code samples that are available for download, I hope that you will now be able to create sites that are straightforward to build, maintain, and modify.

Index